DEMYSTIFYING ISLAM

DEMYSTIFYING ISLAM

Tackling the Tough Questions

HARRIS ZAFAR

ROWMAN & LITTLEFIELD
Lanham • Boulder • New York • London

To Rohan, Zara, Arkan
and all brave seekers of knowledge and truth.
Never stop seeking. Never.

Published by Rowman & Littlefield
A wholly owned subsidiary of The Rowman & Littlefield Publishing Group, Inc.
4501 Forbes Boulevard, Suite 200, Lanham, Maryland 20706
www.rowman.com

16 Carlisle Street, London W1D 3BT, United Kingdom

British Library Cataloguing in Publication Information Available

Library of Congress Cataloging-in-Publication Data
Zafar, Harris, 1979-
  Demystifying Islam : tackling the tough questions / Harris Zafar.
    pages cm
  Includes index.
  ISBN 978-1-4422-2327-1 (cloth : alk. paper) — ISBN 978-1-4422-2328-8
(electronic) 1. Islam. 2. Islam—Doctrines. I. Title.
  BP161.3.Z323 2014
  297—dc23
                                                              2014004827

∞™ The paper used in this publication meets the minimum requirements of
American National Standard for Information Sciences—Permanence of Paper
for Printed Library Materials, ANSI/NISO Z39.48-1992.

Printed in the United States of America

CONTENTS

ACKNOWLEDGMENTS

Truth be told, this book is the culmination of my research, lectures, classes, debates, and conversations about Islam and other faiths over a span of more than fifteen years. After graduating high school, I entered my bachelor's program with a youthful rebellious desire to put my faith to the test. I challenged my faith and sought to determine not only why I should be a follower of this religion but also how to correctly understand and interpret it. This led not only to some memorable conversations with my parents but also to countless conversations and debates with Muslims and non-Muslims—some respectful, some confrontational.

I am most indebted to those who made arguments for which I had no response, as it prompted me to challenge my assumptions in order to determine whether Islam could provide a clear and cogent answer. Although they may be nameless memories, each person I challenged and disagreed with during those years has a part to play in my study, scholarship, and understanding of Islam. And because I assuredly offended some Muslims and non-Muslims on my journey toward higher learning and understanding of God and His teachings, I pray that God forgives me and blesses those people for unknowingly supporting my search for truth. I am truly grateful for those experiences.

In the wake of September 11, 2001, my local mosque—the Portland Rizwan Mosque, which stands as the first and oldest mosque built in Portland, Oregon—was flooded with requests for speakers to come and discuss Islam at various settings. I am grateful that our mosque leaders at that time trusted a zealous twenty-two-year-old to represent Islam at some of these gatherings. The countless talks and lectures I now so enjoy giving have their birth during these tense times after 9/11, when I was given an opportunity to share what I knew about the religion of Islam.

My love for the study of Islam and other religions would never have been so strong if I did not have my parents there to inspire this quest for finding and understanding God as well as His teachings. No amount of thanks can capture my gratitude for what they have done to set their son on the path toward enlightenment and higher education. Their love, instructions, and prayers—and their willingness to address my questions instead of simply telling me to believe as they believe—has brought me to where I am today. Additionally, their work in finding and translating many passages from Urdu into English during my painstaking research for this book has enabled me to introduce an English-speaking audience to references they otherwise would never find.

Undoubtedly, the biggest influence on not only my understanding of Islam but also my passion for greater study is Mirza Ghulam Ahmad, the founder of the worldwide Ahmadiyya Muslim Community. He claimed to be that Messiah who was foretold in Quranic and biblical scriptures as well as that long-awaited guide and reformer whom the Prophet Muhammad had said would come to unite humankind, raise God consciousness, and trigger a renaissance of Islam. He called people to faith through logic and reason—a call that continues to resonate in my heart and mind. From him, I learned how reason and faith can live together in perfect harmony. He penned more than eighty books in order to elucidate the teachings of Islam in a rational and reasonable manner. He wielded only the pen in the clear explanation of faith and, thus, inspired me to also turn to scholarship and writing for the same purpose. His fifth and current successor—His Holiness Mirza Masroor Ahmad, the only Khalifa of Islam today—has provided me with endless inspiration and guidance, for which I am eternally grateful.

During my exhaustive research for this book, I relied on many people to help me find literary gems hidden in libraries across the country. Their willingness to find these books, and even at times look up references for me, saved me from having to fly around the country myself and proved to be incredibly vital to my research and theses. Thank you sincerely for your time and support. Many others dedicated their time discussing and debating the many topics of this book with me and reviewing the multiple drafts of my chapters. Dr. Nasim Rehmatullah, Imam Ayyaz Mahmood Khan, Imam Mubasher Ahmad, Dr. Faheem Younus, Amjad Mahmood Khan Esq, Sardar Anees Ahmad, Saliha Malik, Aziza Rahman, Dr. Shanaz Tejani-Butt, Ronald Abdul Rahim Hubbs, and Rasheed Reno all provided insightful and valuable feedback after reviewing the contents of this book, for which I am very thankful.

What I learned through the process of researching and writing this book is that doing so is an incredibly selfish pursuit when you are married and have three beautiful young children. Without the support of my wife and best friend, Yasemin, I simply would not have been able to complete this book. Not only did she patiently allow me to live in the library when I should have been helping with our children, but she also provided invaluable support and feedback on every chapter of the book. She taught me the true meaning of the term "soul mate."

Finally, I am grateful for the support and opportunity given to me from my editor, Sarah Stanton, and the entire team at Rowman & Littlefield. They believed in the vision and value of this book in confronting the hot topics about Islam and were very supportive and patient throughout this process. They set a bar for me that I pushed myself to my limits in order to meet, and the end product is all that much better for it.

The views expressed by Harris Zafar do not necessarily reflect the official views of the Ahmadiyya Muslim Community.

INTRODUCTION

Do you find yourself unable to understand the religion of Islam or certain aspects of its teachings? Certainly, it feels like endless books, commentaries, articles, and speeches have been written since September 11, 2001, that offer either an opinion about Islam and Muslims, or a basic introduction to Islamic teachings and history. There are many Muslim and non-Muslim writers who have painted Islam as a beautiful and peaceful religion, founded by a prophet who sought to reform people and restore their connection with God. At the same time, there have been a growing number of publications in the past several years opining that Islam is a vile, violent, and oppressive religion that is incompatible with the values of the modern world.

These combating views have created a difficult landscape for the study of this rapidly growing religion. For the average reader, it can be a challenge to grasp even the basic tenets of Islam, let alone the more advanced and deeper topics about its theology. What complicates matters even further is that media reports from Middle East nations have shaped opinions or judgment regarding the teachings of Islam. It is no secret that there are Muslims—as well as nations that are predominantly Muslim—who have said or done some very shocking things over the past several years. Such incidents of irrationality, savagery, ignorance, and barbarity have not only shocked people in the West; they have also caused many to feel conflicted on the justification for these actions within the teachings of Islam.

Although Muslim groups in America and abroad have condemned or rejected such acts of violence, injustice, and inequity, a growing number of non-Muslims feel at least conflicted on several matters they see as Islamic practices. Even worse is the growing resentment in the West toward behavior and beliefs perceived to be inspired by Islam, which is built upon misconceptions about the faith that have never been properly addressed.

Understanding that this opinion has as much to do with the behavior and words of Muslims themselves as it has to do with baseless allegations made by anti-Islam groups, I, through this book, *Demystifying Islam*, will focus on debunking myths about Islam by providing honest, well-researched information on topics about Islam that stir up the most anxiety or confusion. The purpose of this book will be to finally "demystify" this religion and remove these shrouds of confusion by providing detailed analyses on subjects that puzzle people the most.

Each chapter of the book begins by identifying a topic of confusion—and even highlighting Muslim confusion on the matter—and then proceeds to shed light on the subject by referencing Islamic teachings and historical data as evidence. Where there may be differing Muslim viewpoints, you will learn about this diversity of thought, and then I will elucidate the viewpoint that is most consistent with Islamic scripture and the practice of the Prophet Muhammad. You will not only learn the diversity of views within the Muslim world; you will also learn how to analyze the veracity of these differing views.

Through this book, you will discover the religion of Islam and how to make sense of the breadth of its teachings. This book is not simply an introductory piece about Islam's central tenets. In addition to elucidating the basic teachings of Islam, *Demystifying Islam* takes a very frank and honest approach to focus specifically on the hot topics about this religion that stir the most controversy and debate—topics that are often the more misunderstood concepts within the Islamic community as well. The subjects chosen for these hot topics are the result of not only my lifelong journey toward understanding Islam as an adherent and representative of the faith but also my sixteen years of deeply focused study of the faith and, in particular, my dialogue with those seeking to understand Islam.

Demystifying Islam contains everything you need to know about Islam, and more. It is your single source to answer your common questions about Islam, with references to Islamic scripture and scholarship. A religion provides humankind with guidance through spiritual law and, thus, cannot be defined by the widely diverse—and often conflicting—actions and words of those who profess belief in it. Rather, a religion can only truly be defined and understood by looking to its scripture and its prophet, which provide the very foundation of the faith and a practical example of how to put it into action. This book is written to address this need to understand the principles of the Islamic faith. It is not merely based on opinion but, rather, on documented teachings of Islam as well as on how these teachings have been expounded by scholars of various ages.

A note about references to the Quran: every chapter of the Quran—Islam's Holy Scripture—begins with the verse "In the name of Allah, the Most Gracious, the Most Merciful" with the exception of just one chapter. In the entire length of this book, the numbering of Quranic verses follows the practice of citing "In the name of Allah, the Most Gracious, the Most Merciful" as verse no. 1 since that verse was revealed to the Prophet Muhammad at the beginning of every chapter. Some published translations of the Quran use a slightly different numbering system in which this first verse is not numbered. Readers should keep this in mind when cross-referencing any Quranic verses from this book with a copy of the Quran they may have. If the reader's Quran does not mark "In the name of Allah, the Most Gracious, the Most Merciful" as verse no. 1, its verses will be off by one as compared to the references provided in this book.

Now, on to chapter 1!

1

BEGIN WITH THE BASICS—
BEFORE WE CAN DEMYSTIFY

Although so much information is available regarding Islam, some remain confused about Islamic teachings on a variety of subjects. It is, thus, important to demystify these subjects in order to clarify and understand Islam's teachings. Before diving into specific topics about Islam that require clarification, however, it is important to take a step back and introduce Islam and its fundamental beliefs and practices. This will provide a solid framework with which to understand Islam and its individual teachings.

BASIC TERMINOLOGY

Islam

At its root, "Islam" is an Arabic word meaning "peace and submission." It is derived from the Arabic root word "*salema*," which means peace, purity, submission, and obedience to God. According to the Quran—Islam's Holy Scripture—Islam is the name given to God's one and only religion: "This day have I perfected your religion for you and completed My favour upon you and have chosen for you Islam as religion."[1] This means that the only true religion prescribed for humankind is the practice of entirely submitting to the will of God and fostering peace within ourselves and in the world around us. This practice is given the name "Islam."

It is important to note that "submission" alone is an inadequate translation of the word "Islam." Some detractors commonly use this translation to argue that Islam advocates the use of force or coercion to make people submit or surrender to Islam. This is not at all what the word means. The submission that the word "Islam" refers to is only the submission of humans to God; it does not connote any form of submission or surrender to other human beings or earthly institutions. "Islam" refers to the act of submitting to God through one's free will—not through any compulsion. (See chapter 5, "Demystifying Islam's View of Religious Freedom," for more explanation.)

Muslim

Thus, "Islam" refers to the path of those who are obedient to their Lord and who establish peace with Him and His creation. One who follows this path and accepts Islam as one's religion is referred to as a "Muslim," which is an Arabic word meaning "one who submits to the will of God." Although the word "Muslim" in itself does not differentiate between followers of one prophet versus another, it is a term that has come to be seen as referring to those who accept and follow the religion of Islam. So, whereas the word "Islam" refers to the religion, the word "Muslim" refers to the person who practices that religion. Some have the false notion that Muslims are Arabs. The truth is that Muslims are not confined to one geography or ethnicity. The followers of the religion of Islam are spread across hundreds of countries in all continents throughout the world, making Muslims ethnically diverse. (See chapter 9, "Demystifying the Sects of Islam," to further explore the ethnic and theological diversity among Muslims.)

Allah

"Allah" is an Arabic name used in Islam to refer to God and literally means "The God" or "The Only God"—the prefix "Al" in Arabic is defined as "the" and is connected to the suffix "ilah," which means "god." It is the name of the One Supreme Being also known as "Elohim" or "Yahweh" by the Hebrews, "Elah" in the Aramaic language of Jesus Christ, "Deus" in Latin, "Theos" in Greek, and "God" in the English language. In the Arabic language, the word "Allah" has never been used to refer to anyone or any entity other than the One God and is considered the only proper personal name of God. Islam teaches that He is a living God; alive even now, just as He was alive before. He speaks even now, just as He spoke before. He hears even now, just as He heard before. So Islam advances the concept of belief in the same One God that others have always accepted; He is the same God of Abraham, Moses, Jesus, and Muhammad.

Prophet Muhammad

Muhammad is considered the founder of the religion of Islam. Even though Muslims do not consider Islam to be a new faith—rather, to be a continuation of previous faiths (see chapter 2, "Demystifying the Origins of Islam")—Muhammad is the prophet who was sent with this final message about peace and submission to God. He is a messenger and prophet of God, born in Mecca (in present-day Saudi Arabia) in the year 570 AD. He was forty years of age when he received the call to prophethood (i.e., received the first revelation from God of being an appointed prophet). In the Quran, prophets are said to fulfill two vital tasks—receiving and conveying messages from God. Thus, prophets receive messages that are revealed from God, and they are commissioned to convey and spread that message among their people. Muhammad brought the message of the absolute unity of God, as well as guidance for mankind on living a moral and spiritual life. He was granted the title "*Kha ta man na biyeen*," which means "the Seal of the Prophets," sent with the final law from God in the form of the Quran.

The Prophet Muhammad holds a special place in the hearts of Muslims and is a source for much inspiration for his followers. What makes Muhammad unique is the amount of his life that has been recorded, which details the way he interacted with others—whether they were his followers or not. World religions scholar Sir Muhammad Zafrulla Khan wrote about the Prophet Muhammad: "His was a truly historical personality. He lived his life in the full light of day. Enough is known of his early life to enable one to form a fair idea of his qualities and character. After he received the Divine Call his every word, act, and gesture were observed, and a complete record of them has been preserved."[2] Muslims look to him as a perfect exemplar whom they can emulate. As Sir Zafrulla Khan noted,

> Muhammad was a human being—no more, no less—and therefore he could serve as an example for mankind. He possessed no supernatural powers, nor did he claim any. He was subject to the same conditions and limitations as his contemporaries. He suffered more than most and achieved outstanding success in his lifetime. His life had many facets and passed through many phases. Like other men, he was a son, a husband and a father. He had been a servant employed by a master, and was a citizen subject to the authorities of his town. God appointed him a teacher and a guide. He immediately became an object of scorn and derision, and soon of bitter persecution. He was a loving and watchful shepherd of his little flock. Through bitter persecution and hard fighting he gave proof of the highest courage, endurance and perseverance.[3]

Sir William Muir was a nineteenth-century orientalist, who held very strong Evangelical Christian views that fueled his passion for preaching the superiority of Christianity to Muslims. According to Dr. Avril Powell, lecturer and emeritus reader in the School of Oriental and African Studies at University of London, Muir tirelessly engaged in attempts "to persuade the *ulama* [Muslim scholars] that testimony to the truth of Christianity is to be found in the Quran."[4] With that motivation, he was very critical about Islam and the Prophet Muhammad, but even he had to concede about Muhammad's character. Muir spoke reverently about the character of the prophet, writing:

> A remarkable feature was the urbanity and consideration with which [Muhammad] treated even the most insignificant of his followers. Modesty and kindliness, patience, self-denial, and generosity, pervaded his conduct, and riveted the affections of all around him. He disliked to say *No*; if unable to answer a petitioner in the affirmative, he preferred silence. . . . He possessed the rare faculty of making each individual in a company think that *he* was the favoured guest. When he met any one rejoicing he would seize him eagerly and cordially by the hand. With the bereaved and afflicted he sympathised tenderly. Gentle and unbending towards little children, he would not disdain to accost a group of them at play with the salutation of peace. He shared his food, even in times of scarcity, with others; and was sedulously solicitous for the personal comfort of everyone about him. A kindly and benevolent disposition pervades all those illustrations of his character.[5]

Quran

"Quran" is the name given by God Himself to the book revealed to the Prophet Muhammad. The word means a book that is meant to be not only read but also conveyed to people. It is the most trusted source of religious knowledge for Muslims because it is believed to be the literal, direct words of God, revealed to Muhammad through the angel Gabriel. Muhammad would receive these revelations, which were not only memorized by Muhammad and several of his followers but also recorded in written form by those appointed by Muhammad for this purpose, over a span of twenty-three years. From the moment these revelations were received until the present, the Quran has never been altered or changed (i.e., the text is still in its original form), which makes it the most authentic source of knowledge about Islam.

The Quran states: "This is a perfect Book; there is no doubt in it; it is a guidance for the righteous."[6] If one accepts that this book came from

God—who Himself is perfect—it only stands to reason that His words would also be perfect. So it comes as no surprise for God to reveal within the text of the Quran that it is perfect. This is a sufficient response to those Muslims and non-Muslims who advocate for the flawed abrogation theory—they allege that some verses in the Quran abrogate (or cancel out) previously revealed verses from the Quran. This is a patently absurd idea to think that God (the Perfect and All-Knowing) would make one statement that He would then have to reverse later. This theory is typically cited by extremists to justify their violence by alleging that the peaceful verses in the Quran were abrogated by the verses about fighting. (See chapter 3, "Demystifying Jihad," for a more-detailed discussion about fighting.)

Sunnah and Hadith

After the Quran, the next highest source of knowledge within Islam is called the "Sunnah," which are written accounts of the actions of the Prophet Muhammad (what his disciples witnessed him do). Following that is the Hadith, which are written maxims of the prophet (what his disciples heard Muhammad say). The life of Muhammad is a living embodiment of the teachings of Islam and is, thus, replete with guidance for how to live one's life. Therefore, traditions recollecting the actions and words of the prophet are considered very valuable and are very similar to the Gospel accounts of the life and teachings of Jesus.

It should be noted that there are many reported stories about what Muhammad said and did, which were passed down orally for many years before finally being captured in written form. Therefore, a large number of Sunnah and Hadith are considered inaccurate or even fabricated, but since the word of God recorded in the Quran has never been altered, the Quran is considered the highest and more trustworthy source of knowledge about Islam. For this reason, any such Sunnah or Hadith that contradicts the teachings of the Quran are to be considered invalid.

THE ESSENCE OF ISLAM

Within Islam's twofold meaning of peace and submission lies the spirit of this religion, which provides instruction both on one's relationship with God and on one's relationship with fellow human beings. Its meaning of submission provides the guidance on the attitude one must have with God, whereas its meaning of peace establishes the attitude people must have not only within themselves but also with other people. Thus does Islam provide the recipe for one to establish a relationship with God based on submission to His will, as well as to establish inner peace and a loving, peaceful relationship with all mankind.

Muhammad emphasized this point when he characterized the essence of Islam with the following words to his disciples: "You will not enter Paradise until you believe, and you will not believe until you love one another, shall I tell you of something which if you do it, you will love each other? Spread peace among yourselves."[7] Within all teachings of Islam can be found this underlying spirit of establishing peace (within oneself, between one and God, and between people and even nations) as well as fostering love and concern for others.

FIVE PILLARS OF ISLAM

At the foundation of Islam is what is referred to as the "Five Pillars of Islam," which are the principle acts of worship required in order to practice Islam. Islam not only requires its followers to believe in certain matters but also requires them to put their faith into action by performing certain duties. According to Islam, the goal of every person is to establish love for the Creator as well as a love for His creation. If that love is merely in thought and not in action, however, that profession of love is vain lip service only. Islam teaches that the love one professes must have visible expression. Each pillar of Islam, thus, has a physical form but also contains a spirit behind that form. According to Islam, when the act is combined with an awareness of its significance, it fosters and breeds higher levels of spirituality and righteousness.

Declaration of Faith

The first and foremost pillar of Islam is the declaration of faith. The first step to implementing faith is to declare it. In Islam, this is done with the following declaration: "I bear witness that there is no god but Allah, and I bear witness that Muhammad is His Servant and Messenger." Declaring this belief is the only step necessary for one to become a Muslim, as it forms the foundation of Islamic belief.

This pillar also serves as a baseline for the remaining four pillars, as it establishes that everything we do is for God. Everything comes together by putting all of our trust in the One God and establishing an undying conviction that love for, and from, Him is all we need.

With so many similarities between the two faiths, this pillar presents a point of distinction between Islam and mainstream Christianity. Declaring that Muhammad is the Servant and Messenger of Allah is not meant to be an assertion of superiority of Muhammad. Rather, God requires this to be a part of our declaration of faith in order to constantly remind us that Muhammad was only a human. Repeatedly declaring that someone is a servant of God prevents us from making what Islam declares is the grave mistake made by many Christians who deified the Prophet Jesus. Always declaring that Muhammad—no matter how noble, blessed, and special he may be—is but a servant of God prevents any possibility of making a deity of a man.

Thus, God established this declaration and reminded all Muslims that Muhammad is a servant of the one and only God. This one God is the One with Whom we are to establish a personal, loving relationship by communicating with Him and following His commandments.

Salaat (Daily Prayer)

The second pillar of Islam is Salaat, which is the five daily prayers performed by Muslims around the world. It is considered the most important means by which to communicate with God and establishes a direct and personal relationship between every person and God, with no intermediary. A personal relationship cannot be established without constant communication. It is for this reason that Muslims are instructed to pause from their daily routines at the following five times every day and to communicate with their Lord:

1. Fajr prayers—morning, before sunrise;
2. Zuhr prayers—early afternoon;
3. Asr prayers—late afternoon;
4. Maghrib prayers—just after sunset; and
5. Isha prayers—later in evening, before going to sleep.

The Quran states that regular prayer protects against evil and indecency. There is a formulaic aspect of Salaat, with specific postures and prayers—both of praise of God and of seeking His guidance and forgiveness. There is no question that such consistent worship establishes love with one's Creator. But this also cultivates love for His creation not only because Muslims are encouraged to pray for others but also because they are advised to pray together in congregation. Standing, bowing, and prostrating toward God, shoulder to shoulder with others, cultivates a feeling of community and togetherness. It removes rancor and replaces it with feelings of unity, which serves to foster more care and consideration for other people, irrespective of whether or not they are related.

Fasting

The third act of worship meant to foster love for God and a love for His creation is fasting, especially during the month of Ramadan, which is one full month within the Islamic year calendar when fasting is prescribed for the entire month for all healthy adults who are neither sick nor traveling. During the fast, one abstains from all food, drink, and conjugal relations from dawn to sunset. The Quran states that the ultimate objective of fasting is to become righteous and, thus, gain nearness to God.

This is one of the ultimate displays of love for one's Creator, since it is only one's love for God that leads one to listen to His commandment to refrain from all food and drink all day. Muslims do it only because God tells them to, and they have a strong desire to obey His commands and earn His pleasure and love. The Prophet Muhammad advised that all other virtues have their own reward, but God Himself (and His nearness) is the reward for fasting.

This is not the only value of fasting, however. The core of fasting is empathy for others. During the fast, as one regularly feels the discomforts of hunger and thirst, one gains a glimpse into what it is like for those who have no choice but to be hungry and thirsty every single day. Such people exist not just across the world but also across our own country, and fasting helps us feel their pain, suffering, loneliness, poverty, and hunger. This is meant to foster more care and love for those who are often neglected and forgotten, thereby cultivating love for God's creation. This is why Muslims are advised to be more charitable—with their time, wealth, and general attitude—while fasting during the month of Ramadan. One's love for God's creation should compel them to make whatever effort necessary to provide relief and comfort to others. Islam teaches that to love others, one must be willing to serve humankind.

Zakaat (Almsgiving)

The fourth pillar of Islam is *zakaat*, which is charity or almsgiving. Charity in general is instructed almost as many times as prayer in the Quran and is the cornerstone of a truly Islamic society. The word "zakaat" itself means "that which purifies" because Islam teaches that the act of giving money to the less fortunate segments of society in the name of God purifies one's heart from selfishness and greed. It is an expression of sacrifice of worldly possessions in preference to obtaining God's love and pleasure, by spending one's wealth to help those who need it most.

Almsgiving is a commandment of God found throughout the Quran. As with the other pillars of Islam, one of the purposes of this form of worship is to foster love for our Creator by sacrificing that which mankind covets the most (wealth) simply because God tells us to do so. But it also fosters love for His creation by not only being aware of the suffering and inconvenience of others but also donating from our own wealth to remove that suffering from their lives and, thus, ensuring the well-being of the greater community. This is considered a form of worship of God because it is a sacrifice in accordance with God's instructions and is a benefit to society.

The recommendation given to Muslims is to donate 2.5 percent of their wealth toward relieving poverty and distress and helping those in debt. The wisdom of taking from one's wealth (as opposed to income) is that it doesn't impose difficulties on those who earn such little income that they can barely cover their own expenses. Instead, the 2.5 percent applies to wealth that one has accumulated that is above and beyond what they need. In Muslim-majority countries, there are systems in place that allow Muslims to easily contribute this 2.5 percent. Here in the West, Muslims typically work with their local mosque on the collection and usage of these funds.

This is diametrically opposed to the philosophy and financial system here in the Western societies. The Western economic system breeds selfishness and greed, as it rewards those who hoard money for themselves. The system of interest creates a scenario of money making money by itself when it sits in a savings account. The more money people accumulate for themselves, the more they are rewarded by that interest. This not only discourages money from being in constant circulation in society but also continually puts more money into the hands of the rich. Islam fundamentally disagrees with such a financial system of rewarding the greedy. Instead, it teaches that wealth must remain in constant circulation among all sections of the community and should not become the monopoly of the rich.

Hajj (Pilgrimage to Mecca)

Finally, the fifth and final principle act of worship in Islam is Hajj, which is the pilgrimage to Mecca that all Muslims are told to make some time in their life, when their medical, economic, and political conditions allow them to go. The significance of the practice and tradition of the pilgrimage revolves around the story of the Prophet Abraham and his family. The focal point of the pilgrimage is the Kaaba, a very large cube-shaped structure that is understood to be the first-ever house of worship, originally built by the Prophet Adam and then rebuilt by Abraham and his firstborn son, Ishmael, some four thousand years ago.

The pilgrimage is one of the greatest expressions of one's love for one's Creator. It requires leaving one's entire life behind and traveling great distances to Mecca, due to the single fact that God requires it of us. Muslims go through this worldly inconvenience in the pursuit of God's love. The pilgrimage was prescribed by God as a means for people not only to renew their faith by going back to where God spoke to man but also to cultivate a spirit of sacrifice in the quest for nearness to God.

Furthermore, the pilgrimage was prescribed in order to nurture within us a love for His creation by emphasizing brotherhood and equality of all human beings. Each Muslim sheds symbols of his or her culture, social status, wealth, and education and puts himself or herself on the same level as all fellow Muslims in being equal in the sight of God. It can have a transformative effect on people, who may come to the pilgrimage for the sake of strengthening their bond with God but end up also strengthening their bond with fellow humans.

One of the greatest examples of this phenomenon is that of Malcolm X. Malcolm is understandably known for his role, as a minister and national spokesperson for the Nation of Islam, in advancing the belief that the white man is the devil. It is incredibly unfortunate, however, that the world forgets about the man he became before his life came to an abrupt end. Malcolm completely changed his outlook, and it was due to his pilgrimage to Mecca.

After separating from the Nation of Islam in 1964, Malcolm went in search of an understanding of the true religion of Islam. This prompted him to take the pilgrimage to Mecca in April of that year, and the brotherhood and equality he witnessed changed his entire view of not only Islam but also races other than his own. He wrote a letter home from Mecca, in which he stated:

> Never have I witnessed such sincere hospitality and the overwhelming spirit of true brotherhood as is practiced by people of all colors and races here in this Ancient Holy Land, the home of Abraham, Muhammad, and all the other prophets of the Holy Scriptures. For the past week, I have been utterly speechless and spellbound by the graciousness I see displayed all around me by people of all colors. . . . There were tens of

thousands of pilgrims, from all over the world. They were of all colors, from blue-eyed blonds to black-skinned Africans. But we were all participating in the same ritual, displaying a spirit of unity and brotherhood that my experiences in America had led me to believe never could exist between the white and the non-white. America needs to understand Islam, because this is the one religion that erases from its society the race problem. . . . You may be shocked by these words coming from me. But on this pilgrimage, what I have seen, and experienced, has forced me to re-arrange much of my thought-patterns previously held, and to toss aside some of my previous conclusions. . . . During the past eleven days here in the Muslim world, I have eaten from the same plate, drunk from the same glass, and slept in the same bed (or on the same rug)— while praying to the same God—with fellow Muslims, whose eyes were the bluest of blue, whose hair was the blondest of blond, and whose skin was the whitest of white. And in the words and in the actions and in the deeds of the "white" Muslims, I felt the same sincerity that I felt among the black African Muslims of Nigeria, Sudan, and Ghana. We were truly all the same (brothers).[8]

This is the transformative effect that the Hajj can have on people. Malcolm X left for this pilgrimage with a love for his Creator and came back with a love for His creation.

ARTICLES OF FAITH

In addition to these foundational acts of worship in Islam, there are the principles and beliefs of faith that Muhammad brought, which are often referred to as the "articles of faith." These are the core beliefs in Islam that must be professed by anyone desiring to be a Muslim and, as such, are universally accepted by members of every sect of Islam. Aside from the first article of faith, which is the most important, the remaining are presented in no particular order.

Unity of God

The first of these articles of faith is the absolute belief in the unity of God (i.e., the belief that there is only one God, with no partner). With Islam's definition of submitting to the will of the One God, this article of faith is the foundation of Islam, with all other beliefs springing from it. This doctrine of Islam declares that the unity of God is absolute, with no room for adding any other entities or beings to the Godhead. It is for this reason that the very first pillar of Islam is the declaration of this belief in the absolute oneness of God. Muhammad taught that God has neither a mother, father, spouse, nor child. The Holy Quran makes this absolutely clear when it instructs us to not only believe, but also constantly remind others, that "He is Allah, the One! Allah, the Independent and Besought of all. He begets not, nor is He begotten; And there is none like unto Him."[9]

Islam very clearly and directly disagrees with the concept of Trinity and with the claim that God ever had a son or partner. This is why Muslims are forbidden to even consider Muhammad to be anything more than a man. Muslims do not pray to Muhammad nor consider him a deity or partner of God. For God to have a son or partner implies that God requires the assistance of another being in order to carry out His work, which undermines His glory and magnificence. As the one and only Supreme Being, He is called the "All Knowing" and "All Powerful" in the Quran.

Muslims believe that God is the sole Creator of the universe, including all life forms in this world, and Islam presents Allah as not only a Perfect Being but also a living God who manifests Himself to His creation every day. He communicates with mankind today just as He did before and hears and answers prayers, just as He did before. God says in the Quran: "And when my servants ask thee about Me, say, 'I am near. I answer the prayer of the supplicant when he prays to Me. So they should hearken to Me and believe in Me, that they may follow the right way.'"[10]

Whereas some other faith traditions may teach that people should seek help from a holy person to intercede or pray on their behalf, Islam fundamentally disagrees with this concept because it implies that personal avenues of communication with God are closed. Islam emphasizes the principle that everyone can and should establish a personal relationship with God, without the need of an intermediary.

Belief in Angels

The second article of faith is the requirement for Muslims to believe in angels, but Islam presents a different concept of angels from what may be understood by others. Islam does not subscribe to the fantasy tales of angels being like fairies, flying with wings. Such depictions of angels flying with wings are likely a result of taking literal interpretations to metaphorical language in religious texts about angels. The Quran also refers to angels' having wings but also uses wings in relation to a child's attitude toward elderly parents by instructing to "lower to them the wing of humility out of tenderness."[11] Thus, use of the word "wing" simply refers to a particular attribute—in this case, the attribute of humility and tenderness. The word "wing" also refers to one's power. For example, Arabs say that one "had his wings clipped" as an expression to mean that one "lacks power, ability, or strength." In this context, Muslims understand angels as having power and ability granted to them by God and possessing the attributes necessary for carrying out their assigned task(s).

Angels are spiritual beings who carry out various duties assigned to them by God. Their primary duty is to transmit messages from God to humans, which explains why, in Hebrew, angels are called מלאך (*malach*), which translates to "messenger." Even the English word "angel" is derived from the Greek word αγγελος (*angelos*), which also translates to "messenger." Accordingly, angels are also referred to as "messengers" in the Quran.

In order to make it easier to envision angels, religious books often describe them as appearing in human form. But some people, even within Islam, have misunderstood this to mean that angels have a human shape or form. According to Islam, all material and spiritual matters of the universe are governed by spiritual powers known as "angels." They are a creation of God given specific tasks, which they carry out with no free will—unlike humans, who have free will to choose whether or not they follow God's commandments.

Although some specific angels—such as Gabriel, Michael, and Israel— are mentioned in religious texts, the teachings of Islam help one understand that there are countless angels in existence. The reference to specific angels by name indicates they are the respective leaders of a particular function who govern the work of a multitude of angels. Muslims do not worship angels; rather, Muslims acknowledge their existence and that they are created by God to govern every minute aspect of the material world, as well as individual matters of spirituality.

Belief in Books of God

The third article of faith is the requirement for Muslims to believe not just in the Holy Quran as a revealed book but also in all such divine revelations granted to other prophets. Thus, one cannot call oneself a Muslim if one does not believe in the divine origin of other books, and the Quran specifically mentions the *suhuf* (Scrolls) of Abraham, the *taurat* (Torah) of Moses, the *zabur* (Psalms) of David, and the *injeel* (Gospel) of Jesus. This remarkable tenet of faith is unique to Islam and builds a foundation for interreligious harmony and respect, which is necessary in order to unite all of mankind.

As part of the belief in the evolution of religion, Muslims believe that God gave these sacred scriptures to different prophets over time, but one of the reasons the Quran was necessary is because all of these previous scriptures have been at least altered—and, thus, have lost their original purity—if not lost altogether. This is why, for the sake of guiding mankind, all previous scriptures culminated in the Quran—the final book revealed to the Prophet Muhammad.

With the exception of the Quran, none of the earlier scriptures mentioned above were recorded during the lifetime of the prophet for whom it was sent, which certainly affects the validity and absolute authenticity of those texts. Some scriptures have been lost altogether, including the Scrolls of Abraham. The injeel (Gospel) was never recorded during the lifetime of Jesus, and attempts were made after his life to capture his teachings in written form. After several attempts by various writers to record the teachings of Jesus, the early church selected the following four Gospels to represent the account of the life of Jesus, which are not the injeel mentioned in the Quran:

- Gospel according to Matthew,
- Gospel according to Luke,
- Gospel according to Mark, and
- Gospel according to John.

Muslims will refer to other scriptures for historical information and as a source of supplementary knowledge that can provide more wisdom to mankind. If, however, any contradiction is found between the scriptures, then that indicates evidence of alteration to the text. After all, if these scriptures came from, or were inspired by, the same perfect Source of Light (God), certainly He would not contradict Himself.

Belief in Prophets of God

The fourth article of faith is the requirement for Muslims to believe not just in Muhammad as a divinely sent messenger of God but in all previous prophets as well. This is a logical conclusion to the belief in all books, since both articles of faith embody the same philosophy that is unique to Islam, where all of God's messengers must be accepted and revered as prophets of God. The Holy Quran is clear that God has sent prophets to all people over the course of history: "And We did raise among every people a Messenger with the teaching, 'Worship Allah and shun the Evil One.'"[12]

God reiterates this point in the Quran when speaking to Muhammad about his own prophethood and stating that by this time, all people have been sent a prophet and no people have been left without a messenger: "Verily, We have sent thee with the Truth, as a bearer of glad tidings and as a Warner; and there is no people to whom a Warner has not been sent."[13]

Thus, in addition to the belief in prophets mentioned in the Quran and Bible, Muslims accept and revere the prophets of other religions, such as Moses, Jesus, Zoroaster, Confucius, Krishna, Ram Chandar, Buddha, Socrates, and so on. No people have been left without divine guidance. No other divine book of any religion bears testimony regarding the truth of the founders of other religions. Islam stands apart by firmly declaring that the institution of prophethood is universal, and Islam requires of its followers to equally believe in all other prophets as they believe in Muhammad.

Muslims, therefore, admire and respect all prophets of God, beginning with the Prophet Adam and ending with the Prophet Muhammad. Adam—popularly believed to be the first man created by God—was, in fact, not the first man created but, rather, the first man to whom God spoke. He was, thus, the first prophet sent by God in mankind's history. So Islam disagrees not only with the account of Adam as the first human on earth but also with the claim that Adam and Eve knowingly committed an unforgivable sin for which they were removed from heaven's lush garden. Instead, Adam and Eve are accepted in Islam as humans living here on earth, and the Quran states that Adam inadvertently made a mistake, which was not deliberate: "And verily, We had made a covenant with Adam beforehand, but he forgot, and We found in him no resolve to disobey Us."[14]

Like all other prophets before him, Muhammad is considered a prophet of God. The distinction given to Muhammad, however, is that he was sent with the final law from God—not just for one people or one era; rather, for all people and for all time to come. Muhammad came as the culmination of prophethood and has, thus, been granted the title the "Seal of Prophets." This is not only because he came encompassing all previous laws into the final law in the Quran, but also because he came bearing testimony to the truth of all previous prophets. The Prophet Muhammad was not sent to compete with, or devalue, his predecessors. Rather, he was sent to honor all those previous prophets and connect their teachings together.

Belief in the Day of Judgment

The fifth article of faith is the firm belief in the Day of Judgment—the day in which all souls will meet their Creator and answer for their deeds in this world. This day is referred to by many different names in the Quran, such as the "Day of Judgment," "Last Day," "Day of Distinction," "Day of Resurrection," "Day of Gathering," "Day of the Meeting," as well as others. The belief in the Day of Judgment serves to inculcate two lessons for all Muslims.

First, this belief serves as the reminder that every soul will be raised after death and held accountable for his or her life in the current world. God says in the Quran: "Allah burdens not any soul beyond its capacity. It shall have the reward it earns, and it shall get the punishment it incurs."[15] In Islam, there is no simple blueprint for attaining salvation by doing or believing in one thing. Rather, Islam teaches that the determination of whether one earns salvation/heaven/paradise is made based on how one lived one's life in this world. Good deeds are recognized by God and will be rewarded abundantly, whereas evil deeds will be punished when done deliberately and consciously. The lesson is to avoid sin and perform good deeds.

Second, this belief in the Day of Judgment serves as a lesson to the true nature of our existence, which is not simply confined to this world. God says in the Quran: "How can you disbelieve in Allah? You were without life and He gave you life, and then will He cause you to die, then restore you to life, and then to Him shall you be made to return."[16] Therefore, according to Islam, death is not an end to one's life; it is simply the end to our earthly existence, since God will allow our souls to continue on to another life in a spiritual world.

In the next world, based on how we have been judged, we will be either in heaven or in hell, but the concept of heaven and hell is different in Islam from what may be generally understood. First, heaven and hell are not understood to be physical locations (i.e., heaven is not in the clouds, nor is hell a pit of fire in the center of the earth). Like the concept of angels, the afterlife has been sorely misunderstood due to the symbolic and metaphoric nature of the language used to describe heaven and hell.

Heaven is often misunderstood—even by some Muslims—to be, literally, an infinitely large garden with beautiful rolling hills and trees, underneath which rivers flow. They believe the garden bears endless fruits and drink for those in this land of bliss. People in this garden do not need to work or labor. Rather, they live a life of total indolence. This is a gross misunderstanding.

In reality, all such material descriptions of heaven are metaphorical depictions of a spiritual existence that will not have any carnal aspect. Rather than considering heaven or hell to be physical abodes, Islam describes heaven and hell to be a state of mind of one's soul in the afterlife. Those judged to be granted "heaven" will gain a peace of mind knowing that their Lord is well pleased with them. Those judged to be sent to "hell" will live in a painful and torturous state of mind, due to the countless opportunities that they had forsaken to obey God and do good in this world. In essence, each individual creates one's own heaven or hell, which will be unique to him or her.

Islam does not subscribe to the self-righteous belief that only followers of this religion can be granted heaven. Rather, God states very clearly in the Quran: "Surely, those who believe and the Jews and the Christians and the Sabians—whichever party from among these truly believes in Allah and the Last Day and does good deeds, shall have their reward with their Lord, and no fear shall come upon them, nor shall they grieve."[17] Therefore, Muslims are taught they will not have a monopoly over paradise. People of other religions can still be rewarded with heaven. With the diversity of thought and interpretation within the Muslim world, there certainly are other interpretations that exist about allegorical issues such as heaven and hell, but the above teachings are widely accepted by many Muslims around the world and are grounded in the teachings of the Quran. Muslims who believe non-Muslims cannot go to heaven must study Islam more.

Whereas heaven will be an eternal existence, Islam is clear that hell is not an eternal damnation as described by some faith traditions. It is a painful, yet transient, phase a troubled or sinful soul must endure in order to reach its ultimate destiny in heaven. In this state of hell, the soul is cleansed of its sinful nature and gradually progresses to a higher level of spirituality. It is where souls go to be reformed but from where every such soul will eventually exit. Explaining this, Muhammad once said that a time will come in Hell when not a single person will be left in it, and its doors and windows will rattle to the blowing wind.

Belief in God's Decree

Some Muslims include the belief in Divine Decree as a sixth article of faith. This is the belief that humans are given free will to choose everything they do and say but that God's order and law controls the eventual outcome of all such actions. Each person chooses the course to follow but God creates the boundaries of possible paths. Islam disagrees with the view held by some that God has predetermined everything large and small and that each person has no control over his or her own life.

Islam advances the understanding that each soul has not only the ability and freedom but also the obligation to choose between good and bad or between right and wrong. People do not, however, have control over the consequences of their actions. Humans have control over only a finite area of life, and God controls the rest.

Each of the five fundamental acts of worship and basic articles of faith presented by Islam is deeply rooted in the mission to enable people to establish love with God, as well as a love for His creation. This is a presentation of how Muslims are instructed to live their lives, in accordance with the teachings of Islam, which provides the framework with which Islam can be understood, from both a historic perspective and a theological perspective. With this foundation presented, further topics about Islam will be explored in the remainder of this book that draw from this introduction to the faith of Islam.

2

DEMYSTIFYING THE ORIGINS
OF ISLAM

Some people claim that Islam is a new religion that was founded in Arabia by Muhammad. The teachings of Islam and claims of Muhammad, however, do not agree with this view. An important claim made by Islam is that it is not a new religion nor does it deviate from the teachings of Abraham, considered the father of monotheistic religions. Rather, Islam is a natural and expected continuation of the religious teachings brought forth by prophets that came before Muhammad. So, not only does Islam call people toward the worship of the same One God of Abraham, Moses, Jesus, and all other prophets, but it also claims to be an extension of the messages brought by these prophets of the past. Thus, to study the origins of Islam, one needs to go back further than the life of the Prophet Muhammad.

EVOLUTION OF RELIGION

As mentioned in chapter 1, Islam does not consider itself a new religion. It is, in essence, the same message and guidance revealed by the same One God to all prophets before Muhammad. Thus, when it is stated that Muhammad is the founder of the religion of Islam, it is only true in the sense that he was the messenger through whom this final message was sent to humankind. Islamic teachings indicate that God sent prophets to all people in order to guide them toward Himself and provide instructions on how to live a righteous life. This is why a fundamental tenet of faith for Muslims requires them to believe and accept all of these prophets. The Quran repeatedly mentions a selection of these prophets for this very purpose. For instance, it states: "Say, 'We believe in Allah and in that which has been revealed to us, and that which was revealed to Abraham and Ishmael and

Isaac and Jacob and the tribes, and in that which was given to Moses and Jesus and other Prophets from their Lord. We make no distinction between any of them and to Him we submit.'"[1]

Islam's followers are, thus, required to believe in all of God's prophets, regardless of the country, race, or community to which they came. This is a point of significance, as it underlies the concept of the evolution of religion that has occurred throughout time. According to Islamic teachings, divinely commissioned messengers were sent to different parts of this world at various times throughout history in order to raise God consciousness among their people and deliver God's instructions on living moral and spiritual lives. God did not send these messengers with competing or contradictory messages. They were sent both to spread God's guidance throughout the world and to remind a people who have lost sight of the guidance already brought to them.

Over time, some of these prophets brought new laws from God in order to progressively extend religious teachings for mankind, in step with general human progress. So, as humans achieved greater ability to understand God's instructions, God sent additional guidance to build upon what had already been revealed.

Consider the way we are taught math in school. Why is it that children are not taught advanced vector calculus in first grade? The reason is that they do not yet have a foundational understanding of mathematical principles with which to understand advanced vector calculus. This is why children begin with basic arithmetic such as addition and subtraction, and they build on that understanding to then learn multiplication and division. With this foundation, they then progressively learn basic algebra, then geometry, then advanced algebra, then trigonometry, and then calculus. After understanding these principles over years of study, students can then begin to understand advanced concepts such as differential equations, multivariable calculus, and vector calculus.

This is precisely how God implemented our study of His religious teachings. From the moment God began to speak with mankind through the Prophet Adam, Islam teaches that God progressively revealed more lessons and wisdom over time. As humans physically and intellectually evolved—achieving an increased capacity to understand—God progressively revealed additional philosophies and principles for their spiritual evolution. Certainly, this does not mean that earlier religions were primitive or simpler. After all, the Vedas of the Hindu faith is one of the oldest known set of religious laws and is very comprehensive and multifaceted. The applicability of the teachings, however, needed to be reevaluated and connected with the various teachings around the world in order to examine the full breadth of God's teachings.

There is only one religion that was gradually rolled out over time through the advent of various prophets, and Muhammad simply came with the final law, building upon—and building connections between—the messages of Abraham, Moses, Jesus, and other previous prophets. The advent of Muhammad completed the evolution of religion by bringing the final chapter in God's progressively revealed law.

CONNECTION WITH ABRAHAM

Thus, the origins of Islam are the same as the origins of other religions practiced before its advent. All of the Semitic faith traditions trace their origins back to the Prophet Abraham, as their prophets were descendants of his sons, Ishmael and Isaac. Ishmael, his firstborn, had twelve sons of his own, who are called the "twelve princes" in the Bible.[2] Isaac, Abraham's second son, had two twin sons—Esau and Jacob. Jacob, in turn, also was given twelve sons, who have become known as the twelve tribes of Israel. From Jacob's lineage we discover other prophets, most notably the prophets Moses and Jesus.

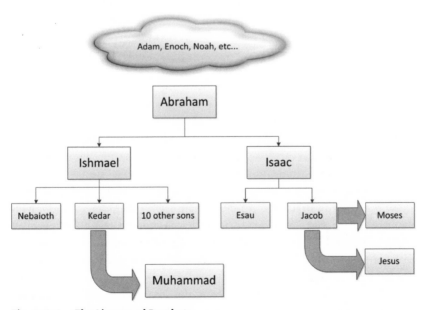

Figure 2.1.   The Lineage of Prophets

Ishmael's firstborn (first of the twelve princes) was named "Nebaioth" (also spelled "Nebajoth"), and his second son was named "Kedar." Those who trace Kedar's lineage discover that among his direct descendants is Muhammad, the Prophet of Islam. Muslims are descendants of Abraham's firstborn son, Ishmael, just as Jews and Christians are descendants of Abraham's second son, Isaac. For this reason, some Muslims, Jews, and Christians refer to one another as cousins.

If we accept that God's one religion slowly evolved over time through these many prophets, surely there should be evidence from previous prophets of future prophets to come who would take God's message further. From this knowledge that the Semitic faiths descend from these two brothers, one can understand the prophecies from previous prophets about the coming of the Prophet Muhammad. This further advances the concept of an evolution of religion, by presenting evidence from previous prophets about the coming of Muhammad as a pivotal future messenger of God.

PROPHECIES IN THE HEBREW BIBLE

In the Old Testament, God speaks to the Prophet Moses and says while referring to Israelites: "I will raise them up a Prophet from among their brethren, like unto thee, and will put my words in his mouth; and he shall speak unto them all that I shall command him."[3] There are three main points of significance with regard to this prophecy.

First, God tells Moses that He will bring a prophet to this world who will be raised among the brethren of the Israelites. If God meant that the prophet would be an Israelite himself, would it not have been sufficient for God to simply state that He will raise up a prophet "from among them?" God, instead, stated that this prophet would be raised "from among their brethren," meaning among the brethren of the Israelites, and as discussed above, the brethren of the descendants of Isaac are the descendants of Ishmael.

This prophecy could not be speaking about Jesus; not only because Jesus never claimed to be the prophet prophesized in this verse but also because Jesus was an Israelite and a descendent from the lineage of Isaac. Muhammad, as discussed earlier, was indeed a descendent of Ishmael through his second son, Kedar. Thus, Muhammad's advent as a prophet fulfilled the first part of this prophecy for the coming of a great prophet from among the brethren of the Israelites.

The second point of significance in this prophecy is that God says He will bring a prophet to this world who is like Moses. There is deep wisdom in this statement. Would it not have been enough for God to simply say that He will raise up a prophet? Stating that this prophet will be "like unto" Moses indicates that a certain type of a prophet will be raised.

There are two types of prophets: those that come to bring a new religious law or revelation and those who come to spread or revive the existing law among their people. For example, Adam, Noah, Abraham, Moses, and Muhammad were law-bearing prophets; they were not only divinely sent messengers but also came with new religious law, new commandments. Other prophets—such as Isaac, Ishmael, David, Job, Jesus, Krishna, Socrates—were non-law-bearing prophets; rather than coming with new commandments or laws, they spread existing laws and/or revived those laws in various places around the world. Some people—including Muslims—may be surprised to see Socrates and Krishna in this list of prophets. Readers are invited to read *Revelation, Rationality, Knowledge and Truth* by Mirza Tahir Ahmad for further exploration of Socrates and Krishna.

So when God tells Moses that He will raise up a prophet like him, this refers to the coming of a law-bearing prophet, just like Moses. The reason this prophecy cannot be referring to Jesus is due to the simple fact that Jesus Christ was not a law-bearing prophet. Jesus clearly stated that he did not come to change the Law of Moses; rather, he came to fulfill and revive the Law of Moses. He is quoted in the Bible as saying: "Think not that I am come to destroy the law, or the prophets: I am not come to destroy, but to fulfill. For verily I say unto you, Till heaven and earth pass, one jot or one tittle shall in no wise pass from the law, till all be fulfilled."[4] He was clear that—far from making even the slightest change to the law—he came to fulfill the prophecies made about him. As the Messiah, since Jesus came to gather the lost and bring the teachings of Moses to them, he could not be considered to be a law-bearing prophet like Moses.

A prophet with a new law must present a comprehensive set of beliefs that incorporate basic principles and detailed tenets. Muhammad did bring a new law containing detailed teachings, which is preserved in the Quran. This contains the direct word from God, revealed through the angel Gabriel. And this Quran has expressly stated that Muhammad is that messenger God spoke of to Moses when it states: "Verily, We have sent to you a Messenger, who is a witness over you, even as We sent a Messenger to Pharaoh."[5] This is mentioned again later in the Quran when God instructs Muhammad to tell the people that "a witness from among the Children of Israel bears witness to the advent of one like him,"[6] thereby further establishing the claim that Muhammad indeed is the law-bearing prophet about whom God had spoken to Moses.

The third and final point of significance of this prophecy given to Moses about the coming of a great prophet is that God says He will put His words into this prophet's mouth, who will, thus, speak all that God commands him. This cannot refer to Jesus because the Gospels of the New Testament do not contain the words of God that were put into Jesus' mouth. Rather, the Gospels are stories and accounts of the life of Jesus and his disciples as recorded some decades after the events of the crucifixion.

Muhammad, on the other hand, made the claim to only speak that which is revealed to him from God. The Quran was the direct word received from God, and the claim is recorded in the Quran that it is the word of God. Since the Quran was his law that he spoke with, Muhammad thus only spoke the words of God that were revealed to him. This is a direct fulfillment of the great prophet foretold by God to Moses.

Further evidence about the coming of the Prophet Muhammad exists in the Hebrew Bible's Song of Solomon (Song of Songs)—one of the smallest books in the Bible—where Muhammad is mentioned by name. The interpretation and significance of this book has been widely lost in modern day, as many consider it to be a love poem between a man and a woman. But Rabbi Shlomo Yitzhaki (commonly referred to as "Rashi")— an eleventh century commentator who not only authored a thorough commentary on the Hebrew Bible and Talmud but has also been called "the most influential Jewish exegete of all time"[7]—has correctly asserted that the narrator of this poem is God, speaking to the people of Israel. Chapter 5, verse 16 reads as follows: "His mouth is most sweet: yea, he is Muhammad. This is my beloved, and this is my friend, O daughters of Jerusalem."

If this does not look familiar, that is because the word "Muhammad" was translated in printed Bibles. The word "Muhammad" is not only an Arabic word but also a Hebrew word and means one who is most praised and entirely splendid, respectively. The translation one will find in Bibles reads as follows: "His mouth is most sweet: yea, he is altogether lovely. This is my beloved, and this is my friend, O daughters of Jerusalem."[8]

The Hebrew word used in this verse is מחמדים (pronounced "Mahammad-im"). The suffix "im," also used in the Hebrew word "Elohim" to refer to God, in this word expresses respect and greatness. Without "im" the name becomes "Mahammad" which was translated as "altogether lovely" in most versions of the Bible. Thus, when using the word "Muhammad" in either Arabic or Hebrew, it is understood to be something that is praiseworthy and lovely. Translators knew not that this spoke of an actual name and, thus, translated it to the equivalent found in various languages. Yet, if one were to listen to the original Hebrew recited, one would clearly hear Muhammad's name mentioned in this verse.

In this song, God repeatedly refers to the subject as "My beloved," which is one of the names that Muhammad was known by. In addition to being called Muhammad, during his life he was known by other names or titles, such as "Sadiq" and "al-Ameen," meaning "one who is most truthful." One of the other titles he was given was "Habibullah," meaning "the beloved of God." Thus, the Song of Solomon is not merely an expression of love between two lovers. Rather, there is divine wisdom to be found when it is understood to be the words of God.

PROPHECIES IN THE NEW TESTAMENT

As would be expected, evidence can also be found in the New Testament for the coming of a later prophet, who is believed to be none other than the Prophet Muhammad.

Coming of the Comforter

The book of John captures prophecies made by Jesus Christ when he says to his followers: "If ye love me, keep my commandments. And I will pray the Father, and he shall give you another Comforter, that he may abide with you for ever."[9] A couple of chapters later, it is recorded that Jesus gave more detail around the circumstances surrounding the coming of this Comforter:

> Nevertheless I tell you the truth; It is expedient for you that I go away: for if I go not away, the Comforter will not come unto you; but if I depart, I will send him unto you. And when he is come, he will reprove the world of sin, and of righteousness, and of judgment. . . . I have yet many things to say unto you, but ye cannot bear them now. . . . Howbeit when he, the Spirit of truth, is come, he will guide you into all truth: for he shall not speak of himself; but whatsoever he shall hear, that shall he speak: and he will shew you things to come.[10]

Jesus speaks of someone to come after him, whom he refers to as "the Comforter" and "the Spirit of truth," who will not be sent until after Jesus is gone. Jesus is very clear that he must go away first in order for this Comforter to be sent later. This foretells of the coming of a great prophet who will comfort and provide guidance to mankind while bringing a message that Jesus says his people are not yet ready to hear.

These words by Jesus, a noble and divinely sent messenger, refer to the coming of the Prophet Muhammad, who, history records, was also known by the title of "Rehmatal Lil Aalameen" (translated as "a mercy for all peoples"), a title granted by God in the Quran.[11] This is because the message he was sent to deliver was meant to provide mercy, comfort, and guidance to the world. As Jesus foretold, Muhammad admonished people away from sin and toward righteousness. He came not only to guide mankind to the truth but also, by bringing and teaching the Quran, to fulfill Jesus' prophecy to not speak on his own authority but, rather, to speak that which he hears. Muhammad spoke only what he heard from God in the form of revelations that are preserved in the Quran. On this point, the Quran says about Muhammad: "Nor does he speak out of his own desire. It is nothing but pure revelation, revealed by God."[12]

Some have argued that this "Comforter" or "Spirit of truth" is none other than the Holy Spirit, but there are clear reasons that this cannot be the case. First, by saying, "It is expedient for you that I go away: for if I go not away, the Comforter will not come unto you," Jesus makes it clear that he must leave first in order for this Comforter to arrive. The Holy Spirit, however, is known to have already been present during the lifetime of Jesus.

The New Testament says that John the Baptist was filled with the Holy Spirit even before he was born. The Gospel of Luke states: "But the angel said unto him, Fear not, Zachari'ah: for thy prayer is heard; and thy wife Elisabeth shall bear thee a son, and thou shalt call his name John. And thou shalt have joy and gladness; and many shall rejoice at his birth. For he shall be great in the sight of the Lord, and shall drink neither wine nor strong drink; and he shall be filled with the Holy Ghost, even from his mother's womb."[13] This establishes the presence of the Holy Spirit even before the birth of John.

The New Testament also speaks of the Holy Spirit being with Jesus during his lifetime. It states that Jesus received the Holy Spirit in the form of a dove on the day he came to John to be baptized: "And Jesus, when he was baptized, went up straightway out of the water: and, lo, the heavens were opened unto him, and he saw the Spirit of God descending like a dove, and lighting upon him."[14] It is also stated that the Holy Spirit guided him into the wilderness: "Then was Jesus led up of the Spirit into the wilderness to be tempted of the devil."[15]

According to the New Testament, the Holy Spirit was even present before the birth of Jesus, as it is recorded in the story of when the angel came to tell his mother, Mary, that she will give birth to a special son: "And the angel answered and said unto her, The Holy Ghost shall come upon thee, and the power of the Highest shall overshadow thee: therefore also that holy thing which shall be born of thee shall be called the Son of God."[16]

It becomes evident that the Holy Spirit was already present before and during the life of Jesus. So his prophecy about the coming of a future Comforter can in no way refer to the Holy Spirit. The departure of Jesus is absolutely necessary for the coming of this Comforter. Moreover, by using the words "another Comforter," Jesus establishes that just as he has been a Comforter, God will send "another Comforter." This clarifies that the coming Comforter, like Jesus, will be mortal; not a spiritual being. Furthermore, Jesus referred to the Comforter as "he" as opposed to "it," which also prevents the Comforter from being the Holy Spirit. Instead, every aspect of these prophecies matches the life and description of the Prophet Muhammad.

Coming of That Prophet

It is also recorded in the book of John that the people of that time knew about the expected arrival of a future prophet other than the Messiah. The book of John states:

> And this is the record of John, when the Jews sent priests and Levites from Jerusalem to ask him, Who art thou? And he confessed, and denied not; but confessed, I am not the Christ. And they asked him, What then? Art thou Elias? And he saith, I am not. Art thou that prophet? And he answered, No. Then said they unto him, Who art thou? that we may give an answer to them that sent us. What sayest thou of thyself? He said, I am the voice of one crying in the wilderness, Make straight the way of the Lord, as said the prophet Esaias. And they which were sent were of the Pharisees. And they asked him, and said unto him, Why baptizest thou then, if thou be not that Christ, nor Elias, neither that prophet?[17]

In this profound story, John the Baptist is confronted by the priests, asking who he was and with what authority he baptizes others. Two things become clear from the line of questions the priest raise to John. First, it is clear these priests knew that only someone in a position of divinely commissioned authority could perform such an act. Second, and more important, it is clear they knew that their Scriptures foretell about the coming of three figures in the future, as they then proceed to ask John if he is any of those three figures.

John begins by denying that he is the Christ, who is the Messiah for whom everyone has been awaiting. Ruling out the possibility of John being that much-awaited Messiah, the priests then ask if he is Elias, the advent of whom had been foretold in the Hebrew Scriptures. To this question, John responds that he is not Elias. Hearing John deny being either the Messiah or Elias, the priests then proceed to ask him if he, then, is "that prophet" who had been prophesized. It becomes clear that this other prophet they refer to is certainly not the same as either Elias or the Christ. That prophet is another figure for whom they await.

After John denies being "that prophet," the Pharisees challenge John's authority to then baptize people, asking him, "Why baptizest thou then, if thou be not that Christ, nor Elias, neither that prophet?" It, thus, becomes evident that at the time of Jesus, there were three prophecies known to the people and their priests. The first was regarding the second coming of the Prophet Elias. The second prophecy was regarding the birth and advent of the Christ. Finally, the third prophecy was regarding the coming of that prophet who had been mentioned in the Hebrew Bible to come in the future. As previously explained, the Book of Deuteronomy had spoken about the coming of a prophet like Moses, who would be raised among the brethren of the Israelites.

It cannot be claimed that the third authority about whom these priests spoke (i.e., "that prophet") is Jesus of Nazareth, for this verse makes it abundantly clear that Elias, the Christ, and "that prophet" were three distinct and different individuals whose advents had been foretold in earlier Scriptures. Since Jesus came fulfilling the prophecies of the Christ, this signifies that someone else would have to be "that prophet" yet to come. Muhammad becomes the one whose claim to prophethood fills the void of this third authority who had been promised to come.

Thus does the coming of Muhammad fulfill the evolution of God's religion, including the prophecies made by previous prophets of the coming of a great prophet from among the descendants of Ishmael who will be the beloved of God and will bring a new law not of his own words but of the direct word of God in order to provide guidance, truth, and comfort to mankind.

UNITY THROUGH RELIGIOUS EVOLUTION

The understanding of how the one set of religious laws from God evolved throughout the course of time—and slowly expanded, as appropriate—

provides the framework to understand why and how Muslims accept all prophets of the past as true messengers of God. The belief in Muhammad is the belief that all previous messages have culminated in this final holistic set of religious laws from God, which verifies and unites the teachings of previous prophets.

This is not said with any semblance of superiority, for certainly this is not a matter of competition. Rather, this system of evolution of God's one religion is testament to the infinite wisdom of God and proof of God's intention for mankind to be united under His teachings that He revealed over time. The differences and disagreements between people are not due to God's revelation of His laws; rather, such differences are due to human-kind's mistakes and weaknesses. The Quran states: "Mankind were one community, then they differed among themselves, so Allah raised Prophets as bearers of good tidings and as warners."[18] Thus, the disagreements and arguments prevalent among people of various religious and cultural backgrounds are man-made differences—because God created humans in unity.

It is for this reason that many consider not only all prophets but also all of their followers to be Muslims. This does not mean that previous prophets were followers of Muhammad. As mentioned in the opening chapter, although the word "Muslim" has been understood and accepted to be a label that applies to those who accept Muhammad as a prophet of God, the word has deeper significance. Whereas other religious labels have been used to distinguish and differentiate people (e.g., Christian, Jew, Hindu, Sikh, etc.), the term "Muslim" is holistic in nature. It does not simply apply to those who follow Islam and the Quran. The word "Muslim" means one who submits to the will of God, which is a description that applies to all God-fearing people.

This is why the Quran states: "He [God] has chosen you and has laid no hardship upon you in the matter of religion; so follow the faith of your father Abraham; He has named you Muslims both before and in this Book, so that the Messenger may be a witness over you, and you may be witnesses over mankind."[19] The Quran makes it clear that the name "Muslim" is not a new term, nor is it invented to further divide an already divisive people. It is a term that has applied to all those who submit to God and His will, dating back to the Prophet Abraham.

The term "Muslim" is the only name ever given by divine scripture for a people. God had never sent in a scripture for people to refer to themselves as "Jews," "Christians," and so on. Islam is unique in its claim that God has divinely named the people who follow His religious teachings, and that name He gave is "Muslim." So, although the term seems new because of God's designation, it comes with God's guarantee that all those in the past who follow the faith of Abraham and, thus, submit to God's will have the right to call themselves "Muslims." This seems to be an appropriate fulfillment of the prophecy found in the Book of Isaiah in the Hebrew Bible, which states: "And the Gentiles shall see thy righteousness, and all kings thy glory: and thou shalt be called by a new name, which the mouth of the Lord shall name."[20]

3

DEMYSTIFYING JIHAD

Perhaps the most misunderstood and manipulated teaching of Islam is Jihad—by non-Muslims and even some Muslims—and, as such, has been a subject of great controversy in recent years. Often translated as "holy war" by pundits in the media—a wholly inaccurate and incomplete translation of this word—Jihad has come to be seen by many as something dangerous, scary, and barbaric. This is due not only to fear mongering from the critics of Islam but also to the alarming words and actions of various Muslim individuals and groups around the world.

There have been violent and radical acts perpetrated by some Muslims in the name of Jihad for several decades, but they have received greater global attention and caution since 9/11. Media reports often speak of acts of terrorism committed by those calling themselves "Muslims," which are accompanied by images of Muslims depicted as angry, violent, aggressive, closed-minded, and backward. They are seen burning flags and effigies, rioting, shouting, and celebrating a violent or deadly attack against "non-believers." The media cannot entirely be blamed for this. After all, they are not manufacturing such images and videos. Of course, the way this information gets reported is often misleading, but if Muslims were not acting in such ways or committing acts of terrorism, the media would not be able to depict them in such a manner.

The actions of such Muslims—especially in the name of Islam—are entirely antithetical to the teachings and belief structure of Islam. As discussed in the opening chapter, the term "Islam" itself means "peace," and, as such, Muslims are expected to be obedient to Allah and establish peace with Him and His creation. Far from causing chaos and disorder, Muslims are required to establish peace and order in society. Thus, do we have instructions in the Holy Quran such as "And create not disorder in the earth after it has been set in order,"[1] and "Commit not iniquity in the land, causing disorder."[2] So the behavior of such Muslims who create chaos and disorder in the land violates very clear commandments found in the Quran.

The consequence of these repeated incidents is that many non-Muslims have assumed the worst about this term "Jihad." If one were to type "What is Jihad" into Google, above all search results is presented a dictionary-like definition of the word, which states the primary definition to be "(among Muslims) A war or struggle against unbelievers." Some of the staunchest critics of Islam—purporting to be scholars of this faith—go further by claiming that Jihad is defined as an offensive "holy war" meant to extend the power of a Muslim sovereignty. The prevalence of this inaccurate translation has often been seen in news reports that use the word "Jihad" followed by the short explanation "or, holy war." The term has been shrouded in such confusion and debate, that a fair and accurate clarification is warranted.

"Jihad"—as defined by Islam—is an infinitive noun describing the process of making an effort or endeavoring for a particular cause. It is derived from the root word "*jahada*," which is a verb meaning to strive, labor or exert oneself or one's power; the process of diligently employing oneself towards some cause.[3] Also derived from this same root is the noun "*juhd*," which means an effort. So the word "Jihad" refers to the process of striving or struggling for some purpose. Over the centuries, however, the meaning of "Jihad" has somehow been distorted to mean a "holy war," which is an incomplete and inaccurate translation of the word.

There have been many figures in the Muslim world who have called for violence and suicide attacks (or "martyrdom operations" as they call it) as a response to occupation of some land or territory. Although mostly a fight against occupation—and, thus, a geopolitical endeavor—they draw upon Islamic sources of knowledge in order to rigorously incite people to join their cause. This is where any religious teaching can be hijacked for nefarious purposes. As will be presented later, verses from the Quran and traditions of the Prophet Muhammad have been twisted in order to justify incredibly despicable behavior. Muslims have themselves to blame for allowing the profound and meaningful understanding of Jihad to be altered over the centuries to somehow mean "holy war."

In the current age, many Muslims finally have been attempting to reconnect with the original, pure meaning of the word "Jihad." This is due to the realization of just how far this perverted view of Jihad has proliferated. Jihad has been cited as justification by those accused of 9/11, the 2009 Fort Hood shooting, the 2009 Christmas Day attempted bombing on

Northwest Airlines flight 253, the May 2010 failed Time Square bombing, the 2010 Black Friday attempted bombing in Portland, Oregon, and many other incidents. Prominent figures such as Osama bin Laden, Ayman al-Zawahiri, Sheikh Omar Abdel-Rahman (also known as "the Blind Sheikh"), and Anwar al-Awlaki have been cited numerous times calling Muslims toward violence and aggression under the name of "Jihad." Videos have emerged showing Arab clerics calling a crowd of Muslims toward violence and killing—particularly of either Jews or Americans—all in the name of "Jihad." Muslims have, thus, necessarily begun reconnecting with the original meaning of "Jihad" in order to counter this wave of dangerous misinterpretation.

According to the teachings of Islam, there are three types of Jihad, and each must be understood in order to recognize the true meaning of "Jihad." According to the Quran and the Hadith (recorded maxims of the Prophet Muhammad), the three types of Jihad are Jihad-e-Akbar (the greatest Jihad), Jihad-e-Kabeer (the great Jihad), and Jihad-e-Asghar (the lesser Jihad). Each will now be examined in detail.

JIHAD-E-AKBAR (THE GREATEST JIHAD)

The term "Jihad-e-Akbar" is used to describe the greatest form of Jihad in which Muslims must engage. Deriving from the root word كبر (*kabara*)—which is a verb meaning "to become large or great"—the Arabic word "*akbar*" is an adjective and refers to something that is greater than all other things and, thus, is translated as "the greatest" or "the greatest of all greats."[4] Hence, the term "Jihad-e-Akbar" can be translated as "the greatest Jihad" or even "the greatest of all great Jihads." Therefore, no matter what other forms of Jihad in which Muslims may be encouraged to participate, they would necessarily be of lesser importance and significance to the greatest Jihad.

This "greatest Jihad" is defined as "the process of striving or struggling within one's own self to improve one's character." It is the effort of purifying oneself by striving, struggling, or fighting against one's evil tendencies and vices and curbing any inclination or temptation toward immoral or sinful behavior. Because this struggle is an internal battle with one's own self, it is the most difficult form of Jihad, which would explain why it is referred to as "the greatest"—for, the greater the effort, the greater should be the reward. Muslims are instructed to exert the greatest amount of effort on using the teachings of Islam to purify themselves and rid their souls of every indecency and vice. Muslims must strive their entire lives and continually work to improve their moral and spiritual existence for as long as they live.

The Quran makes this clear in chapter 29, which was revealed during the life of Muhammad when he still lived in Mecca. The time of its revelation is significant because the verses in this chapter referring to Jihad or "*jahada*" (its root word) were revealed at a time when permission to physically fight was out of the question. That permission would only be granted many years later when Muhammad and his followers were in Medina. In this chapter, the Quran states "whoso strives (*jahada*), strives only for his own soul; verily, Allah is Independent of all His creatures. And as to those who believe and do righteous deeds We shall, surely, remove from them their evils, and We shall, surely, give them the best reward of their works."[5] These verses makes it clear that doing this Jihad serves no other benefit than self-purification by removing vices from one's life. One could not translate this instance of jahada to mean "fight" since the idea of fighting hadn't even entered into Islamic teachings yet. But even if one were to maliciously translate this verse as "fight," it would no longer make any sense because a physical resistance was only permitted to selflessly help society as a whole (see section entitled "Jihad-e-Asghar" below) and never to selfishly help one's own self. The above verses define "to strive" as the acts of believing and doing righteous deeds, thereby eliminating evil from oneself.

The Quran further elucidates that the highest objective is to purify one's soul, which establishes the fact that this is the greatest of all pursuits in Islam. The Quran states "by the soul and its perfection—and He revealed to it the ways of evil and the ways of righteousness—he, indeed, prospers who purifies it, and he is ruined who corrupts it."[6] The wisdom granted here is for us to understand that in the sight of God, the one who truly prospers and succeeds is the person who purifies his or her soul. A soul without purification is ruined. Hence, the objective of the greatest Jihad is to purify our souls in order to be saved from ruin and, instead, achieve true success in our lives.

Included in this effort to purify oneself is the striving to overcome one's ego or evil desires. This is why the greatest Jihad is often described as the Jihad against one's own ego. It is the struggle to humble ourselves and sacrifice our own carnal desires in preference to the pursuit of God's pleasure. This is why the Quran instructs: "As for him who fears to stand before his Lord, and restrains his soul from evil desires, the Garden shall surely be his abode." Our endless struggle, thus, is to fight our own soul and ego from impure desires and vices in order to receive a heavenly reward.

This was, in fact, one of the missions the Prophet Muhammad was sent with: to guide mankind on the path of purification of their souls and attaining higher levels of God consciousness. God says in the Quran that it is a "perfect Book," which has been sent to reform mankind. Its philosophies have the ability to teach even savages the rules of conduct and manners of humanity. Muhammad was sent at a time when the world had already been corrupted, due to man's disconnect from God. The Quran says, "Corruption has spread on land and sea because of what men's hands have wrought,"[7] which necessitated divine guidance to bring people back to the path of God.

In this state of loss and corruption among mankind, the Arabs of the seventh century were arguably the most steeped in indecent and immoral behavior. When referring to the magnificence of God, the Quran states: "He [God] it is Who has raised among the unlettered people a Messenger from among themselves who recites unto them His Signs, and purifies them, and teaches them the Book and Wisdom though before that they were in manifest error."[8]

This verse refers to seventh-century Arabs as "the Unlettered people," because the people of Arabia were immersed in barbarism. Far from social responsibility, they took pride in sin and transgression. Arabs indulged in excessive consumption of alcohol and were often seen drunk in the streets, which was a socially accepted norm. Men were known to marry as many wives as they desired, with little-to-no care or consideration given to them. Some would kill and bury female infants due to their desire for male children. They would even murder innocent orphans in order to consume their property. Many did not believe in God nor in the afterlife. The qualities of modesty and shame were foreign concepts to them. Their ignorance on matters of civility, humanity, and spirituality earned them the distinction of being called "the unlettered ones."

According to this verse, Muhammad was sent as a messenger to people of such ignorance and spiritual depravity in order to purify them by teaching them the ways and wisdom of God. He taught them how to purify themselves through the teachings that God had revealed to him. In a well-known Hadith, Muhammad is quoted as saying, "The *mujahid* [striver] is he who makes jihad against his ego for the sake of obeying Allah" (Tirmidhi). Thus, before anything else, he taught his followers how to wage a Jihad-e-Akbar against their lower selves for purposes of self-purification. He brought spiritual life into those who were spiritually dead by raising their God consciousness and delivering to them God's instructions to refrain completely from alcohol, to speak the truth, to compete with one another in doing good deeds as opposed to improper deeds, to enjoin justice and forbid indecency, to treat one's wife with love and fairness, to enjoin good and forbid evil, to observe justice, to avoid breaking oaths after making them firm, to take care of the poor and orphans, to refrain from slandering or speaking ill of others either overtly or covertly, and to observe many more commandments for living a morally upright life. Muhammad taught the Arabs how to attain dignity and self-respect born from humility and a pursuit of God's nearness through worship and upright behavior.

The pursuit of these noble characteristics is a lifelong endeavor, which is why the greatest Jihad is a struggle that Islam orders for all people to persistently endure all throughout their lives. This greatest Jihad directly relates to the belief in life after death and the Day of Judgment, since the effort to continually struggle to purify ourselves is grounded in the understanding that each soul will be held accountable for the life it lived on this earth. The wisdom offered by Islam is to prepare for that fateful day by continuously seeking more ways to live a moral and spiritual life. Islam teaches that the struggle to rid ourselves of impurities and instill good manners and spiritual practices within ourselves is recognized by God and will be rewarded accordingly, and our ultimate goal for this struggle is to earn God's reward.

The Quran speaks highly about those who reprove themselves in order to become better people, using the term نفس اللوامة (*nafsi lawwamah*)[9]—meaning the self-reproving and self-accusing soul—to describe those who reproach themselves and seek repentance every time they make a mistake or fall into error and from the path toward God. This is the awakened state in which people are conscious of their bad deeds and, thus, make full efforts to restrain themselves so that they may purify their souls. Islam guides its followers to evolve from the unrefined state of the soul that is prone to evil into this awakened state of the soul that wishes to recognize within itself higher moral qualities and is, thus, appalled with its own weaknesses and defiance. In its place, the soul is instructed to undertake good, moral behavior based on the firm belief in God.

JIHAD-E-KABEER (THE GREAT JIHAD)

The second type of Jihad is called Jihad-e-Kabeer. The Arabic word "*kabeer*" derives from the root word كبر (*kabara*)—the same verb from which the word "*akbar*" (the greatest) derives—and is an adjective that refers to something great. Whereas "*akbar*" is the superlative form of the root word and, thus, means "the greatest of all greats," "*kabeer*" is the derivative of this root verb and means something that is "great and noble."[10] Hence, the term "Jihad-e-Kabeer" can be translated as "the great Jihad" or "the noble Jihad" and is considered to be an excellent and highly revered effort for one to make. Although the aforementioned greatest Jihad is the most significant and greatest matter that a Muslim can strive for, this great Jihad (Jihad-e-Kabeer) is also given a great deal of importance.

This great Jihad is defined as the process of striving or struggling to spread the word of God found in the Quran. This entails spreading the true message of Islam—based on the teachings in the Quran—through logic and reason. This serves two purposes. First, it serves to preach and, thereby, spread the teachings that Muslims firmly believe to be directly revealed by God. If anyone feels they have a true message, their love and concern for fellow human beings should compel them to share that message with others. There is nothing wrong with proselytizing one's beliefs, as long as it is done with respect and without any compulsion.

The second purpose that this great Jihad serves is to defend Islam against attacks levied against it. In this day and age, Islam and its prophet are continuously under a barrage of verbal attacks and allegations. Islam's teachings are not only twisted and misconstrued but are also falsified in order to paint the religion of Islam as backward, barbaric, and incompatible with the twenty-first century. The character and honor of Muhammad is frequently dragged through the mud, and this noble messenger of God—who was sent as a mercy for mankind—is unjustly and inaccurately abused by the harsh critics of Islam. Aside from absurd films and cartoons that are blatantly designed to ridicule and defame Muhammad and his followers, there is a ceaseless onslaught of accusations made against Islam (e.g., that it promotes the worship of some false deity that is different from the God of Moses and Jesus, advocates for terrorism, oppresses and abuses women, endorses violence as a means of spreading the faith, endorses a theocratic form of government, cultivates a hatred for Jews and Christians, etc.).

This Jihad-e-Kabeer (great Jihad) commands Muslims to fight these attacks and allegations by preaching the true word of God. Far from riots, threats of violence, or displays of anger, the teachings of Islam call its followers to use the commandments of the Quran as a sufficient tool to dispel these myths about the religion and to advance the truth about Islam through sound arguments. This is why the term "Jihad-e-Kabeer" is used in the Quran when it states, "So obey not the disbelievers and strive against them by means of the Quran with a mighty striving."[11] The term "Jihad-e-Kabeer" appears at the very end of the verse and is translated as the "mighty striving" and defined as striving against such antagonistic forces by preaching the message of the Quran. Other translations of the Quran translate this verse as saying to "fight" against them by means of the Quran rather than to "strive" against them, but even in such a translation, the same message applies. Use the Quran and the true teachings of Islam as the defense of one's faith.

It takes courage to defend against powerful enemies who continually defame and slander one's faith, which is why the effort to strive in this path is considered a great and noble endeavor. In Islam, God has placed the expectation upon all believers to make their maximum efforts to take a step forward and propagate the true message of Islam. The Quran states, "Those of the believers who sit at home, excepting the disabled ones, and those who strive in the cause of Allah with their wealth and their persons, are not equal. Allah has exalted in rank those who strive with their wealth and their persons above those who sit at home. And to each Allah has promised good. And Allah has exalted those, who strive above those who sit at home, by a great reward."[12] This verse is meant to inspire Muslims to not simply accept the truth of Islam while taking no part in defending or spreading its message. Instead of sitting still, Muslims are told to strive in the cause of their faith by not only living up to Islam's teachings but also participating in the work of defending and propagating those teachings. This verse states that those who do so are exalted in rank in the sight of God and shall, thus, be rewarded for their efforts. The reasonable exception is made for those who are not able to make such efforts due to circumstances beyond their control. This verse can also be interpreted to refer to the act of physically defending one's faith, which will be discussed in the section below entitled "Jihad-e-Asghar."

Fighting enemies of Islam by means of the Quran certainly does not mean to use the Quran as a weapon with which to physically strike someone. Rather, it means that the Quran is sufficient as a means to defend Islam, as it is the "perfect Book"[13] that contains all truths about Islam's teachings. The Quran also instructs Muslims to "call unto the way of thy Lord with wisdom and goodly exhortation and argue with them in a way that is best."[14] This further establishes the commandment for Muslims to defend and even preach their faith by relying on sound argument that is grounded in dignity and rationality. The Arabic word حكمة (*hikmah*) is translated in this verse as "wisdom," but its full meaning goes much deeper. This word refers to knowledge and science (as in the matters of religion), equity and justice (to avoid unlawful behavior), forbearance or clemency (including to control one's temper when angered), and something that prevents or restrains one from ignorant behavior.[15] Thus, according to the Quran, these are the qualities a Muslim must have when arguing with critics of Islam.

So, when Muslims respond to insults against their religion or their prophet with anger, protests, riots, burning flags in the street, or even through violence, they are violating a very clear commandment in the Quran—and, thus, violating the very word of God. Muslims are never given permission to burn, pillage, and maim in response to insults or criticism. Much to the contrary, Muslims are instructed to turn to logic and reason in order to rationally defend their faith and teach its true message. That is the impetus of this book—to dispel false myths about Islam and replace those myths with the truth of Islam based on the teachings recorded in the Quran. So technically speaking, by writing this book, I am waging a Jihad on you as we speak. But there is no need to fear. This is the Jihad-e-Kabeer, which is the noble struggle to not only speak about Quran's instructions but also to act upon its teachings.

This is the Jihad that all Muslims must continue to wage: to use the teachings of the Quran in order to demystify the religion of Islam for those who do not understand it and to strive against evil or negative forces in order to bring about a spiritual revolution in the world and bring people toward God. This must be done with intelligence and integrity. The fact that the Quran makes it clear that "there is no compulsion in religion"[16] points to the reality that included in this teaching of arguing in a manner that is best is the expectation that the argument can only advance a point of view that is backed with knowledge, evidence, and rationality. The argument cannot be made so forcefully and confrontationally that it borders on forcing someone to accept your point of view.

The example of the Ahmadiyya Muslim Community is noteworthy here. The founder of this worldwide community, Mirza Ghulam Ahmad, made it clear that the Jihad he calls his followers toward is what he called the "Jihad bil Qalam" (Jihad by the pen). Understanding that what people knew as the "Jihad by the sword" (which is explained in greater detail in the below section entitled "Jihad-e-Asghar") was a temporary condition in which Muslims had no choice but to physically stop religious persecutors, he declared over 120 years ago that such conditions do not exist in the current world. As such, he called Muslims toward Jihad-e-Kabeer to defend Islam. He wrote: "In the present age, the pen has been raised against us (Muslims), and it was through the pen that Muslims had been caused so much pain and suffering. Therefore, the pen should be the weapon of the Muslims. . . . In this age, God wants us (Muslims) to defeat critics by using the pen as our weapon to refute their allegations. Therefore allegation by pen against Islam should not be responded by sword, but pen."[17]

Mirza Ghulam Ahmad taught Muslims that the only recourse Muslims had in defending Islam against the onslaught of verbal attacks is to take to the pen and engage in a rigorous intellectual debate to rationally defend Islam and its prophet. He made it clear that those who misuse the term "Jihad" as an excuse to kill and hurt others commit a grave sin: "The tradition prevalent among Muslims of attacking the people of other religions, which they call *jihad*, is not the *jihad* of Divine religious Law (Shariah). Rather, it is a grievous sin and a violation of the clear instructions of God and His Prophet."[18]

JIHAD-E-ASGHAR (THE LESSER JIHAD)

The third and final type of Jihad is called "Jihad-e-Asghar." Deriving from the root word صغر (*saghar*)—a verb that means "to be smaller or lesser"—the Arabic word "*asghar*" refers to something smaller, lesser, smallest, or least, in terms of body, material substance, rank, or dignity.[19] As such, the term "Jihad-e-Asghar" can be translated as "the lesser Jihad" or "the smallest Jihad" or even "the lowest rank of Jihad." Thus, when compared to efforts that are called the "greatest Jihad" or even the "great Jihad," this lesser Jihad is easily understood as being an effort that certainly has some importance but one of much lower ranking and priority.

It is ironic, then, that so much time and attention is afforded to this lesser Jihad than to the great Jihad or the greatest of all great Jihads. Jihad-e-Asghar refers to the physical struggle or resistance that Islam permits under very strict and clear guidelines. This is an external, physical effort to halt the progress of those who are enemies of freedom of religion and freedom of conscience. It is the effort of fighting back against those who have already begun a physical assault on purely religious grounds.

This is the notion of a "just war" within Islam, where fighting is deemed abnormal and destructive but is permissible only in the instance when one has been physically attacked first—and that, too, only if one was attacked because of one's religious beliefs. Thus, fighting in Islam is allowed only in self-defense, and purely for the sake of God—not for any political or territorial purposes. Considered a last resort within Islamic teachings, Muslims are permitted to physically defend the right to practice their faith, and they must fight if failure to do so promotes war and jeopardizes peace.

Regarding this permission for a physical self-defense, the Quran states, "Permission to take up arms is given to those against whom war is made, because they have been wronged and Allah, indeed, has power to help them—those who have been driven out from their homes unjustly, only because they said, 'Our Lord is Allah.' And if Allah had not repelled some people by means of others, cloisters and churches and synagogues and mosques, wherein the name of Allah is oft remembered, would surely have been destroyed. And Allah will, surely, help him who helps Him. Allah is, indeed, Powerful, Mighty."[20]

There is much to be said about this deeply meaningful selection from the Quran. First, and perhaps foremost, is that this verse lays out the principle of a defensive war—which is the only war allowed in Islam. There is no concept of a preemptive war in Islam, for it considers war to be a destructive activity that should only be considered as the last resort. The verse explains that such people who have been attacked have permission to defend themselves because they have been wronged. By stating that permission to fight is given to those who have been attacked unjustly due only to their religious beliefs, this verse clarifies that the only type of self-defense that can be religiously sanctioned in Islam is when one is defending oneself from religious persecution. There may be other times when an individual or community must defend oneself from attack for various other material, political, or societal reasons, but that is more of a commonsense self-defense. The only religiously sanctioned self-defense is the physical defense against religious attacks or wars.

The verse then proceeds to explain the wisdom of this just war by stating if God had not permitted righteous people to physically defend freedom of religion, then the enemies of different religions would be able to destroy churches, cloisters, synagogues, and mosques. All of these places are considered houses of worship for God and, as such, it is necessary to protect them from the violent acts of religious persecution. Thus, God permits a physical resistance against those who try to inflict harm on those with whose religious beliefs they may disagree. This is deeply rooted in divine wisdom. If God did not permit good people to physically resist and fend off the wicked people, then the wicked people would have free reign to inflict any and all atrocities against religious communities. As a result, these houses of worship—where God is glorified—would be targets of assault. This concept is repeated in the Quran, when it states: "Had not Allah repelled some men by others, the earth would indeed be full of mischief. But Allah is Lord of grace to all peoples."[21] Again, if God did not permit a section of mankind to protect religious freedom against an aggressive party or army of people, the earth would surely be filled with disorder.

The Quran depicts war as a fire and affirms God's intention to extinguish such fires as soon as possible, thereby indicating that the believers must wage the self-defense battle in such a way so as to put an end to the persecution as quickly as can be done, while also minimizing its damage (to life and property). This is why the Quran states, "Whenever they kindle a fire for war, Allah extinguishes it. And they strive to create disorder in the earth, and Allah loves not those who create disorder."[22] So, far from promoting or advocating for war, Islam considers war a very dangerous and destructive matter that causes disorder in the earth—something Muslims are explicitly told to avoid. But fighting becomes necessary in order to cease the aggression of those who persecute other communities purely due to their religion.

The Quran continues by commanding to "fight in the way of Allah against those who fight against you, but do not transgress. Surely Allah loves not the transgressors."[23] Here Muslims again are told to fight against those who have already waged a war against them (a defensive war), but the rules of war Islam has prescribed dictate that Muslims can never exceed the limits prescribed by God. Muslims are only allowed to wage a self-defense war, and if they were ever to be transgressors in any conflict, this verse affirms that such Muslims would be violating the law and, thus, would be seen as transgressors in the sight of God.

Just a few verses later, the Quran continues this teaching of the lesser Jihad by instructing to "fight them until there is no persecution, and religion is professed only for Allah. But if they desist, then remember that no hostility is allowed except against the wrongdoers."[24] This verse reminds Muslims that hostility is only permitted against those who are the aggressors and who have initiated violence and war. Hostility is not permitted in Islam against those who have not initiated violence in the name of religion. It also establishes the limit of fighting for Muslims by stating that fighting can only last so long as religious persecution remains. Once the aggressors desist and, thus, their persecution comes to an end, Muslims are no longer permitted to fight them. This same sentiment is repeated almost verbatim later in the Quran when it states, "And fight them until there is no persecution and religion is wholly for Allah. But if they desist, then surely Allah is Watchful of what they do."[25] Taking all of the aforementioned verses together establishes the fact—not simply an opinion—that fighting in Islam is only permitted as a response to religious persecution so that anyone's practice of faith is exclusively due to one's worship of God, not due to any societal or governmental pressure or compulsion.

There are, indeed, some misguided Muslims in the world who would argue with this point and make the claim that fighting for political or geopolitical reasons is justified by Jihad-e-Asghar. This is patently false. There are some Muslims who have attempted to classify the fighting between Palestinians and Israelis as a Jihad. Some Muslims have attempted to classify the fighting between Pakistanis and Indians over Kashmir as a Jihad, but these can only be considered territorial wars. Whatever justification such Muslims may feel for these battles, they simply cannot be called "Jihad," as the Quran is abundantly clear that this lesser Jihad is only justified as a self-defense in the face of physical persecution due exclusively to one's belief in Islam. It is solely meant to protect houses of worship from being destroyed and from followers of any religion being persecuted for their faith.

WHAT ABOUT THE "VIOLENT VERSES"?

Many of the harshest opponents of Islam draw attention to what they call the "violent verses" in the Quran that they claim prove that Jihad in Islam is purely a violent call to kill non-Muslims. The most cited verse comes from chapter 9 of the Quran, which states: "And when the forbidden months have passed, slay the idolaters wherever you find them and take them captive, and beleaguer them, and lie in wait for them at every place of ambush. But if they repent and observe Prayer and pay the Zakat, then leave their way free. Surely, Allah is Most Forgiving, Merciful."[26] This verse has been seen as a matter of great concern for those who have not studied Islam or its instructions about Jihad. Some cite this verse to prove their point that Islam is a violent religion, bent on the massacre of non-Muslims.

This matter requires careful consideration and analysis in order to clarify that this verse is not a call for Muslims to hunt down and kill all non-Muslims. In order to understand the context of this verse in the early part of chapter 9, one must begin with the latter part of chapter 8 of the Quran, for these two chapters are connected. Of all 114 chapters in the Quran, chapter 9 is the only one to begin without the verse "In the name of Allah, the most Gracious, most Merciful." This is the verse that begins every new chapter, and in the life of a Muslim, this verse is recited before beginning any task, meal, job, travel, and so on. The reason chapter 9 does not begin with this verse is because it is, in fact, a continuation of chapter 8.

The end of chapter 8 speaks specifically about the time of war when hostilities were high between the Meccans (idol worshippers) and Muslims (who had been violently chased out of Mecca several years earlier). From about verse 51 until 61, the Quran speaks about the sanctity of treaties and promises because it was at this time when the Muslims and the Meccans agreed to sign a peace treaty where neither side would attack the other for ten years. As the chapter continues, not only are Muslims instructed on the importance of living up to the requirements of every treaty; they are also given a stern warning to never preemptively attack the idol worshippers (with whom they entered the treaty) even if the Muslims feared a breach of the peace agreement.

The Quran then states in chapter 8, "And if they incline towards peace, incline thou also towards it, and put thy trust in Allah. Surely, it is He Who is All-Hearing, All-Knowing."[27] So, if the peace treaty is broken and Muslims are attacked and killed by Meccans and, thus, find themselves in the midst of hostilities and war, and then the idol worshippers suddenly offer peace again, that offer cannot be rejected. Muslims must incline toward peace. But the Quran goes even further in the very next verse, saying, "And if they seek to deceive thee, then surely Allah is Sufficient for thee."[28] That is to say, in the course of the ensuing battle, Muslims are required to accept an offer to make peace, even at the risk of being deceived. Even if they feel this is a false offer for peace that is meant to deceive them, Muslims are to put their trust in God and accept the offer for peace. Peace is so highly emphasized in Islam that Muslims must accept the offer of peace, even from an enemy who has violated a previously established peace treaty.

The remainder of chapter 8 of the Quran is spent reassuring Muslims not to fear the enemy and to, instead, fight bravely and with fairness, for God is watchful of what they do and has already established that fighting is only allowed in self-defense for the freedom to practice one's faith. The chapter states that during this time of war, if anyone from the opposing army is taken as a prisoner of war, Muslims must treat that person kindly and even provide them consolation that God has power to provide for them and forgive them.

When chapter 8 comes to a close, the subject matter still being discussed is how to behave during a time when war has been forced upon them. It is not speaking about regular days; it only refers specifically to times of war when a group, with whom Muslims had a peace treaty, betrayed and killed Muslims while the Muslims were living up to the obligations of the peace treaty.

Chapter 9 of the Quran thus begins by speaking about four sacred months in which Muslims are to cease fighting, even at a time when they are in a state of war against those who broke the truce. Muslims are told to stop fighting and even let the opposing army travel the land. The commandment to stop fighting is not only because the months are considered sacred but is also meant to give the idolaters time to mend their ways and discontinue their hostilities. After this period, fighting would only resume if the enemy continued its hostilities and devious ways. It is made clear that the enemy is only the party of people who have broken the peace treaty. All idolaters are not to be considered enemies, and Muslims are not allowed to exhibit any hostility against those who have not played a role in attacking Muslims. This is why verse 4 of chapter 9 states: "except those of the disbelievers with whom you have entered into a treaty and who have not subsequently failed you in anything nor aided anyone against you. So fulfill to these the treaty you have made with them till their term. Surely, Allah loves those who are righteous."[29]

Then it states that once the sacred months are over, Muslims should continue to battle them. This is where the verse in question is found that says to kill them and lie in wait for them. These are the same instructions any military commander would give to his soldiers (i.e., when you are on the battlefield itself and confronted by your enemies, who have betrayed you and seek to kill you, be not hesitant to kill them). But the Quran does something that no other military commander would do in the very next verse.

The very next verse states, "And if any one of the idolaters seeks protection of thee, grant him protection so that he may hear the Word of Allah; then convey him to his place of security. That is because they are a people who have no knowledge."[30] So it becomes clear that Muslims are not instructed to indiscriminately kill all idol worshippers specifically or all non-Muslims in general. If that were the case, then why would Muslims be expected to protect such people from opposing armies who ask for protection? This establishes the fact that the so-called violent verse is simply guidance for soldiers in battle. The Quran affords great mercy even at a time of war by stating that even when Muslims are fighting for their lives, if the enemies suddenly ask for protection, Muslims must not continue to fight them. Rather, Muslims must protect them and take them to a place of security. And why? So that hopefully they may hear and understand the word of the One God. This is what Islam expects of its followers—to bring about a change in people through their hearts and minds, not through force.

SUICIDE BOMBING

Moreover, in Islam's instructions to maintain peace and order in society— in addition to its instructions that fighting is only religiously permissible when it is a last-resort self-defense—Islam takes a clear stance against those who utilize tools of terrorism to further their agenda. Suicide attacks are unequivocally condemned and forbidden in Islam. Irrespective of how they seek to justify their actions, those who turn to suicide bombs violate clear, essential teachings of Islam. As discussed earlier, the Quran has clearly laid out the philosophy that no hostility is allowed in Islam except as a physical self-defense against the aggressors (i.e., those who have initiated physical violence). Suicide attacks violate this Islamic injunction, as the victims of such attacks are innocent, nonaggressive people.

As mentioned at the very beginning of this chapter, the Quran also instructs on numerous occasions to avoid creating disorder or chaos in any society. In its stead, peace and order is to be established and maintained at all times. Those who implement suicide attacks violate this Islamic injunction by using themselves as tools for spreading chaos and fear in the land, whereas the Quran instructs "and cast not yourselves into ruin with your own hands."[31]

Going further, the Quran contains a categorical rejection of suicide bombings when it states, "And kill not yourselves."[32] This verse has many applications against killing oneself, including as a clear instruction against the idea of suicide altogether. So taking one's own life—for any purpose—is seen as a sin in Islam, and taking one's own life for the purpose of inflicting harm, taking other lives, and creating chaos and disorder is a sin of a higher severity. This is what prompted His Holiness Mirza Masroor Ahmad—the worldwide Khalifa (spiritual leader) of the Ahmadiyya Muslim Community—to boldly state during a 2009 speech in front of three thousand Muslim youth in the UK: "Those who instruct and indoctrinate suicide bombers claim they are acting righteously. They are doing nothing of the sort. Suicide bombing is not based on righteousness; it is based solely on evil."[33]

All of the aforementioned verses from the Quran give supplemental understanding to the true concept of Jihad not only in the greatest context of striving or struggling for a cause but also in the lesser context of a self-defense physical battle—when necessary—that can only be waged with the intention of repelling physical attacks against religious freedom.

VEERING OFF COURSE

When one reads and studies the true nature and intention of Jihad according to Islam's scripture, one cannot help but ask how the radical clerics justify their form of violent Jihad, which finds no support in Islam's original teachings. When we hear of a cleric promoting the indiscriminate murder of Jews and Christians or the subjugation of non-Muslims under threat of violence, it is only fair to ask from where such philosophy is born.

It must be stated clearly that such acts of violence—and even such calls for violence—are due to a failure to understand the philosophy of Jihad. There truly is no basis for such brutality and wanton violence or murder in Islam. Such vicious actions are extreme manifestations of a false ideology claiming that the Prophet Muhammad spread Islam by force and violence and, thus, current-day Muslims can (or must) do so as well. This is perhaps one of the most unfair and erroneous allegations made against the Prophet Muhammad: that he spread his faith by force; this claim is not grounded in reality. Yet, we see this claim used as the foundation of political movements established by some Muslims as well.

Maulana Abul A'la Maududi

Perhaps the most significant modern example of this is Maulana Abul A'la Maududi (1903–1979), who was the founder of the controversial Pakistani political party called "Jamaat-e-Islami." Maududi began his career as a journalist during his teenage years and became a prolific writer and editor of several publications. His tenacious and unique ability to write quickly and eloquently earned him popularity and prominence. He had a deep animosity toward India's British rulers at that time and had a growing interest in Islam—both strongly influenced by his father, who also had an aversion to British schools and professions and, thus, employed homeschooling for his son, which focused on the study of Islam, the Quran, and foreign languages such as Arabic and Persian. Maududi was less than twenty-five years of age when he employed his writing talents to publish his first book, entitled *Al-Jihad fil Islam* (Jihad in Islam), which advanced his theories about the laws of war and peace in Islam.

As the founder of a political party in 1941, Maududi's focus was on politicizing Islamic teachings, and, as such, he was the first to coin the term "Islamic state" in the same year he founded Jamaat-e-Islami. He was not an Islamic scholar but was a gifted and incessant writer, and his ability to advance an argument has been mistaken for scholarship. The late professor Fazlur Rahman—a well-respected Islamic scholar and Harold H. Swift Distinguished Service Professor of Islamic Thought at the University of Chicago—staunchly opposed the views of Maududi, stating,

> [Maududi] was by no means an accurate or profound scholar, but he was undoubtedly like a fresh wind in the stifling Islamic atmosphere created

by the traditional madrasas. . . . Being a journalist rather than a serious scholar he wrote at great speed and with resultant superficiality in order to feed his eager young readers. . . . Not one of Maududi's followers ever became a serious student of Islam, the result being that, for the faithful, Maududi's statements represented the last word on Islam—no matter how much and how blatantly he contradicted himself from time to time on such basic issues as economic policy and political theory.[34]

Maududi's book *Tahfim-al-Qur'an* (Toward Understanding the Quran) "has been the most widely read commentary of the Qur'an in the Urdu language."[35] Promoting ideas that are truly antithetical to the teachings of Islam, his vast popularity has caused many Muslims to completely misunderstand the teachings of Islam with regard to Jihad. He claims that Muslims must fight unbelievers until they accept Islam or are killed, asserting that force not only can, but should, be used against non-Muslims. He made the appalling statement that the Prophet Muhammad spread Islam with the Quran in one hand and the sword in the other—a claim made throughout history only by staunch opponents of Islam.

We need not look any further than his own book, *Al-Jihad fil Islam*, in which Maududi presents this astonishing claim, stating: "I find it necessary to say that there is a connection between the expansion of Islam and the sword. There is no doubt that the sword plays no role in preaching Islam, but along with preaching there are some other elements which are helpful in spreading Islam and the sword can be helpful in those elements."[36] This begins his carefully crafted argument that teaching Islam may not require violence but spreading Islam and its acceptance does require violence. This is a dangerous ideology, deeply opposed to Islam's view that the sword is only to be used to protect the freedom of religion when it is physically attacked. Maududi then continues by stating:

> The Messenger of Allah invited the Arabs to accept Islam for 13 years. He used every possible means of persuasion, gave them incontrovertible arguments and proofs, showed them miracles and put before them his life as an example of piety and morality. In short, he used every possible means of communication, but his people refused to accept Islam.
>
> When every method of persuasion had failed, the Prophet took to the sword. . . . That sword removed evil mischief, the impurities of evil and the filth of the soul. The sword did something more—it removed their blindness so that they could see the light of truth, and also cured them of their arrogance; arrogance which prevents people from accepting the truth, stiff necks and proud heads bowed with humility.

As in Arabia, other countries accepted Islam so rapidly that within a century, a quarter of the world accepted Islam. The reason for such rapid growth was that the sword of Islam tore away the veil which had covered men's hearts.[37]

It is true that the Prophet Muhammad received the revelation to physically defend the right to freedom of religion after thirteen years of persecution, but as has already been established above, the instruction was entirely for a defensive war. The sword was never meant to be used in response to an alleged failure to convince people by sound argument and reasoning, nor was it meant to remove spiritual blindness or arrogance through apparent intimidation. By stating that the conversion of people to Islam took place due to violence and intimidation, Maududi is guilty of the most heinous form of intellectual dishonesty that can be imagined. His claim is not grounded in reality. How could the Prophet Muhammad turn to the sword as a reaction to an alleged inability to convince people of Islam's truth? After all, God directly forbids this in the Quran when He says to Muhammad: "Admonish, therefore, for thou art but an admonisher; Thou art not appointed a warder over them."[38] Here, God has instructed the Prophet Muhammad to only use arguments and reason to persuade people; he has been forbidden from compelling anyone to accept Islam. Maududi's claim that Muhammad explicitly disobeyed God is patently absurd.

Maududi advanced the theory that Jihad should be used to eliminate non-Islamic rule and that the Islamic "state" is not limited to simply the homeland of Islam—a dangerous point of view that has unfortunately deceived many Muslims over the past several decades. His views have been rejected by many Islamic scholars, who view his writings as an abomination. Mirza Tahir Ahmad spoke about Maududi in his book *Murder in the Name of Allah*, when he wrote:

> Maulana Maududi was not convinced of the inherent beauty of Islam or that it could conquer hearts by its spiritual force alone, either in the past or present. He said: "Human relations and associations are so integrated that no state can have complete freedom of action within its own principles, unless those same principles are in force in a neighboring country. Therefore, Muslim groups will not be content with the establishment of an Islamic state in one area alone. Depending on their resources, they should try to expand in all directions. . . . If their Islamic state has power and resources it will fight and destroy non Islamic governments and establish Islamic states in their place.[39]

Here, Ahmad quotes from Maududi's own writings to illustrate Maududi's flawed belief that Islam is some sort of a state with no borders, thereby granting "Islamic states" justification to preemptively attack other nations in order to spread Islam by force. Ahmad gave a pointed response to Maududi, stating:

> No sword can change a heart and turn belief into disbelief. There was a long chain of prophets before the Prophet of Islam and it is an historical truth that every prophet was opposed by force. Every time a prophet taught the true religion he was opposed by the sword and yet true religion spread and the sword failed to cut it back. If all past prophets and their followers could stand against the sword's might, how is it possible that Muhammad could have adopted a different approach and taken to the sword—the instrument of oppression, not truth? There is no greater injustice than to accuse him of using force to change people's beliefs.[40]

Those who were drawn to Maududi's writings never seriously studied Islam enough to validate the veracity of his claims. As has been demonstrated, those who pursued true scholarship of Islam wholly condemned Maududi's words. It is for this reason that Maududi was imprisoned on multiple occasions due to upsetting the law and order of society, including his role in the 1953 Lahore riots. Many other Muslim leaders have opposed Maududi and his writing, including Muhammad Yusuf Banuri, Sheikh Muhammad Yusuf Ludhianvi, and several others. Although many of the aforementioned Muslim scholars and leaders have disagreed with one another on different matters, they were in agreement in regard to the illegitimacy of Maududi's views.

The Islamic historian and *NY Times* bestselling author Karen Armstrong has spent a considerable amount of time, as a scholar outside of the faith of Islam, studying and chronicling the teachings of the Prophet Muhammad. Upon studying his teachings, she concluded: "Maududi argued that jihad was the central tenet of Islam. This was an innovation. Nobody had ever claimed before that jihad was equivalent to the five Pillars of Islam, but Maududi felt that the innovation was justified by the present emergency. The stress and fear of cultural and religious annihilation had led to the development of a more extreme and potentially violent distortion of the faith."[41]

Yet, after facing such opposition and even being given a death sentence for his words and actions, Maududi's views have gained much popularity after his demise. Although his reputation through his life had been rocky at best and he had been rejected by religious and political figures, Maududi's fortunes began to turn just before his demise in September 1979, helped by support and funding from Saudi Arabia. He was the very first winner of the King Faisal International Prize—awarded by the king of Saudi Arabia himself during a ceremony in Riyadh—just months before his death. The prize comes along with gold and a significant financial award. His political party began to increase its circle of influence. Soon after, Maududi began to be praised as a twentieth-century Islamic reformer. Thus, unfortunately, many began to more deeply accept his words when he said: "Islam wishes to destroy all states and governments anywhere on the face of the earth which are opposed to the ideology and programme of Islam, regardless of the country or the nation which rules it. The purpose of Islam is to set up a state on the basis of its own ideology and programme. . . . Islam requires the earth—not just a portion, but the whole planet."[42]

In short, Maududi's posthumous growing popularity has been spurred by his own followers who gained positions of authority through the support that was given to him. As a result, his impact has grown to the point where it is now said that "his influence on contemporary Islam is so pervasive that whether one agrees with him or not, no modern Muslim discourse on the social, economic, and political teachings of Islam can avoid using the terms first coined by him. . . . His books have been translated into all the major languages of the world and are widely read in most Muslim countries."[43]

Sayyid Qutb

Another major player in spreading a radical ideology among Muslims is Sayyid Qutb (1906–1966), a contemporary of Maududi, who shared some of Maududi's beliefs and carried them forward in other countries. He was an Egyptian author and intellectual and eventually became a leading member of the Muslim Brotherhood in Egypt before being hanged to death. According to the *Encyclopaedia of Jihad*, "His views exercise considerable influence over the militant movements, which are active in many countries of the Islamic world. . . . He says Islam must be guaranteed freedom of propagation otherwise Muslims can go to war against those who put obstacles in their way." But neither he nor Maududi "would agree to allow the same freedom of propagation to those of other religions in their Islamic states."[44]

Philip Jenkins—author, professor of humanities in history and religious studies at Penn State University, as well as Distinguished Senior Fellow at the Institute for Studies of Religion at Baylor University—explained the link between the writings of Maududi and Qutb. As the "critical link" between all political Islamic movements, Maududi "was a principal founder of what became a global revolutionary cause . . . [and] found faithful pupils in Egypt, where . . . by the early 1940s, Al Banna (founder of the Muslim Brotherhood) was reading Maududi. So was Sayyid Qutb, a [Muslim Brotherhood] alumnus who built on Maududi's stark picture of a civilizational clash between Islam and its enemies."[45] As Maududi's writings became more popular in Egypt, Qutb was able to expand on his theories on the social and political role of Islam.

Qutb began as an educator in Egypt, preferring to learn mostly from Western and secular philosophies, as he was turned off from the traditional religious schools and programs in Egypt. Although well versed in religious education and the memorization of the Quran, his passion was education, and he disagreed with the manner in which people were educated in religious studies programs. In Cairo, he earned his bachelor's degree in education, became a professor, and even took a job in the Ministry of Public Instruction (Education), while continuing his passion for writing as a journalist and editor.

During the 1940s, Qutb grew increasingly critical of the United States, taking great exception to the manner in which President Truman dealt with Jewish immigration into Palestine. As a result, Qutb wrote in a 1946 article: "How I hate and despise those Westerners! All without exception: the British, the French, the Dutch and now the Americans who were at one time trusted by many. . . . And I do not hate or despise these alone. I hate and despise just as much those Egyptians and Arabs who continue to trust Western conscience."[46] Despite his growing animosity toward the West and the United States in particular, he accepted a two-year scholarship to visit the United States in order to inspect the American education system.

Historians agree that Qutb established his religiously political ideology during his stay in the United States, where he grew disgusted by his experiences of the American culture—and what he saw as materialism and indecency. He was also incensed by U.S. support for the foundation of the state of Israel at the cost of land that belonged to the Palestinians, which "he perceived as a rejection of the rights of the Arabs to self-determination and a rejection of their equality to Western man."[47] The weakness of the then-current governments in Egypt and other Arab nations—especially as he witnessed during World War II and the subsequent loss of Palestine—coupled with injustices implemented by Western nations, stimulated not only his frustration but also a desire to empower Arab nations toward a stronger political system. Understanding his seething hatred for the West, how could anyone claim he was a man of faith who reached any form of religious scholarship?

By the 1950s, his transformation had been complete from a literary educator to a political activist and leader. When he returned from the United States back to Egypt in 1951, he joined the Muslim Brotherhood and used religious texts and teachings to justify his political mission. Two years later, Qutb was assigned the prestigious and powerful post of editor in chief of the Muslim Brotherhood's publication section, where his prolific ideological agenda received a greater platform for recruitment. Like Maududi, Qutb's ability to write eloquently and forcefully garnered much admiration.

To further his political agenda, Qutb turned Islamic teachings to gain followers. He defined Jihad as more than simply a spiritual struggle or a self-defense for the purpose of defending freedom of religion. He claimed that Jihad is an offensive tool meant to preemptively attack non-Muslim states in order to spread Islam. Referring to the aforementioned so-called "violent verse," he wrote: "Concerning the polytheists and the hypocrites, it was commanded in this chapter that Jihad be declared against them and that they be treated harshly."[48]

Qutb claimed that Muslims should fight to destroy worldly, man-made political systems and, in their place, institute a system in which God is the authority. To provide justification of such a belief, Qutb refers to a verse from the Quran as stating: "The command belongs to God alone. He commands you not to worship anyone except Him. This is the right way of life."[49] Here Qutb asserts that since God alone is worthy of commanding us, no human can take a position of authority. In a later publication of this same book, this verse is maliciously changed to further this flawed conclusion: "Legislation (*hukm*) is not but for Allah alone. He has commanded that you worship not except Him. That is the correct religion, but most of the people do not know."[50] With this amazingly erroneous presentation of the verse, Qutb argues that only God can legislate in this mortal world. Thus, according to him, this verse means to eliminate "all those systems and governments which are based on the rule of man over men,"[51] for he argues that only God should rule over people.

By only presenting the first half of the above verse and twisting the definition of one word to mean legislation, Qutb alleges that the Quran calls for earthly legislation to be administered by God alone. The problem for him, however, is that this is not what the verse states. The verse in its entirety states: "You worship nothing beside Allah, but mere names that you have named, you and your fathers; Allah has sent down no authority for that. The decision rests with Allah alone. He has commanded that you shall not worship anything save Him. That is the right religion, but most men know it not."[52] This verse deals with worshipping other "gods" besides the One God. It states that God has not given authority to worship anything or anyone but Him and that the decision (not legislation) of whom we should worship belongs only to God alone, but Qutb clearly misrepresents this verse in order to deceptively advance his point of view, which disregards the Quran's instruction to "obey Allah, and obey His Messenger and those who are in authority among you." So, of course, Muslims are commanded to obey God and the words of the prophet, but Muslims are also commanded to obey those who are placed in positions of authority.

He advances Maududi's theory of an Islamic state with no borders that can and should infiltrate neighboring lands that are under a different system of law. He called it "immaterial whether the homeland of Islam—in the true Islamic sense, Dar ul-Islam—is in a condition of peace or whether it is threatened by its neighbours."[53] He supports this theory by distorting the history of Islam with patently false assertions. Qutb writes: "God held back Muslims from fighting in Mecca and in the early period of their migration to Medina, and told them, 'Restrain your hands (from fighting) and establish regular prayers, and pay Zakat.' Next, they were permitted [to fight] when war was made, because they were oppressed . . . [and] expelled from their homes without cause, except the next stage came when the Muslims were commanded to fight against those who fight against them. . . . And finally, war was declared against all the polytheists."[54]

Like Maududi, Qutb was widely rejected by those who knew the truth of Islamic teachings. The authorities at al-Azhar University in Cairo declared Qutb to be a heretic. He has been identified as having little-to-no real scholarship of Islam by many Muslims. Khaled M. Abou El Fadl—author and professor of law at UCLA with particular focus on Islamic jurisprudence—called Sayyid Qutb "an extremist . . . [who] attempted to offer a description of the genuine Islamic society and the true Islamic faith, but in reality, Qutb's book did nothing more than attempt to add an Islamic veneer to a thoroughly fascist ideological construct."[55] He went further, stating, "Neither Qutb nor Maududi were trained jurists, and their knowledge of the Islamic jurisprudential tradition was minimal."[56]

After analyzing Qutb's life and message, Karen Armstrong concluded: "By making jihad central to the Muslim vision, Qutb had in fact distorted the Prophet's life. The traditional biographies make it clear that even though the first *ummah* (community) had to fight in order to survive, Muhammad did not achieve victory by the sword but by a creative and ingenious policy of non-violence. The Koran condemns all warfare as abhorrent, and permits only a war of self-defense."[57]

Considering that Qutb's views are in stark contrast to the teachings of the Quran, it seems that he expected the inevitable conflict between his views of Jihad and that of true Islamic teachings. Perhaps for this reason, he made considerable effort to disgrace those Muslims who view fighting as a temporary defensive mechanism. In one example, in order to discredit those who spoke the truth regarding Jihad, he wrote:

> Islam is not a "defensive movement" in the narrow sense which today is technically called a "defensive war." This narrow meaning is ascribed to it by those [Muslims] who are under the pressure of circumstances and are defeated by the wily attacks of the orientalists, who distort the concept of Islamic Jihaad. . . . As to persons who attempt to defend the concept of Islamic Jihaad by interpreting it in the narrow sense of the current concept of defensive war, and who do research to prove that the battles fought in Islamic Jihaad were all for the defense of the homeland of Islam . . . against the aggression of neighboring powers, they lack understanding of the nature of Islam and its primary aim. Such an attempt is nothing but a product of a mind defeated by the present difficult conditions and by the attacks of the treacherous orientalists on the Islamic Jihaad.[58]

His treacherous rhetoric matches that of Maududi, and like Maududi, Qutb's teachings have trickled down to the present-day issues around the world. Ayman al-Zawahiri—leader of al-Qaeda following the death of Osama bin Laden—has been an ardent follower of Sayyid Qutb all his life. His uncle, Mahfouz Azzam, a lifelong friend and eventual personal lawyer of Sayyid Qutb, had filled Zawahiri's mind with stories of Qutb's courage and wisdom, since he was a child. Lawrence Wright, the Pulitzer Prize–winning author who chronicled the rise of al-Qaeda, explains that the stories Zawahiri heard about Sayyid Qutb all his life provided "an abiding mission in his life: to put Qutb's vision into action."[59] Zawahiri would later be known as the mentor to Osama bin Laden.

Sayyid Qutb became even more influential due to the assistance of his brother, Muhammad Qutb, who moved to Saudi Arabia in 1972 after his release from prison in Egypt and edited and published his famous brother's writings in that society, where he also taught as a university professor. Wright found that while Muhammad Qutb "was jealously defending his brother's reputation"[60] in Saudi Arabia, he caught the attention of one Osama bin Laden, who "usually attended his public lectures"[61] at the King Abdul Aziz University in Jeddah during the late 1970s.

Thus, there is a profound connection between Sayyid Qutb's ideology (influenced by Maududi) and the radicalism seen today. This is what led Karen Armstrong to affirm, "Every Sunni fundamentalist movement has been influenced by Qutb."[62] Even Anwar al-Awlaki—the notorious American-born Yemeni cleric with alleged connections to some of the most infamous modern-day acts of terror against the United States—was incredibly influenced by the writings of Sayyid Qutb. The *New York Times* reported in 2010 just how enchanted al-Awlaki had become of Sayyid Qutb, quoting him as having said: "Because of the flowing style of Sayyid I would read between 100 and 150 pages a day. . . . I would be so immersed with the author I would feel Sayyid was with me in my cell speaking to me directly."[63]

So, Jihad went from its original meaning for Muslims—a struggle to improve one's character, to preach the word of God, and to fight against those who physically attack freedom of religion—to becoming used as a highly politicized system of violence and oppression made prevalent by men who have become the most widely revered modern-day figures of extremists. What began as a small radical following of politically minded Muslims grew to a worldwide phenomenon due to few charismatic followers attaining positions of influence. Regretfully, some modern-day Muslims defend people like Maulana Maududi and fruitlessly argue that he was a reformer, but his writing speaks for itself. Regardless of the impact of such politicized leaders who had an ax to grind, the original definition and teachings of Jihad cannot be altered and, thus, maintain the same significance for Muslims worldwide today.

4

DEMYSTIFYING SHARIAH

In recent times, the term "Shariah" (sometimes called "Shariah Law") has generated a great deal of fear of Muslims. Simply translated as "Islamic law," Shariah has become the veritable boogeyman in political discourse about Islam and Muslims. As a result, this term oftentimes generates confusion, uneasiness, and even concern in the hearts of many non-Muslims who know this term only from what they hear in the news and from anti-Islamic activists. This is primarily because Shariah, much like the concept of Jihad, has been twisted and misrepresented not only by critics of Islam but also by Muslims themselves, who have implemented ruthless forms of governance that they have branded "Shariah."

Countries such as Saudi Arabia, Iran, Afghanistan, Pakistan, and Sudan all purport to have implemented Shariah as their system of governance, even though each has implemented it differently from one another. And in such countries, some of the most brutal, misogynistic, and unjust acts imaginable have been witnessed. The governments of these nations have enacted laws that restrict not only freedom of conscience but also freedom of religion and equal access to what should be inalienable rights. There have been reported incidents of death by stoning, honor killings, limited access to education for women, religious policing, and death penalty sentencing for apostasy, as well as other reports of punishments due to the nations' prevailing laws. Such laws have adversely shaped Western views of Shariah.

In March of 2013, a Pakistani soldier, Anwar Din, was publicly stoned to death for allegedly having an affair with a local woman.[1] In 2008, thirteen-year-old Somali teenager Aisha Ibrahim Duhulow was sentenced to death by stoning because, in admitting to being raped, she conceded to charges of fornication against her.[2] In 2007, twenty-seven Iraqi Kurdish women were victims of honor killings in a span of just four months.[3] Saudi

Arabia has the *mutaween* (a religious police) who arrest unrelated men and women for socializing, seize products deemed "un-Islamic," and enforce Islamic dress codes and dietary laws. In March 2002, they caused the death of fifteen schoolgirls and serious injury to fifty more by forcibly barring them from escaping a burning school in Mecca because the girls were not wearing head scarves and black coats nor were they accompanied by a male guardian at the time.[4] In 2007, seven Saudi men abducted and gang-raped a teenage woman whom they found with an unrelated man in a mall. The seven were sentenced to two-to-nine years in prison, but the woman was also sentenced to six months in prison and two hundred lashes for not having a male guardian with her and, instead, being alone with an unrelated male.[5]

All of these stories are appalling and disgusting to anyone with a conscience, but they are particularly infuriating to Muslims grounded in the reality of Islamic law, because all such incidents violate Islamic teachings. Islam does not promote nor condone any such punishments, and yet these punishments are implemented by so-called Muslim states. It is no wonder that non-Muslims observing this state of disrepute in the governance model of these countries have judged Shariah to be a barbaric and frightening institution not compatible with the twenty-first century.

At the same time, there are Western activists and political leaders—such as Ayaan Hirsi Ali, Robert Spencer, Geert Wilders, Newt Gingrich, David Horowitz, Frank Gaffney, Pamela Geller, and many more—who have fanned the flames to provoke hysteria about Shariah. They have adamantly stated that Shariah, at its core, is barbaric, brutal, and a direct contradiction of human rights. They claim the purpose of Shariah is to eliminate and subsequently take over the government of any nation around the world. They paint Muslims as eager to implement Shariah as the form of government everywhere they live, using violent Jihad as the means to achieve this goal.

Shariah has been given such a fearful stigma that those who protested the 2010 construction of an Islamic center in Lower Manhattan would often do so with a sign that simply read "Sharia" in dripping red text. Some have gone as far as to place billboard ads on highways and buses to warn everyone that Shariah threatens America. The prosecutor in the case in Murfreesboro, Tennessee, who was charged with the responsibility of trying to halt the construction of a mosque in that city, did not argue against the legality of building the mosque. Rather, he rested his entire case on attempting to prove that Shariah is a dangerous, misogynistic, and anti-American concept, which should lead the government to prevent any mosque from being built. The Shariah hysteria has incited some to deny Muslims the right to have a house of worship.

In his failed 2012 presidential bid, Newt Gingrich made Shariah a cornerstone of his campaign, claiming that if elected president, he would enact a federal law banning Shariah from entering the United States. He had previously referred to Shariah "in its natural form" as "totally abhorrent to the Western world" and "a mortal threat to the survival of freedom in the United States and in the world as we know it."[6] At the 2013 Conservative Political Action Conference (CPAC), former attorney general Michael Mukasey furthered the cause of instilling fear of Muslims and Shariah by claiming that the "vast majority" of Muslims around the world want to impose Shariah on others. In the past few years, there has been a marked increase in legislative efforts to ban Shariah from entering state court systems. In 2012 alone, more than forty bills were introduced in twenty-three states around the country to prevent the imposition of Shariah[7] and, thus, solve a problem that does not yet exist (i.e., a supposed threat of Shariah usurping the U.S. Constitution).

With such brutality witnessed in parts of the Arab and African world, plus the incessant fearmongering of political figures who fan the flames with outlandish statements, there is no wonder that Shariah has become a thing to be feared in the minds of those who do not understand its role and significance in the life of a Muslim. These two forces have exacerbated many Americans' anxiety and generated hysteria about Shariah in the United States. But according to Professor Noah Feldman—author and professor of law at Harvard Law School, who is well versed in international and Islamic law—there is absolutely no reason for Americans to be afraid of Shariah. He said, "There's no reason for an American living under our constitutional system of government—that protects us against an established religion—to fear the introduction of Shariah in our country. It literally cannot happen . . . and there is no danger of any court saying that Shariah law could be established as the law in the United States." He concluded that "the fear of Shariah can only be explained in terms of a broader fear of Islam, and that fear comes—in some part, reasonably—out of September 11th, when people who described themselves as Muslims, and said they were acting on behalf of Islam, attacked the United States and killed 3,000 Americans. And it's inevitable that, as a result of that, there will be some backlash against Islam. But it is a very far cry from recognizing the threat of terrorism, to imagining—to fantasizing—the possibility of some sort of Islamic takeover in Tennessee or any other American state."[8]

SHARIAH DEFINED

The study of Shariah must begin with an understanding of the word itself. "Shariah" is an Arabic word that derives from the root word شرع (shara'a), which is a verb that has as its primary meaning the act of making something (particularly a pathway) plain, clear, or manifest. The many uses of this root verb are to indicate the bringing of one onto the path toward water, entering into water, and drinking water.[9] Thus, the word "Shariah" can be understood to mean a very clear, distinct, and manifest pathway often understood to indicate a path toward life-giving water because it has been defined to mean not only "the road to be followed" but also "the way to a watering place."[10]

Imam Raghib Asfahani was a twelfth-century Muslim scholar, well known for his exegesis of the Quran, in which he explained deep meanings of its Arabic terms. He concluded that the word "Shariah" not only means "a straight path, which is clear" but also "as a metaphor, this word is used to refer to the divine path." His detailed analysis of this word expounded why it is equated to be a path toward water, stating, "And divine law is called Shariah because if an individual attains a true understanding of it, he becomes satiated and pure . . . [which] means to acquire Divine understanding." Imam Raghib concludes that this refers to "the path of religion, which Allah the Exalted has appointed for the people, and He has commanded that every individual should tread this path of his own free will."[11] Furthermore, Dr. Abdullah Abbas al-Nadwi—a twentieth-century Muslim scholar who focused his study and writings on the Arabic language and Islamic theology—also wrote a comprehensive lexicon of Quranic Arabic and explained that Shariah means "a religion, or a way of belief and practice in respect of religion."[12] Thus is it made clear that Shariah itself is not a governmental law; it is the set of guidelines with respect to following one's religion, which is to be done by everyone's free will. The word itself defines it as something that cannot be imposed on someone else.

The reason for much of the confusion about Shariah is because it is a very broad term covering a wide range of matters. Being a practical path of life, it not only covers religious matters but also encompasses all aspects of society. In addition to religious, moral, and spiritual guidance, it provides direction on economic, social, cultural, legal, and even political matters. For this reason, Shariah not only can be defined as "the religious law of God; consisting of such ordinances as those of fasting and prayer and pilgrimage and the giving of the poor-rate and marriage, and other acts of piety, or of obedience to God, or of duty to Him and to men"[13] but can also be defined and understood as "a law, an ordinance, or a statute."[14] Thus, legal codes and ordinances are also one part of the broad arena that is known as Shariah. When some exhibit a fear of Shariah due to the errors in its implementation seen in various countries, what they truly fear is the legal aspect of Shariah, which is only one aspect of a very broad spectrum of subjects that comprise Shariah. For this reason, it is important to understand the greater definition of Shariah, and not simply its legal codes.

Such a holistic meaning accurately illustrates the intention and purpose of Shariah, for Shariah is the Islamic code that guides all Muslim beliefs and actions. It is meant to be that path that has been clearly defined and manifest by God and, thus, upon which all God-fearing people are to walk. The Quran makes this clear when it states, "Then We set thee on a clear path (*shariah*) concerning the Affair; so follow it, and follow not the vain desires of those who do not know."[15] Here, the word "*shariah*" is used directly and translated to mean a clear path. It connotes, more specifically, the religious path set forth by God for mankind to tread.

This makes Shariah the collection of principles and tenets that regulate a Muslim's life, which is why it is referred to as Islamic law—because it comprises laws and statutes by which Muslims are to live their lives, as well as laws to help govern a society. When Muslims break away from their daily routines five times a day to turn toward Mecca and pray, they do this as part of the process of living their faith, a process that is called "Shariah." When Muslims refrain from drinking alcohol or eating pork, that is Shariah. When Muslims refuse to lend money with interest, they do so according to Shariah. When they greet each other by saying "Asalaamo Alaikum" (peace be with you), that is Shariah. Shariah furnishes principles that Muslims follow when they get married, have children, get divorced, or bury family members. It is a code for all public and private aspects of life.

This concept is not unique to Islam. There are Jews and Christians who also adhere to their religious code in their daily lives. For example, the Halakha (also spelled Halacha) is a comprehensive set of religious laws for Jews, which includes customs, traditions, and laws from the Torah and the Talmud. Not ironically, just like the meaning of "Shariah," the word "Halakha" (often translated as "Jewish Law") is a Hebrew word that is translated to mean a path or a way of walking and represents God's instructions on how to live one's life.[16] This is precisely the meaning and significance of Shariah for Muslims. In fact, this is the significance of any religious law in the life of an adherent of that religion. It should shape who they are and provide a basis for the moral code each individual uses to determine right from wrong.

Religious laws themselves are defined within the religious texts of each faith tradition. As described in the opening chapter of this book, there are known to be three primary sources of knowledge within Islam. The Quran is the most trusted source of religious knowledge for Muslims because it is accepted to be the literal revealed word of God. After the Quran, the two supplemental sources of knowledge in Islam are the Sunnah and the Hadith—the written accounts of the Prophet Muhammad's actions and words. Since Muhammad was the living embodiment of the revelations given to him, Quranic commandments are further understood and clarified by his example and model behavior. Thus, these same three sources also form the universal basis of the Shariah. Through the great diversity within any religion, however, such religious texts are interpreted in a variety of ways by people of the same faith. It is, thus, no surprise that there is no one universal understanding or interpretation of the laws that constitute the Shariah. What complicates matters further is that, in addition to the three primary sources of knowledge listed above, the consensus of learned Islamic jurists (known as "Ijma") and the individual reasoning and analogical deduction of scholars (known as "Ijtihad" and "Qiyas," respectively) often are considered legitimate sources for the implementation of Islamic law. The varying opinions from jurists and scholars (referred to as "juristic preference" or "juristic discretion," known as "Istihsan") bring even more varying interpretations of the Shariah.

This explains the varying opinions or versions of Shariah implemented in the world today: they are based on the opinions, discretion, preference, and interpretations of the scholars and jurists in each country. Although these jurists are formulating interpretations from the same three sources of knowledge, opinions of human beings will invariably differ and lead to different interpretations. When these different interpretations become established and agreed upon, they form a particular brand or school of Islamic jurisprudence, referred to by the Arabic word "Fiqh." So when people speak about the legal code or legal aspect of Shariah, they are really referring to Fiqh, which is certainly a very important aspect of Shariah but still only one part of it. What this means is that a particular Fiqh represents a particular body of law as an interpretation of Islamic law. It is considered a comprehensive set of derived legal rules. So, whereas Shariah is the overall code of conduct and life found in Islamic teachings, a particular Fiqh is a set of laws that are derived based on a particular interpretation and scholarly opinion. Consequently, what some refer to as the implementation of Shariah in various countries around the world are actually implementations of the particular Fiqh that the rulers of each country use for their legislation.

So when someone asks for an opinion on Shariah, one is left to wonder which Shariah they are speaking about. Is it the Shariah of the Hanafis,
or the Shariah of the Ismailis? Or perhaps it is the Shariah of the Malikis, or
maybe the Shafi'is? Or is it the Ja'faris? These are just some of the schools of
jurisprudence (Fiqh) within Islam, all of which may agree on several matters but have considerable differences of opinion on several other matters
of interpretation as well. So the study of Shariah is confined to the same
rules of the study of any set of religious tenets; it is an interpretation of
how religious instructions—as taught by a prophet—can and should apply
to our current age. The diversity of interpretations indicates the true nature
of these laws—to provide a foundation and influence over individual un-
derstandings of God's law and shape moral codes for individuals of diverse
cultures. One people's interpretation cannot be forced upon those who do
not share that interpretation, as religion will then be misused as a force of
oppression.

Tragically, however, this is precisely what has happened in many
countries around the world today. Governments have chosen to legislate
their local scholars' interpretations of Shariah and make it the law of the
land, thereby subjecting their citizens to a particular interpretation of God's
laws, regardless of their religious diversity. Consequently, Shariah has become known to many as a form of government that enacts laws based on
local religious leaders' interpretations of Islamic teachings. As already described above, this is certainly not the intention of Shariah. In fact, Islam
does not require nor promote any particular brand of governance other
than a representative form of government in which its representatives vote
to implement laws and establish order by adhering to absolute justice.

ABSOLUTE JUSTICE

The basis of Shariah, therefore, is absolute justice—a concept that can be
understood by looking at the Quran. The Quran uses two different words
when commanding its followers to observe justice. Both the Arabic nouns
عَدْل (*adl*) and قِسْط (*qist*) describe the philosophy by which people should live
not only individually but also collectively as a society. The word "adl" is
defined as "equity, justice, or rectitude (righteousness, morality, integrity)"
and "a thing that is established in the minds as being right."[17] It derives
from the root word عدل (*adala*), which is translated as "to act and deal
justly, equitably, with fairness" and to "establish justice."[18] The word "qist"
is defined the same, to mean "equity" and "justice"[19] and in its verb form

means "to act justly" and "to be just."[20] The Quran instructs Muslims to observe complete justice and equity so much—the words appear in their various verb and noun forms dozens of times—because it is a principle that forms the foundation of all personal and societal peace.

Relating to law, the Quran states: "Verily, Allah commands you to give over the trusts to those entitled to them, and that, when you judge between men, you judge with justice (adl). And surely excellent is that with which Allah admonishes you. Allah is All-Hearing, All-Seeing."[21] This verse mainly refers to matters that concern the governance of a state. First, it establishes the instruction to entrust authority only to those people who have the characteristics and abilities needed to be a leader. The verse then turns its attention to the leaders who are entrusted with the authority to rule by instructing them that the only manner in which they are allowed to govern is with justice. That is, all people entrusted with the administration of the state are required to be equitable and just and to exercise their authority fairly. God could have very easily said "when you judge between men, you judge with God's law," but that is not at all what God says in this verse. Rather than religion, God has made it incumbent upon leaders to use the universal principle of justice as their golden rule.

Elsewhere, the Quran states, "If thou judge, judge between them with justice (qist). Surely, Allah loves those who are just."[22] Here, the Quran places the religious obligation upon its readers to maintain the standard of justice and fairness in order to earn God's love. It teaches that God loves those who are just and coaches everyone to strive to earn God's love in everything they do in order to raise one's God consciousness. And since observing justice will be rewarded with God's love, absolute justice must be the guiding principle used not only individually but also by any Muslim leader or administration. Again, the Quran does not call for religion to be used as the governing authority of a nation. It calls those entrusted with leadership to rely entirely on absolute justice, equity, and fairness as the governing body's guiding principles.

The standard for justice is set so high in Islam that its followers are instructed to give precedence to fairness and objectivity over selfish considerations of protecting one's own self, family or community. It is stated in the Quran: "O ye who believe! be strict in observing justice (qist), and be witnesses for Allah, even though it be against yourselves or against your parents or kindred. Whether he, against whom witness is borne, be rich or poor, Allah is more regardful of them both than you are. Therefore follow not your low desires that you may be able to act equitably (adl). And if you hide the truth or evade it, then know that Allah is Well-Aware of what you do."[23] Here both Arabic terms for justice are used to teach Muslims to be so meticulous about observing justice that they should speak the truth in all circumstances, even if that means they must testify against themselves, their parents, or their people.

Since truth and justice are inseparable, the Quran wisely calls Muslims toward justice by commanding them to be honest in all matters. Regardless of whether they are in a position of authority or not, Muslims must testify with honesty, even if it means that their honest testimony will incriminate those closest to them—including their own self, other Muslims, their children, parents, relatives, and so on. Even if a Muslim's honor or property is at stake, they are still required to be fair, just, and honest. The Quran clearly articulates honesty as incumbent upon Muslims when it says, "And confound not truth with falsehood nor hide the truth knowingly."[24]

Some falsely allege that Islam only provides these instructions for fairness and justice on those occasions when Muslims are already being treated well by others. In such a case, reciprocating equity with equity is no challenge. But the teachings of Islam have set a higher standard for Muslims. The establishment of justice for all people is so critical in Islam that Muslims are required to observe and maintain justice and equity even when confronted by hostility and antagonism. The Quran thus commands, "O ye who believe! be steadfast in the cause of Allah, bearing witness in equity (qist); and let not a people's enmity incite you to act otherwise than with justice (adl). Be always just (adl), that is nearer to righteousness. And fear Allah. Surely, Allah is Aware of what you do."[25]

So Shariah provides the framework for true justice—to do what is fair, regardless of one's emotions or personal sentiments. Even if one has been offended, attacked, or otherwise victimized by another person's hostility and enmity, Islam coaches one to be resolute in observing justice. God then provides a warning to those who let another people's hatred incite them to bear false testimony or otherwise act unfairly; God says that He is well aware of all that we do. This is a warning that everyone will be held accountable before God if they depart from the path of justice and fairness.

This is the concept of absolute justice to which Islam calls governments of nations to adhere.

RELIGION AND STATE

Whether one considers Shariah a set of guidelines and tenets Muslims must use to govern their lives, or a system of government used to rule a nation, the one thing that can be agreed upon is that the underlying principle of Shariah is absolute justice. The oft-repeated commandment in the Quran to establish a rule of law that is based on justice and equity instead of religion, thus, clarifies that Islam provides the essential framework for the separation of religion and state.

In the aforementioned verse from the Quran, Muslims are told to "give over the trusts to those entitled to them."[26] As mentioned earlier, this verse offers the wise counsel that people should only entrust authority to those who are well suited to be just leaders. Beyond that, however, this verse lays the foundation for a democratic society by placing the responsibility in the hands of the people to select their leaders. The verse does not instruct people to seize control over a nation themselves. Rather, it addresses the people of the society and instructs them that it is their duty to choose the leaders of their nation. The ultimate responsibility is vested in the people of a nation to mutually select those who will be given the authority to govern the land.

Sir Muhammad Zafrulla Khan—a distinguished scholar in world religions and deeply experienced in the world of politics and governance as the very first foreign minister of Pakistan (1947) and, later, president of both the General Assembly of the United Nations and the International Court of Justice—had made the same point regarding the wisdom in this verse from the Quran when he wrote:

> In this verse, governance has been described as a trust, and the implication is that the authority of governance is vested in the people who should entrust it to those most competent among them for the discharge of such trust. Those who are so trusted must discharge their trust equitably and justly. This is illustrated by a well-known *hadith* (maxim of the Prophet Muhammad) comprised in the compilation of Muslim (considered an authentic collection of Muhammad's maxims), in which it is narrated that Abu Dhar, one of the principal Companions of the Holy Prophet (Muhammad), having begged him to be appointed a governor, was told, "Abu Dhar, you are a weak person; governance is a trust which, on the Day of judgment, may prove to have been a source of humiliation and remorse, except in the case of a person who discharges all its obligations to the full." In another hadith reported by Muslim it is narrated that the Holy Prophet said, "I do not appoint to public office anyone who asks for it or is desirous of it."[27]

It is, thus, established within the teachings of Islam to empower the people of a nation to select those among them who are well suited to lead and govern the nation. People are not allowed to demand a position of authority; rather, they have to be selected by the choice of the people. This wonderful principle laid out by Islam can be seen practically by the example of the Prophet Muhammad himself. In the Hadith quoted above, one of the companions of the prophet sought a position of authority and begged to be appointed a governor. Muhammad's response to forbid such a person from being put into that position of authority is profound. He reminded that governance is a trust, and as mentioned in the Quran, it is a trust that the people of the nation collectively choose to put into someone, which brings with it a heavy obligation to rule justly. Muhammad maintained his principle to never appoint anyone into a position of authority who desires to be in office. This attacks the root of corruption—the lust for power. Muhammad's philosophy was that the citizens of the nation should select their leader based on his or her capability to lead impartially and honorably; not based on how badly he or she yearns to be the leader.

Throughout the Quran, Islam continues to construct this philosophy of empowering the people with regard to the governance of the affairs of the state. Addressing those who have been assigned authority to govern over national affairs, the Quran instructs to consult with the people first. This broadens Islam's protection against despotism and corrupt dictatorship by empowering the people to consult and guide the person they elected as their leader. The Quran states that good leaders are "those, who hearken to their Lord, and observe Prayer, and whose affairs are decided by mutual consultation, and who spend out of what We have provided for them."[28] As usual, this guidance in the Quran applies to a lay Muslim's personal life as well, but the verse more directly provides the basis for a representative form of government that provides for the people's voice to be heard. The head of state is required to seek counsel from representatives of the people before making a decision that affects the state.

These instructions illustrate that the guidance provided by Islam with regard to the governance of a state is for a democratically elected government that operates purely on the principle of absolute justice and seeks consensus from representatives of the people. These principles align with our understanding of the separation of religion from state. The Quran provides such profound and practical instructions that its principles certainly can (or, as some argue, should) be used to derive laws for the land, but in and of itself it is not meant to be a constitution of the government. Rather, legal rulings for a particular country can be derived from its doctrine.

In fact, when Muhammad was given state authority after migrating to Medina, the Quran records revelation he received instructing him to seek consultation in state affairs from non-Muslims and even those people described as hypocrites, who would often turn their back on Muhammad and his followers. In this revelation, God tells Muhammad to "pardon them and ask forgiveness for them, and consult them in matters of administration; and when thou art resolved, then put thy trust in Allah. Surely, Allah loves those who put their trust in Him."[29] Thus, as the ruler over that land, Muhammad was instructed to forgive those who have behaved hypocritically and to seek their consultation as fellow citizens. The reference to put his trust in God serves as a reminder that one must do their due diligence to determine the best course of action, but then, ultimately, the matter rests in the hands of God. This offers guidance for Muhammad to consult others and then make what he considers the right decision. Once the decision has been made, he should leave the matter in the trust of God, who has ultimate power over all things.

This instruction given to the Prophet Muhammad affords valuable insight into the true nature of his character. His traits of mercy, kindness, and fairness were not reserved for Muslims alone; he maintained these qualities toward non-Muslims as well (both those who had treated him well, as well as those who would turn their backs on him and even seek opportunities to prevent his progress). In the historical Battle of Uhud, the leaders of Mecca set out their army to attack Muhammad and the inhabitants of Medina. Knowing that war was upon them, Muhammad assembled an army in Medina to repel the strong force marching toward them. At that time, a body of three hundred men turned their backs on Muhammad and his followers by deciding not to participate in the battle and, instead, return to Medina just hours before the battle commenced. With a small army of seven hundred remaining, the Muslims suffered a defeat at the hands of the three-thousand-strong army from Mecca. Although the above verse contains general advice to seek consultation even from those who are not Muslim, it refers predominantly to those three hundred hypocrites who abandoned Muhammad on the battlefield. As a result, Muhammad not only forgave and pardoned them for their behavior; he continued to consult with them in matters of the state. This illustrates the true nature of Muhammad's character; he not only displayed mercy and forgiveness but also maintained his adherence to justice by continuing to consult with them.

Muhammad's examples put into practice Islam's directives for rulers to refrain from using religion to govern the law of a state. The primary responsibility of any governing body is to protect the rights, dignity, and property of its people. Governments who monitor, enforce, and punish people for their level of adherence to religious practices fundamentally violate the Quran's commandment "There is no compulsion in religion."[30] That is, people must never be forced or compelled in matters of religion. This verse was revealed in Medina, when Muhammad had already become head of a state. The fact that this injunction was sent after Muhammad was already in a position of authority clearly establishes that a governing body must not legislate religion. Considering the pluralistic and multicultural nature of the world's countries today, no country can be ruled by a single religious practice anyway, as that would be outside the dictates of justice. One group of people cannot be compelled to abide by the laws of a religion they do not accept.

For Muslims who disagree—that is, they believe that Islam can indeed be legislated and dictated as the law of a nation, irrespective of the number of non-Muslims residing in that country—they must juxtapose their belief with the Islamic injunction of absolute justice. If a Muslim-majority country has the right to impose its law on its entire population, the same logic should be applicable for a Christian-majority country. That country would, too, have the same right to legislate their laws over their citizens. Imagine a world in which that happened in every country. It would lead to immeasurable conflict, as citizens of every country would have the legitimate right to claim that their freedom of religion is being usurped. This simply is not a sustainable model for the world to follow. It is, rather, based on the passion that individuals have for their own faith that sometimes blinds them to the standards of justice and equity. Thomas Hobbes—the seventeenth-century philosopher often called the "founding father of modern political philosophy"—studied human nature and how people deal with matters about which they are passionate. He concluded that humans "naturally denigrate and compete with each other, are quite easily swayed by the rhetoric of ambitious men, and think much more highly of themselves than of other people. In short, their passions magnify the value they place on their own interests."[31]

Mirza Masroor Ahmad—the worldwide spiritual leader (Khalifa) of the Ahmadiyya Muslim Community—is one of the leading Muslim figures of the world to firmly advance this same principle of separating religion from the governance of the state. He has said, "So what does the Holy Qur'an say? It teaches us that religion is a personal matter for each individual to determine for himself. It teaches that religion should be entirely separate from matters of state, and religious differences should not cause you to act unjustly. . . . Allah has said that a requirement for a just government is that it should separate religious matters from matters of State, and every citizen should be afforded his due rights."[32]

PUNISHMENTS FOR CRIME

When people think of Shariah, they often think about brutal forms of punishment they have witnessed in various countries. But as has been established, Shariah is not simply a set of punishments. Shariah is the path on which not only the individual but the entire society can raise its level of morality and good conduct. Islam as a religion and code of life seeks to establish within society an atmosphere of high moral standards so that crimes naturally become very rare and unnatural. Irrespective of the punishments Islam may recommend, there are standards it requires to be established within society before such punishments can even be effective. Without creating that society first—where everyone's needs are met and where honesty, integrity, and safety are accepted principles and crimes are an anomaly—no attempt can be made to institute criminal punishments. Islam does not command to rush for the implementation of punishments. That is analogous to putting the cart before the horse. The practical means to implement Islam's emphasis on improving both individual and societal standards is for both processes to work together. An Islamic penal code cannot be implemented if the moral standard of that society is not being elevated. Simply applying Islam's prescribed punishment in Muslim-majority countries, without an effort to improve the moral and spiritual conditions of the masses, is not only ineffective but counterproductive.

This is a prerequisite to the Islamic penal code because it is directly related to the system of evidence Islam proposes, which is very strict and deeply connected with the level of morality of that society. For this reason, any witness brought to testify against one accused of a crime is required to hold certain moral values so that the testimony can be trusted. Islamic punishments, consequently, cannot be enforced in any immoral society, where witnesses can be bribed or influenced.

Islam calls for first preparing the atmosphere of a nation before attempting to implement any law in accordance with its recommended punishments. This was not only the practice of the Prophet Muhammad but also the practice of all prophets throughout history, and since Muslims believe in all prophets as a part of their own faith, it is important to learn from the holistic approach of all previous prophets. Even a cursory glance at the ministry of the world's prophets will illustrate that they first fostered a strong atmosphere for the law of God to be freely understood and accepted. The prophets never imposed or forced a law upon the people. They slowly taught and educated people about God's instructions for living good, moral, and spiritual lives. They raised God consciousness and self-restraint in people through this process of reformation and provided for their needs. By doing so, the mission of these prophets was to slowly mold that society so that immorality, indecency, and crime would become nearly nonexistent. Such a society would have the right to be called "God's Kingdom on Earth."

Once education and moral guidance has cleaned up a society of indecency, falsehood, inequity, injustice, greed, and crimes such as theft, murder, and rape, it then becomes a much more alarming and grievous incident when a rare crime occurs. A crime is still a crime wherever and whenever it occurs, but when that crime occurs in such a culture that has been morally and spiritually fortified as described above, it jeopardizes the safety, security, and goodwill that pervades that society. For this reason, such crimes are taken very seriously.

Islam does not, however, require any nation to impose certain punishments for these crimes. Instead, Islam prescribes (or recommends) punishments for certain crimes, but such a recommendation is not binding on the elected authority of a nation. Islam suggests punishments that the state can choose to either ignore or bring into law. It is important to remember that even in such a highly enlightened and moral civilization (which does not currently exist in the world today), where the ethical standard has elevated to this degree, the punishments for those criminals who maliciously jeopardize its safety and culture cannot be imposed. It is still a secular state with elected representatives and leaders who must decide what is best for that particular nation. Two different Islamic societies—which have both been reformed to highly moral cultures—will still have independently run administrations that may not select the same punishments for certain crimes.

The fact that these are simply prescribed or proposed laws is made clear in the Quran itself, when it states, "For each of you We prescribed a clear spiritual Law (*shariah*) and a manifest way in secular matters. And if Allah had enforced His Will, He would have made you all one people, but He wishes to try you by that which He has given you. Vie, then, with one another in doing good works. To Allah shall you all return; then will He inform you of that wherein you differed."[33]

This verse solidifies the Islamic injunction of separating religious and secular affairs by stating that God has prescribed two separate paths: one concerning spiritual matters and the other concerning secular matters. When referring to the spiritual law, this verse uses a derived form of the Arabic word "shariah" and clarifies that this law has been prescribed or advised for mankind, who is not coerced or compelled into following it. It states that if God had desired, He could have enforced these laws upon mankind and, thus, made us all one people on the same path. But God did not do so because this is not something to be enforced. He has given humans free will and presented a clear path for us, which everyone ultimately has the choice to follow.

Now that it has been established that the punishments contained in the Quran are prescriptions rather than commandments, it is important to discuss those punishments observed in Muslim-majority nations that cause the most international astonishment, in order to explain Islam's prescribed punishment for the relative crime.

Stoning to Death for Adultery

Death by stoning is arguably one of the most brutal and alarming forms of punishment ever witnessed and, as such, is understandably a matter that causes a great deal of unease and even fear of Shariah. As pointed out by Professor Jan Michiel Otto, professor of Law and Governance in Developing Countries at Leiden University, "The issue is whether it is common practice [in Shariah] to actually administer corporal punishments, such as stoning and amputation. It is readily assumed that these barbaric punishments are regularly executed throughout the Muslim world."[34] By way of example, in Sudan, extramarital sexual relationships are punishable by stoning, and videos often surface from various African and Middle East countries depicting the stoning of a person—most commonly a woman.

In the 2002 meeting in Geneva of the United Nations Committee against Torture, concerning the use of torture in Saudi Arabia, Mr. Soleiman Al-Hogail from Saudi Arabia's Ministry of Higher Education defended the practice of stoning by claiming it was a punishment set forth in the Quran. The problem for Mr. Al-Hogail, however, is that his claim is factually inaccurate. Although the Quran does not explicitly forbid stoning as a form of punishment, it also contains no instruction for its use as a punishment for any crime at all. Even opponents of Islam admit that death by stoning is nowhere to be found in Islam's Holy Scripture.

In the absence of a directive within the Quran calling for stoning, proponents rely on Hadith and Sunnah (reported examples of the narratives and actions of the Prophet Muhammad) in which Muhammad reportedly ordered death by stoning when judging cases of adultery as head of the state in Medina. Knowing that Muhammad would never do anything in contradiction to the Quran, these cases must be analyzed to determine the veracity of the story as well as the justification of the death sentence.

First, there are examples in which the prophet—as head of the state—was asked to judge over the case of Jews living in Medina who had either been found guilty of adultery or confessed to it themselves. Prophet Muhammad's practice was to never impose Islamic law over anyone who wasn't Muslim. He asked the defendant(s) which law they would like to be held accountable to, and if they responded that they would like to be held accountable to their Judaic law, then stoning was applied. This is because the Torah (first five books of the Hebrew Bible) is the only scripture that not only prescribes death for adultery but also specifically calls for death by stoning in some verses.

First, the Torah calls for death by stoning for fornication. When speaking about a woman who is found to have not been a virgin at the time of her marriage (i.e., she had a sexual relationship before marriage), the Bible instructs, "If this thing be true, and the tokens of virginity be not found for the damsel: then they shall bring out the damsel to the door of her father's house, and the men of her city shall stone her with stones that she die; because she hath wrought folly in Israel, to play the whore in her father's house: so shalt thou put evil away from among you."[35] Similarly, it instructs death by stoning for adultery by stating, "If a damsel that is a virgin be betrothed unto an husband, and a man find her in the city, and lie with her; then ye shall bring them both out unto the gate of that city, and ye shall stone them with stones that they die; the damsel, because she cried not, being in the city; and the man, because he hath humbled his neighbor's wife: so thou shalt put away evil from among you."[36] Thus, death by stoning is prescribed in the Torah for both premarital and extramarital affairs.

Muhammad allowed Jews to be judged according to the laws of their faith. Thus, under his judgment, some Jews were sentenced to death by stoning in accordance with Judaic law. The only instances of Muslims being sentenced to death by stoning during the lifetime of Prophet Muhammad occurred before he received a revelation from God about an alternative punishment. Since the Judaic law was the previously revealed law, Prophet Muhammad would defer to it on matters in which he had not yet received a direct revelation. It was always his practice to adhere to the law of the Torah when deciding cases until a new commandment was revealed to him. After receiving revelation from God containing a prescribed punishment for adultery and fornication, there is not a single case in which he sentenced an adulterer to death by stoning.

The Quran—which Muslims accept as the immutable word of God—has prescribed an entirely different punishment for adultery and fornication.

It states, "The adulteress and the adulterer—flog each one of them with a hundred stripes."[37] Hence, the punishment prescribed is one hundred lashes. Stoning those guilty of this behavior is a direct contradiction to the words of the Quran. It is important to note that this verse makes no distinction regarding whether the guilty party is married or not.

There are some scholars, however, who surprisingly contradict the Quran and argue that "if the offender is not married, he should be given one hundred lashes and should be exiled for a period of a year. If the offender is married, he should be given one hundred lashes and stoned to death."[38] People who make this inaccurate claim rely on an unsubstantiated Hadith that has no support from the Quran or the life of the Prophet Muhammad. First, the Prophet Muhammad's example contradicts this claim, as there is not a single episode in which he ordered someone to be both lashed and stoned to death. Furthermore (and more important), the Quran itself dismisses this false claim. The word used in the Quran to describe people who commit this wicked behavior is الزانى (*al-zani*), which refers to someone who either "committed fornication or adultery." This is based on the Arabic term زنى (*zini*) or زنا (*zina*), which means "a single act of fornication or adultery."[39] So whereas adultery is defined as "consensual sexual relations involving at least one married person" and fornication as "consensual sexual relations involving two unmarried people," the Arabic word refers to both. So the lashes prescribed in the Quran are clearly meant for all persons having premarital or extramarital sexual relationships, with no mention of stoning in any scenario.

With that myth dispelled, attention should be directed toward explaining the punishment of lashes for adultery. Remembering that such punishments can only be applied in a society in which the moral standard has reached great heights, one can imagine how rare and serious such an act would be. Since adultery and fornication are significant allegations to make about someone, Islam has set a very high bar of proving one's guilt. Four eyewitnesses of established high morals and integrity are required to have witnessed the act itself. These witnesses must be of very high moral standing and must never have been found to have spoken a lie. Testimony is not accepted of someone who is known to have ever lied. Such a burden of proof makes convictions nearly impossible to prove, since rarely would there ever be four simultaneous and independent morally upright eyewitnesses to such a shameful act.

The only feasible time this could happen is if such a lewd sexual act were to take place openly and publicly. Such open obscenity would then be a matter of societal disturbance. The standard for several eyewitnesses also implies that this punishment applies to the public demonstration or even publication of these lewd sexual acts, as opposed to simply the act itself. It is worthy to note that the Arabic word used (al-zani) refers to one who is "much addicted to fornication or adultery"[40] and thus suggests a particular class of people who have lost all sense of shame, morality, and remorse for their actions and, instead, indulge in such a crime freely and publicly.

When this happens in an exceedingly moral society, Islam prescribes a harsh punishment, which a government can choose to adopt, that can serve not only as a physical punishment but, more important, as a deterrence due to the social implications of the punishment. Within a culture of a high moral standard, the stigma and embarrassment of being caught committing such vulgarity in a public forum—when one becomes exposed in front of family and acquaintances—serves as a deterrent from even approaching or considering this act. Introducing harsh consequences in addition to this social stigma serves not only as a painful warning but also as a further deterrent from the immoral behavior. This philosophy is not far removed from laws in the U.S. criminal justice system, which introduces seemingly harsh punishments for first-time offenders or mandatory sentencing for repeat offenders. The intention is for the punishment to deter people from committing those crimes.

These days, it is deplorable that countries that base their government on Shariah forget the four-witness requirement for adultery and fornication and, instead, impose this requirement on victims of rape in order for them to prove their attacker is guilty. When four eyewitnesses cannot be presented, the victim of the rape herself is punished. This is a cruel misapplication of the four-witness requirement and not supported by Islamic law at all. The Arabic word "zina" does not include rape because "zina" refers to something consensual. Rape is a monstrous crime, which arguably deserves more severe punishment than just lashes.

So Islam does not prescribe a death penalty for adultery, although it leaves room for a government to adopt the death penalty in cases of extremely heinous crimes such as committing rape; publicizing, promoting, and advocating pornography; child pornography; human trafficking; and so on. This is not only because such people are immoral themselves but also because they try to destroy the moral fabric of society by propagating and promulgating such immoral behavior and, thus, ruin people's lives. Islam allows governments to adopt harsh punishments for such heinous acts, if they choose.

Cutting Off the Hand for Theft

Severing the hands of thieves is another punishment people commonly think about when considering Muslim countries that have implemented Shariah. This causes angst for those who consider it a barbaric law and practice. First, it must be reminded that—as explained above—Islam's prescribed punishments can be successfully implemented only in those cultures that are being reformed to the degree that the society as a whole can attain a very high moral standard. Muhammad—like all prophets before him—sought to create a society that adheres to absolute justice, where everyone's needs are provided for and people are of a high moral and spiritual order. Without creating such a society, Islamic punishments simply cannot be implemented anywhere in the world.

As Mirza Tahir Ahmad argued, that would be like trying to grow a cherry tree in the heart of a desert, which is doomed to fail because the atmosphere in the desert does not promote the growth of cherries. Certainly, punishments have proven to serve as deterrents to crime and can help to lower the incidence of crime, but this alone will not create a just society. Islam speaks of cultivating a culture that is capable of living up to high standards for punishments in order to then successfully deter people from crime. This partnership creates a just society. Once that society is God fearing and God loving, the occurrence of such crimes would be very rare, and punishments would apply only to those who have no consideration for the law and order that the rest of society has embraced. And again, even within such a just society, a representative form of government is in place that will decide whether or not to adopt the recommended punishment for each crime.

In regard to the punishment for theft, the Quran states: "And as for the man who steals and the woman who steals, cut off their hands in retribution of their offence as an exemplary punishment from Allah. And Allah is Mighty, Wise."[41] The Arabic word used for "the man who steals" in the above verse is السارق (al-sariqu), and the word used for "the woman who steals" is السارقة (al-sariqat), which are defined not only as "a thief" or "one who comes clandestinely to a place of custody and takes what does not belong to him"[42] but also as "the man addicted to theft" and "the woman addicted to theft" respectively.[43] This would indicate a more grievous criminal than simply a one-time petty thief. Islam takes a firm stance in favor of protecting the rights and property of the innocent, which is undermined by a criminal who steals an innocent person's property. The Prophet Muhammad forbade his followers from taking the lives and property of others, which is firmly supported by the verse in the Quran that commands, "Do not devour your property among yourselves by false means."[44]

Through this verse, Islam commands people to restrain themselves from devouring one another's wealth or property by false means—and without a doubt, theft is purely an act of seizing someone else's wealth or property through illicit means. Such acts create unrest in society and undermine the law and order of the land. Considering the type of just, moral, and safe society that Islam establishes first, it recommends stern measures in the case of one who maliciously usurps the property or wealth of another person. There is much disagreement among Muslim scholars regarding when the punishment of severing a hand can be applied and under which circumstances, but what is commonly understood is that this punishment only applies when the value of the stolen wealth exceeds a certain amount (i.e., petty theft of a small value should receive a lesser punishment). It is also understood that this punishment only applies to a person who is sane (in possession of their senses), is not a child, and is not forced to steal out of hunger. The exception of hunger is put into place so as not to punish a person who steals out of necessity for survival, for that would indicate a failure of the society to provide for the needs of its people.

As consistent with its other crimes, Islam requires an allegation of theft to be accompanied by eyewitness accounts or confession by the criminal in order to be proven without any shadow of doubt. Of the very few cases of hand severing that occurred during the life of Prophet Muhammad, most of the criminals had confessed to the act themselves. Islam requires two eyewitnesses to the actual act of stealing, and as mentioned earlier, any witness brought to testify must be known to hold high moral values so that their testimony can be trusted. If the witness is known to have spoken falsehoods in the past, the witness's testimony will not be accepted. Of course, knowing that most theft is done out of normal sight, circumstantial evidence can also be used for establishing guilt—for example, discovery of the stolen property in possession of an alleged thief.

Such is the high burden of proof within Islam, which makes the occurrence of such sentencing very rare. The standard of evidence required indicates that these punishments can be applied in only a truly virtuous society. In modern-day so-called Muslim societies, which are devoid of virtue, it would be nearly impossible to find eyewitnesses possessing the standard of honesty and integrity necessary for the acceptance of their testimony, as witnesses are often bought or influenced in these countries. The way Shariah is being implemented today is wrong. The important aspects of Islam that needed to be put into place have been ignored.

The wisdom of a harsh punishment, for only those malicious people who jeopardize the peace of a virtuous society, is in the expectation that the punishment will serve as a deterrent to the crime. Unfortunately, these days many in the West have more sympathy for the criminal than they do for the victim. They object to the stern measure—though very seldom applied—that protects the safety and security of society. Instead, they prefer to show kindness to the thieves and muggers who harass the people. But they do so at their own peril because criminals are not stopped or deterred from the crime.

Here in the United States, as part of the U.S. Department of Justice, the FBI's Uniform Crime Reporting (UCR) program monitors most of the crime statistics in the United States. According to its "Crime in the United States 2011" report, there were an estimated 9,063,173 burglaries, larceny-thefts, and motor vehicle thefts in the United States in 2011, which resulted in financial losses estimated at $15.6 billion.[45] The report concluded that a property crime occurred every 3.5 seconds that year. What is more disturbing is that this is the lowest rate of property crimes the country has seen in several years.

Consider for a moment the stories of the families affected by these nine million cases of theft in the United States alone. Consider the pain, suffering, and trouble those innocent families experienced and the daily harassment that victims face at the hands of muggers. The law of a nation is meant to protect the innocent, as the English House of Lords has established, saying that the "overriding objects of the criminal law must be to protect innocent lives."[46] So if a law fails in this purpose to defend and protect the innocent due to its preference for exhibiting compassion to the criminals, there is no other option but to declare that law ineffective. The philosophy of law provided by Islam, on the other hand, aims to protect the innocent from the threat of regular harassment by raising moral standards and deterring would-be criminals from committing the act. The rights of the innocent (who are in the vast majority) must carry more weight than does sympathy for the criminals.

TODAY'S "SHARIAH" COUNTRIES

Versions of Shariah have been implemented so differently by various governments that, despite clamor to put it in place, it cannot and should not be implemented anywhere in the world today. Many of these countries adhere to a jaundiced view of Shariah, which is devoid of its true original intention. Not only have they implemented a form of government that is not in standing with the dictates of justice required by Islam, they have even lost sight of the pristine role that Shariah is meant to play in the lives of Muslims. Instead, they choose to take matters and people over by force.

Much like what happened to the concept of Jihad (see previous chapter), Muslim understanding of Shariah has been corrupted by the same leaders whose influence remains widespread today. Maulana Maududi spread a very dangerous, politically charged, and violent ideology that he branded as Shariah. One need not look any further than Maududi's own writings for evidence of how his influence has corrupted the understanding of Shariah in the minds of many Muslims.

Maududi first states: "Islam wishes to destroy all states and governments anywhere on the face of the earth which are opposed to the ideology and programme of Islam regardless of the country or the Nation which rules it. The purpose of Islam is to set up a state on the basis of its own ideology and programme, regardless of which nation . . . is undermined in the process of the establishment of an ideological Islamic State. Islam requires the earth—not just a portion, but the whole planet."[47]

He then continues:

> This party is left with no other choice except to capture State Authority, for an evil system takes root and flourishes under the patronage of an evil government and a pious cultural order can never be established until the authority of Government is wrested from the wicked and transferred into the hands of the reformers. . . . It is impossible for a Muslim to succeed in his intention of observing the Islamic pattern of life under the authority of a non-Islamic system of government. . . . Hence a person or a group of persons are compelled by the innate demand of their faith to strive for the extirpation of the rule of an opposing ideology and setting up a government which follows the programme and policies of their own faith, for under the authority of a government professing inimical doctrines, that person or group of persons cannot act upon their own belief. If these people evade their duty of actively striving for this end, it clearly implies that they are hypocrites and liars in their faith.[48]

Maududi incites his followers to rise against any non-Islamic government, claiming that a Muslim cannot live out his or her faith under such a government. He calls for such a government to be captured, wrestled away, and extirpated (demolished or destroyed). He finishes this dangerous call to action by alleging that any Muslim not joining this endeavor is a hypocrite and not true to the faith. The absence of Maududi's Islamic credentials has already been explored in the previous chapter about Jihad and does not need to be restated here, nor does the analysis of how far his influence regretfully persists today. This demands that Muslims reconnect with the original teachings of Islam to truly understand the intention, role, and applicability of Shariah not only personally but also societally. Doing so will expose Maududi's ideology as a stark opposition to Islam.

The example of the Prophet Muhammad stands as a clear testament to the fact that he stood for all the principles of freedom, justice, equity, and fairness to all his constituents, with no power being wrestled away from a ruling government by force. He ruled precisely according to the Quranic principle of absolute justice, granted protection to Jews to freely follow their faith and be judged using Judaic laws, and granted protection to Muslims to follow their faith and be judged by Islamic laws. No citizen was subject to a law or teaching to which he or she did not adhere. Muhammad's Charter of Medina stands as a shining testimony to his form of governance and forms the basis of the world's first "Islamic state." This is the example that Muslims are to emulate—that is, to follow Islam's guidance of protecting justice and fairness for all, through peace as opposed to force.

As author Mark Graham wrote after his analyses of medieval history and religious studies,

> One of the most extraordinary events to take place during this time was the drafting of the Covenant of Medina (Sahifat al-Madinah), what some consider to be the world's first constitution. It was a treaty and city charter between the Arabs and Jews of the city. All groups (Muslims, Jews, and non-Muslim Arabs) pledged to live in civic harmony, governed by mutual advice and consultation. The Covenant bound these varied groups into a common defense pact and stipulated that the Jews of the city were one community with the Muslims, that they were free to profess and practice their religion and that they were entitled to all the rights pertaining to the Muslims. This amazingly foresighted document was a revolutionary step forward in civil government.[49]

Muslims who clamor to institute Shariah through a hostile takeover abandon Islam's instructions and sacrifice the true, just nature of Shariah. As Doi and Clarke accurately stated, "The suggestion that the *Shariah* as 'a system' can save us is utterly fatuous, for indeed in the hands of a totalitarian state, even the *Shariah*, which is an embodiment of mercy, can be turned into a tool of tyranny and oppression."[50] Shariah must be understood for what it is—a clear and manifest path to which all people are called, in order to raise their God consciousness, perfect their morals and principles, and refine their behavior to be just, moral, and fair.

5

DEMYSTIFYING ISLAM'S
VIEW OF RELIGIOUS FREEDOM

Freedom of religion is often considered one form of the greater freedom of conscience—the freedom for every individual to hold any belief or idea without fear of persecution, retribution, or discrimination. It is the cornerstone of any free society and provides the basis for protecting the most intimate right for people—the right to personal belief. Religion, in particular, is a very intimately held system of beliefs that influences the way most people view their lives or the world. Any system or individual that seeks to control such an innately private aspect of human beings will inevitably oppress people through intimidation and coercion.

Freedom of religion was a major consideration in the early history of the United States, as many settlers sought migration to America in order to escape religious persecution. For this reason, the very first amendment to the U.S. Constitution protects its residents from any laws "prohibiting the free exercise" of religion. The United Nations Universal Declaration of Human Rights (UDHR) also ensured religious freedom for all by stating in Article 18: "Everyone has the right to freedom of thought, conscience and religion; this right includes freedom to change his religion or belief, and freedom, either alone or in community with others and in public or private, to manifest his religion or belief in teaching, practice, worship and observance."[1]

All fair and just-minded people accept the freedom to choose one's religious belief system to be a right granted to every human being. Unfortunately, there have been many instances in different parts of the world that cast doubt on whether or not this right is granted by the religion of Islam. In 2006, reports came out of Afghanistan about forty-one-year-old Abdul Rahman, arrested on charges of apostasy (converting from Islam to another religion). He faced the death penalty despite the international outcry his case had created.[2] Eventually, he was released due to concerns about his mental stability and was granted asylum in Italy. There was the 2009 case in Egypt about Maher Ahmad El-Mo'otahssem Bellah El-Gohary, also facing the death penalty for converting from Islam to Christianity.[3] News broke in September 2010 from Iran about the death sentence for Pastor Yousef Nadarkhani, for the crime of converting to Christianity from Islam. Initially arrested in 2009, Pastor Nadarkhani received execution orders in February 2012 and was offered mercy only if he recanted his belief in Christianity.[4] After significant international pressure, he was finally acquitted in September of 2012. In March 2012, the Grand Mufti of Saudi Arabia called for the destruction of all churches in the Arabian Peninsula, which understandably sparked wide condemnation from Muslim, Christian, and human rights organizations around the world.[5]

In many Muslim-majority countries around the world, apostasy is considered a crime punishable by the state. This is a major point of difference within the Muslim world, as many Muslims endorse the notion that Islam calls for death of any Muslim who renounces his or her faith. A growing number of Muslims, however, reject this belief on the basis of the teachings of Islam and, thus, argue that there is no Islamic punishment prescribed for one who renounces their faith. This is because the concept of killing a person for choosing a different faith is, in fact, a violation of the teachings of Islam. Islam does not prohibit freedom of conscience and religion and does not prescribe punishments for matters such as apostasy.

Clearly, however, this is not the interpretation held by governments of some Muslim-majority countries. In Saudi Arabia, although there have not been any confirmed cases of apostates being executed in recent history, "conversion from Islam to another religion is considered apostasy and punishable by death."[6] In Pakistan, a Muslim's conversion to another faith is considered an act of blasphemy, punishable under the country's anti-blasphemy laws.[7] Article 126 of Sudan's 1991 Criminal Act criminalizes apostasy and makes it punishable by death,[8] even though it has been some decades since the last known execution. Iran is slightly different in that it does not make apostasy a criminal act necessarily punishable by death, but their courts have been allowed to mete out such a punishment based on the judge's interpretation of religious pronouncements.[9] Aside from state penal codes, several religious authorities have issued a proclamation (fatwa) that apostasy is to be punished by death. For example, even though Morocco's penal code does not forbid apostasy, its higher council of religious scholars (CSO) published a fatwa in April 2013, calling for the death penalty for Muslims who renounce their faith.[10]

MAKING THE CASE FOR THE DEATH PENALTY

The foremost argument advanced by Muslims who are proponents of death for apostasy relies on a Hadith of the Prophet Muhammad in which he is reported to have said, "Whosoever changes his *din* (religion) [from Islam to something else], then kill him." They, thus, claim that the "punishment by death in the case of reneging on Islam has been unanimously agreed upon by all four [Sunni] schools of Islamic jurisprudence."[11] This Hadith is the most commonly used reference when arguments are made in support of the death penalty.

Knowing, however, that Hadith is considered the third source of knowledge within Islam, evidence must exist in the Quran—the most authoritative source of knowledge within Islam—to prove Islam's stance on such a critical issue. Some who have been accepted as scholars within Islam have cited different verses from the Quran to justify the act of killing those who choose disbelief over belief. One such scholar is the late Sheikh Shabbir Ahmad Usmani, who was born in India and strongly supported the creation of the independent state of Pakistan in the 1940s. Even today, some Muslims around the world turn to his writings for their own education.

Example of the People of Moses

Sheikh Usmani argued that Muslims who renounce their faith deserve to be killed. He used the following verse from the Quran to argue that there is a precedent for killing those who once believed but then turned to disbelief: "And [remember the time] when Moses said to his people: 'O my people, you have indeed wronged yourselves by taking the calf for worship; turn ye therefore to your Maker, and kill your evil desires; that is the best for you in the sight of your Maker.' Then He turned towards you with compassion. Surely, He is Oft-Returning with compassion and is Merciful."[12] This refers to the story of when the people of the Prophet Moses began worshipping the calf while he had left them for forty nights to receive commandments on the mountain. When he returned to see his people worshipping the calf as their Lord, he admonished them by telling them to repent for this grievous mistake.

The point in this verse where Muslims debate among themselves is the phrase فَٱقْتُلُوٓاْأَنفُسَكُمْ (*fak-too-loo-an-foo-sa-kum*), translated as "kill your evil desires." This phrase is an instruction for the people to kill their ego, which prevents them from admitting their error in worshipping the calf, and to turn entirely to the One God with humility and seek forgiveness for this transgression. The words used in Arabic literally mean to slay one's own soul or self, which has led to the publication of many incorrect translations of the Quran by Muslim groups who interpret this verse as an instruction for believers to kill those people who once believed but then turned to disbelief. But the actual term used in the Quran describing what to slay is أنْفُسَكُمْ (*an-fu-sa-kum*), which is translated as "your own selves" or, more accurately, "your own souls." This term does not refer to other people or even one's brethren. It only speaks to one's own soul or self.

This is the same term used earlier in the same verse when Moses says to his people "you have indeed wronged yourselves (*an-fu-sa-kum*)." Thus, it is understood that Moses is admonishing his people that they have wronged their own souls by worshipping something other than the One God. When instructing to kill their own souls, he is clearly speaking to those same people who have wronged their souls. Moses is not speaking to those who were loyal to their belief in the One God; rather, he is addressing those very people who committed the sin of idol worship. He, thus, instructs them to slay that very same self or ego that motivated them to perform this sinful act to begin with. Moses commands his followers to kill their own wickedness.

Sheikh Usmani, however, translates this verse as meaning to physically kill others, and he alleges that "it is noted in various related-traditions, thousands of people were slain in front of Prophet Moses due to the offence of apostasy. The situation got to a point where every single one of those people in the nation, who had not worshipped the calf, killed with his own hand any of his close relatives who had been guilty of worshipping the calf."[13] In his commentary of the Holy Quran, Sheikh Usmani comments on this particular verse under the heading "A Commandment to Kill One Another" by stating that this verse commands that "those who did not take the calf for worship should kill those who took the calf for worship."[14]

It is most regrettable that someone seen as a scholar and guide would come to such a dreadful conclusion that is at odds with the words of the Quran. One need look only three verses prior to the aforementioned Quranic verse to see the unconditional claim that God forgave those who had committed this sin of worshipping a calf. It states "And [remember the time] when We made Moses a promise of forty nights, then you took the calf for worship in his absence and you were transgressors. Then We forgave you thereafter, that you might be grateful."[15] Later in the Quran, it states: "Then they took the calf for worship after clear Signs had come to them, but We pardoned even that."[16] So the Quran itself guarantees that those who made this error were forgiven by God because "they were smitten with remorse and saw that they had indeed gone astray."[17] How could God, then, command such people to be killed after they had been forgiven?

This is a brazen mistruth to claim that the people of Moses were instructed to be killed for having chosen disbelief after having believed. It is only the Bible's rendition of this story that claims Moses ordered people to be killed for having worshipped the calf; this is not the Quran. The Old Testament claims that Moses ordered to "put every man his sword by his side, and go in and out from gate to gate throughout the camp, and slay every man his brother, and every man his companion, and every man his neighbor. And the children of Levi did according to the word of Moses: and there fell of the people that day about three thousand men."[18] This is where the Quran disagrees—the people were told to repent and kill their own egos; not to kill three thousand people. For this reason, the very same verse from the Quran concludes with the words, "Then He turned towards you with compassion. Surely, He is Oft-Returning with compassion and is Merciful."[19] Through God's unending compassion and mercy, forgiveness was granted to the people who first committed this sin and then repented by killing their egos and humbly submitting to the One God. Sheikh Usmani cannot reconcile his violent misinterpretation with the Quran's claim that God turned toward these people with compassion.

Equating Apostasy to Waging a War against God

Another strategy of the proponents for the death penalty is to equate apostasy with waging a war against God and His prophet. They argue that anyone who abandons the path paved by God and the Prophet Muhammad effectively has chosen to wage a war against God. They exploit the following verse from the Quran to explain what should happen to such people: "The only reward of those, who wage war against Allah and His Messenger and strive to create disorder in the land, is that they be slain or crucified or their hands and feet be cut off on account of their enmity, or they be expelled from the land. That shall be a disgrace for them in this world, and in the Hereafter they shall have a great punishment; Except those who repent before you have them in your power. So know that Allah is Most Forgiving, Merciful."[20]

They argue that turning one's back on Islam is akin to waging a war with God. This is another blatant misrepresentation of the Quran, as this verse makes no mention of apostasy or renouncing one's faith. Still, this verse has been cited by even present-day Muslim scholars to justify the murder of apostates. Yusuf al-Qaradawi is a Muslim preacher known as the religious advisor for the Muslim Brotherhood who has traveled all over the world to deliver lectures for several decades and hosts a religious television show. Qaradawi has cited the above verse from the Quran and made this exact argument that to "wage war against Allah and His Messenger" refers to those who choose to adopt a different religion after having already been a Muslim.

The argument, however, is fundamentally flawed. The Arabic term used in this verse that translates as "wage a war against God" is مُحَارَبَه (*mu-harabah*), which refers to an instance when one "waged, or contended in, war, one with another; warred, or battled, one with another" or "became hostile."[21] So the very word indicates that it refers to an act of violence and aggression—not an act of changing a belief. This word refers to physical action, not personal belief. The Arabic word for apostasy, on the other hand, is ارتد (*irtida*), which means to "go back, come back, revert" and refers to one who has "rejected, repelled, or averted" from something. It is defined as "an apostasy" or turning away from Islam to unbelief.[22] The above verse, however, does not use this word when referring to those who cause disorder in society.

Instead, this verse defines "muharabah" as those who engage in hostilities and use violence to "create disorder in the land." Twentieth-century Islamic scholar Grand Mufti Muhammad Shafi was the first Grand Mufti of Pakistan and is best known for his eight-volume commentary on the Quran. He wrote:

> The word, *Muharabah* is derived from *Harb* and intrinsically means to [forcibly] wrest or snatch away. In Arabic usage, it is used against *Salm* which means peace and security. Thus, we can see that, the sense of *Harb* (fight) is the spreading of disorder. It is obvious that rare incidents of theft or killing and plundering do not cause public peace to be disturbed. In fact, this happens only when a powerful and organized group stands up to carry out acts of robbery, killing and plundering. . . . The word, *Muharabah* is used in the sense of spreading disorder by employing force and causing the destruction of public peace and safety. Therefore, this word is particularly used to denote high-handed and group-led intrusion into anything relating to the life, property and honour of people which is called highway looting, robbery and rebellion.[23]

Thus, in no uncertain terms, this verse refers to physical disorder, aggression, and war. It does not speak about war in a symbolic or metaphorical manner. Rather, it is clear in its words in depicting an explicit war of violence and injustice committed against those who worship their Lord. Those who twist this verse and allege that it refers to people who change their belief system are committing a grave injustice by attributing something to Islam that is not supported by the faith at all. Mirza Tahir Ahmad—the fourth Khalifa of the Ahmadiyya Muslim Community and world renowned scholar of Islam—so powerfully stated, "To stretch the word *Muharabah* (i.e., waging a war) and taking it to mean *Irtidad* (i.e., apostasy) amounts to a great injustice done to the Holy Qur'an as well as the Arabic language. It is amazing how, despite being called *ulema* [Islamic clerics], they have the audacity to do such things."[24]

Kill Them Wherever You Find Them

Another verse from the Quran taken out of context to justify death for apostates comes from chapter 4, where it addresses the hypocrites: "They wish that you should disbelieve as they have disbelieved, so that you may become alike. Take not, therefore, friends from among them, until they emigrate in the way of Allah. And if they turn away, then seize them and kill them wherever you find them; and take no friend nor helper from among them."[25] This verse has been misread and misused by some to allege that Islam calls for the murder of those who leave the faith in particular, or even more generally, anyone who preaches a different faith to Muslims. Both claims are false.

First, it must be noted that this verse speaks specifically about those who the Quran refers to as "hypocrites." This is clarified by the preceding verse, which states, "What is the matter with you that you are divided into two parties regarding the Hypocrites?"[26] This refers to Bedouin tribes in the desert around Medina who superficially claimed to be believers but would manufacture misunderstandings among Muslims, make false complaints about Islam, and deceptively pull Muslims away from their own faith. They would make public professions of faith, but through their dishonesty, they would create mischief by trying to deceive genuine Muslims.

This verse guides Muslims to not take such deceitful people as friends, nor to turn to them for help, as they are not trustworthy. This verse says nothing about apostasy (i.e., those who openly recant their belief in Islam). In fact, it refers to those who are the complete opposite to an apostate. Whereas an apostate is one who publicly renounces one's faith, a hypocrite is one who deceptively claims allegiance to the faith with the intention of shaking the faith of those who are genuine in their belief. Thus, this verse has nothing to do with apostates.

But even if one mistook this verse as being applicable to apostates, it still cannot accurately be used as a justification for their murder. This verse must be read in combination with the verses that follow to understand the entire injunction. Whereas the verse in question begins the topic of fighting and killing, the next verse clarifies to whom this fighting applies by describing the exceptions: "Except those who are connected with a people between whom and you there is a pact, or those who come to you, while their hearts shrink from fighting you or fighting their own people. And if Allah had so pleased, He could have given them power against you, then they would have surely fought you. So, if they keep aloof from you and fight you not, and make you an offer of peace, then Allah has allowed you no way of aggression against them."[27]

Thus, Muslims are prohibited from fighting and killing anyone who did not attack them first. The injunction to bravely fight is only against those who have been the aggressors and initiated hostility. The verse forbids fighting not only those who extend an offer of peace to Muslims but also those who remain aloof or refrain from fighting Muslims. This is in consonance with general Islamic instructions of war—to only fight those who initiate fighting (see chapter 3, "Demystifying Jihad"). Irrespective of whether they are apostates or hypocrites, as long as they do not attack Muslims, Muslims are not allowed to attack them. Additionally, Islam lays such importance on treaties and pacts that it forbids Muslims from taking disciplinary action against the hypocrites if they are somehow connected to people with whom Muslims have entered a treaty of peace. With so many exceptions listed, the permission to fight becomes incredibly limited in its scope—with seldom applications—applying toward only aggressors and warmongers.

Fight Those Who Break Their Oath

Another blatant misinterpretation of the Quran presented by those who promote the killing of apostates comes in verses 12 and 13 of the ninth chapter: "And if they break their oaths after their covenant, and attack your religion, then fight these leaders of disbelief—surely, they have no regard for your oaths—that they may desist. Will you not fight a people who have broken their oaths, and who plotted to turn out the Messenger, and they were the first to commence hostilities against you? Do you fear them? Nay, Allah is most worthy that you should fear Him, if you are believers."[28] People who read these two verses in isolation can debate its interpretation. But fortunately, the previous eleven verses bear testimony to the context of these two verses.

Reading this verse in context makes it clear that this chapter addresses what Muslims should do once their enemies have broken their treaty of truce and proactively attacked Muslims. Once the enemy has brought war upon Muslims, these verses serve to tell Muslims to bravely stand up for their right to freely practice their religion in peace. First, it must be noted that these verses very directly speak about the idolators who were staunch enemies of Islam and wanted to see this new faith destroyed. It never once speaks about Muslims who renounce their faith. Thus, verse 12 continues to speak about the idol worshipers of Mecca who had once respected the treaty of peace established with Muslims but had now turned back and decided to "break their oaths after their covenant, and attack your religion."

The words "attack your religion" in verse 12 do not merely refer to verbal attacks or criticisms of Islam. Rather, these words refer specifically to those who launch a physical attack against Muslims, which is reiterated in verse 13 when it refers to these same people as those who "were the first to commence hostilities against you." The Arabic word طعن (*ta'ana*) used in this verse and translated as "attack" literally means to "thrust, one another in war" and the "act of piercing or thrusting . . . with a spear or the like."[29] So, once again, this verse refers to a defensive battle to protect the freedom to practice one's religion.

NO PUNISHMENT FOR APOSTASY

Although proponents of the death penalty for apostasy attempt to use verses from the Quran to justify their position, it has now been established that none of the verses cited can accurately be used to justify such a punishment. But the argument does not simply stop there. Not only are the above verses from the Quran not applicable toward the so-called "punishment for apostasy," but also there are several verses from the Quran that proactively establish that no worldly punishment exists for those who change their religion. Since belief is a personal matter between an individual and his or her Lord, each individual is held accountable to God only. A loss of faith can, therefore, only be punished by God (e.g., in the afterlife). No man can play the role of God.

No Compulsion Allowed in Religious Matters

The most fundamental verse in the Quran in regard to freedom of religion comes in chapter 2, when it declares, "There is no compulsion in religion. Surely, the right way has become distinct from error."[30] The Quran holds firmly to the principle that God has certainly made humans capable of understanding His signs and, thus, distinguishing right from wrong. For this reason, God states very directly—and with no ambiguity—that no compulsion is allowed in matters of religion. He Himself has provided all guidance and clear proofs for the right path, and He has provided humans with the free will to follow that path.

Note that this verse was revealed during the Prophet Muhammad's ministry in Medina, when he was already in a position of authority after being asked by its diverse people to be their head of state. There is immense wisdom in God revealing at that time this instruction that people cannot be compelled in religious matters. Had Muhammad received this revelation in Mecca, some would have had the room to allege that this verse only applied when Muslims were in a weak state, being physically and economically persecuted due to their religion. But Muhammad received this revelation after he had gained a position of authority as a commandment to protect freedom of religion for all people. Consequently, we see no example during Muhammad's lifetime in which he ever compelled anyone in matters of religion. He championed freedom of religion, and it is the duty of every living and breathing Muslim today to do so as well.

This is not the only verse in the Quran that forbids Muslims from compelling others in matters of religion. The Quran repeatedly prohibits compulsion in religious affairs. God tells Prophet Muhammad that he is responsible only for delivering the message and warning to all people as a messenger of God. He has not been permitted to watch over people and ensure they are abiding by his instructions. The Quran quotes God's words to Muhammad as "Admonish, therefore, for thou art but an admonisher; Thou art not appointed a keeper over them."[31]

When speaking about those who associate other gods with the one true God, the Quran states, "If Allah had enforced His Will, they would not have set up gods with Him. And We have not made thee a keeper over them, nor art thou over them a guardian."[32] This verse establishes the free will that God has granted to humankind out of His abundant grace. It vouches that God is so powerful that He could have forced people to worship Him alone, but He did not do so because He has made every person a free agent in matters of faith. This verse fittingly ends with an instruction to Muhammad that he has not been given any authority to compel people in matters of personal belief. If God did not compel people to accept the truth, clearly Muhammad would not be permitted to do so. This is repeated later in the Quran where it states, "If the Lord had enforced His Hill, surely, all who are in the earth would have believed together. Wilt thou, then, force men to become believers?"[33] This leaves no doubt that Islam forbids the use of force for spreading the faith. Accordingly, Muslims are forbidden from imposing religion upon anyone, regardless of whether they are Muslim or not.

This is again witnessed when the Quran states, "Whoever follows guidance, follows it only for the good of his own soul; and as to him who goes astray, say, 'I am only a Warner.'"[34] Islam views religion as a personal matter sent to guide humankind on the right path, and any soul who chooses to follow this path does so only for his or her own good. As for those who then go astray by disbelieving or disobeying God's commandments, this verse contains no instruction to punish them. Rather, it instructs believers to respond to such disbelievers by simply saying, "I am only a Warner." Instead of threatening to punish them, believers are instructed to do nothing more than warn and admonish.

Prophet Muhammad is constantly informed by God to tell disbelievers that he gains and loses nothing irrespective of whether or not they follow his teachings. His duty has been confined to delivering the message. As such, the Quran states that Muhammad said to the people: "O men, now has the Truth come to you from your Lord. So whoever follows the guidance, follows it only for the good of his own soul, and whoever errs, errs only against it. And I am not a keeper over you."[35] A true message from God is strong enough to stand on its own merit; he need not compel anyone to accept something that is true.

With so many clear proofs in the Quran and the life of the Prophet Muhammad, it is appalling to hear accusations that Islam prohibits freedom of religion or forces its followers to adhere to it. And the most inexcusable and unthinkable case of transgression is when Muslims themselves claim that Islam permits Muslims to be compelled in matters of religion. Such is the case of Abu Ameenah Bilal Philips—a Jamaican-born convert to Islam who now writes, speaks, and preaches about Islam and even founded an online Islamic university. During a series entitled "Contemporary Issues" on Sharjah Television, Dr. Philips boldly claimed that Islam's prohibition against compelling people in matters of religion only applies to non-Muslims, whereas Muslims could indeed be forcibly compelled.

In regard to the clear Quranic injunction declaring that no compulsion can be applied in matters of religion, Dr. Philips responds: "Yes there is no compulsion in religion in Islam; compulsion in the sense of joining Islam . . . that is, the person is not compelled to become a Muslim. But once a person becomes a Muslim, then they are obliged to stick with it; that this should be a serious and definite decision that was made. . . . If you became a Muslim, you had to be serious; you had to be real. Otherwise, then you would be executed."³⁶ This is an appalling and blatantly non-Islamic statement that finds support in neither the Quran nor in the actions of the Prophet Muhammad.

Who Punishes the Apostate?

The Quran addresses those who disbelieved after having been believers, and it does indeed speak about their punishment. However, the Quran maintains that the punishment for apostasy is only administered by God in the afterlife. It provides no permission or instruction for humans to take the place of God and mete out punishment for someone's loss of belief. The Quran states "Whoso disbelieves in Allah after he has believed—save him who is forced to make a declaration of disbelief while his heart finds peace in faith—but such as open their breasts to disbelief, on them is Allah's wrath; and for them is decreed a severe punishment. . . . Undoubtedly, it is they who will be the losers in the Hereafter."³⁷ Since faith is a matter between every soul and God, the punishment, thus, for apostasy is only in God's hands. Those who disbelieve after believing will face the consequences of their decision on the Day of Judgment.

The Quran provides even further evidence that the punishment for apostasy rests solely in the hands of God when it speaks about those who commit apostasy more than once. It refers to those who committed apostasy, then later came back to Islam and then committed apostasy again. It states: "Those who believe, then disbelieve, then again believe, then disbelieve and then increase in disbelief, Allah will never forgive them nor will He guide them to the right way."³⁸ This verse provides irrefutable evidence that no worldly punishment is prescribed for apostasy in Islam.

Had the death penalty been sanctioned or permitted in Islam for apostasy, how could an apostate even have had the chance to later believe in Islam again as this verse states? If Muslims were required to be guardians over other Muslims and kill those who renounced their belief in Islam, they would prevent this verse from ever becoming a realistic possibility whereby an apostate later decides to believe in Islam again. If apostasy is a grave crime, one can only imagine the gravity of a two-time apostate. Not only does this verse offer no worldly punishment for apostasy, it even avoids any worldly punishment for one who apostates multiple times. Stating that such a person will not be guided on the right way also indicates that they will remain living but without the blessing of divine guidance.

SO WHAT HAPPENED?

Now that it has been clearly established that the Quran does not permit any punishment for renouncing one's faith, it is only fair to ask how so many Muslims and governments of Muslim-majority countries could have strayed so far away from the teachings of Islam by claiming that apostates deserve death. To understand this, one must look well past the history of the Prophet Muhammad and his four rightly guided successors.

After the prophet's death in 632 CE, four leaders followed him in succession in being elected to the position of Khalifa (successor to the prophet). The belief of death for apostasy did not even arise during this twenty-nine-year period of spiritual succession called "Khilafat." Rather, death for apostasy had its birth in Muslim circles during the Ummayyad dynasty—a period from 661 CE until 750 CE—when the spiritual succession ended and was replaced with the establishment of political rulers of the Muslim empire. The Ummayyad dynasty was governed by secular kings who tried to refer to themselves as caliphs (Khalifas) but did not have the same religious position of the previous four pious caliphs.

These secular kings ruled over the empire during the era when force was commonly employed around the world for spreading influence or an ideology, and these kings appointed clergy to leadership positions much like the clergy after Constantine's conversion. Respected for their religious knowledge, the support of these clerics was perceived to be necessary in order to legitimize unpopular political regimes that seized positions of authority irrespective of the desires of the people.

Hassan Saeed and his brother Abdullah Saeed wrote about the rise of the use of these clerics by kings. Hassan Saeed is a former attorney general and presidential candidate of the Maldives, and Abdullah Saeed is a Sultan of Oman Professor of Arab and Islamic Studies at the University of Melbourne and director of the National Centre of Excellence for Islamic Studies in Australia. As they found, in an effort to abolish any form of objection against the ruling regime, politically motivated punishments were meted out by those given "full authority to suppress dissent. This involved brutal force, executions, crucifixions and general control of all those suspected of political agitation. These killings were not religiously sanctioned. Such killing was aimed at using terror to force the population to submit to political authority. In this, the limitations placed by the Quran and the Prophet on taking a person's life were of no interest to these and many other political authorities."[39]

Commissioned by these despotic rulers, clergy justified physical suppression of dissent in religious expressions. They defined any objection against the ruling regime to be an act of rebellion, which they coupled with apostasy as legitimate crimes deserving the death penalty. Thus began the first-ever incidents within the Muslim world of death for those accused of apostasy.

In order to establish credibility for this outlandish claim that Islam commissions death for an apostate, they cited examples of people who were put to death during the life of the Prophet Muhammad. The stories of Ibn Khatal, Musailamah Kazzab, and Maqees bin Sababah were cited to demonstrate that Muhammad put these apostates to death. They ignored the fact that none of these people were killed for their act of apostasy. Each was given capital punishment by the state for their acts of murder.

Ibn Khatal and Maqees bin Sababah are two of the four people who were executed during the occasion of Muhammad's triumphant return to Mecca after having been forced into exile in Medina for eight years. Both had indeed recanted their faith after having accepted Islam earlier, but it is on record that neither was killed on account of apostasy. When Ibn Khatal was sent out by the Prophet Muhammad to collect tax from the people, not only did he recant his faith on that trip, but he then murdered the man who accompanied him. He was ordered to death for the crime of the cold-blooded murder of his companion. Likewise was Maqees bin Sababah put to death for the treacherous murder of another man. In both cases, the men committed the homicide, left Islam, and fled to Mecca where they settled. They were wanted men, guilty of murder, and when Muslims gained control over Mecca, these outstanding punishments were exacted.

Musailamah Kazzab is an even more serious case. Yes, he had indeed left Islam after having been Muslim, but he went many steps further in transgression. He set himself up as equal to the Prophet Muhammad, began to refer to himself as a messenger of Allah, falsely attributed manufactured quotes to the Quran, and began to assemble an army that would eventually attack Muslims in Medina. The Prophet Muhammad did not retaliate nor instruct for Musailamah to be killed. He only became liable to capital punishment after he captured Muhammad's companion, Haseeb bin Zaid, and brutally murdered him and dismembered his limbs. After Muhammad's demise, Musailamah finally mustered a great army to attack Muslims in Medina, and it was this battle that Musailamah was killed.

Each case of capital punishment during the life of Prophet Muhammad and his four pious successors was due to grievous transgressions such as murder—not due to apostasy. During the age when religion became an instrument to garner support for autocratic leaders, new interpretations of these incidents began to emerge. The problem, then, with many modern-day scholars is that instead of examining and comprehending the wisdom of Islam's teachings, they simply rely on these "classical" traditions and interpretations that were made many centuries ago. This is the biggest mistake many people have made with regard to understanding the Shariah of Islam.

The prime example of such pseudo-scholars is Maulana Abul A'la Maududi—the founder of a Pakistani political party who has been mistaken for a scholar by many Muslims. As the Saeed brothers discovered, "For Maududi, belief in Islam is not just a matter of personal faith. It suggests membership in a social order implemented by the state. A change of faith, therefore, is tantamount to treachery, making such a traitor a potential enemy of the state."[40] Maududi very blatantly presented the false doctrine that Islam forbids not only conversion to another faith but also the propagation of other faiths. He wrote: "Since, in our domain, we do not give the right to a person who is Muslim to change his religion and denomination, then likewise, it also means that in the Islamic domain we do not tolerate any other religion propagating and spreading its faith in competition with Islam."[41] Let it be understood that when he says, "we do not give the right" and "we do not tolerate," it does not mean a simple disagreement. He speaks of forcibly barring these things from happening.

To strengthen his political agenda, Maududi went so far as to allege that Muslims who convert to another religion are to be treated as political traitors because he considered Islam and the state to be one. In his opinion, such a traitor of the so-called "state" of Islam must be dealt with in one of two ways. "Either he should be stripped of all rights of citizenship and be allowed to remain alive, or his life should be terminated. . . . Therefore, it is better to punish him with death and consequently put an end to his own and society's misery at the same time."[42]

Maududi took classical traditions from centuries ago—developed during an era when political rulers sought public control—and brought it to the modern era simply because it met his need to provide a firm response to Western powers and influence. Professor Khalid Bin Sayeed—one of Pakistan's most renowned political scientists and an expert on the history of Pakistan—asserted that "thinkers like Maududi, Sayyid Qutb, or Khomeini . . . have formulated their ideas or concepts in response to Western challenges."[43] Maududi's ideas were not born from a pure analysis of Islam. Rather, as the founder and head of a political party, he used religion to inspire people to join his movement. Since his ideas were not grounded in Islamic teachings, Maududi attempted to shake Muslim confidence in their own practice of Islam and wrote: "This gigantic horde that is called 'Muslims,' in reality 999 out of every one thousand of its members neither have any knowledge of Islam nor are they able to distinguish between the truth and falsehood."[44] Ironically, Maududi's words fittingly apply more to himself than to the Muslims he sought to recruit.

PROTECTING FREEDOM OF RELIGION

As discussed in chapter 3, "Demystifying Jihad," Islam allows fighting in order to protect freedom of all religions. No aggressive or preemptive wars are permitted in Islam; the only fighting prescribed is in the defense of every people's right to freedom of religion. God states in the Quran that fighting those who had physically attacked others on account of their faith was necessary in order to prevent such hostile enemies of religion from wreaking havoc in the world. The Quran states, "If Allah had not repelled some people by means of others, cloisters and churches and synagogues and mosques, wherein the name of Allah is oft remembered, would surely have been destroyed."[45] The wisdom here is very clear. If God did not allow the good people to fend off the bad people, the bad people would have free rein to wreak havoc in the land and increase in their hostilities. The only objective of fighting in Islam is to protect the right of every person to practice one's religion—irrespective of what religion that may be. This includes the protection of houses of worship because Islam recognizes their right to worship.

As would be expected, the Prophet Muhammad proved with his own actions that religious freedom is to be honored and protected for all people—not just Muslims. He did this not only when his people were in a state of political weakness and, thus, perhaps had no choice but to advocate for freedom of religion. But rather, Muhammad was a staunch advocate for freedom of religion even after gaining authority as head of the state in Medina. It is there that he established the Charter of Privileges that was delivered to the monks of St. Catherine Monastery in Mt. Sinai—known as the oldest working Christian monastery in the world. This charter represents a pledge of peace and religious freedom for Christians around the world for all times to come.

In this charter, the prophet wrote:

> This is the document which Muhammad, son of Abdullah, God's Prophet, Warner and Bearer of glad-tidings, has caused to be written so that there should remain no excuse for those coming after. I have caused this document to be written for Christians of the East and the

West, for those who live near, and for those of the distant lands, for the Christians living at present and for those who will come after, for those Christians who are known to us and for those as well whom we do not know. Any Muslim violating and abusing what is therein ordered would be regarded as violator of God's testament and would be the breaker of His promise and would make himself deserving of God's curse, be he a king or a subject. I promise that any monk or wayfarer, etc., who will seek my help on the mountains, in forests, deserts or habitations, or in places of worship, I will repel his enemies with all my friends and helpers, with all my relatives and with all those who profess to follow me and will defend him, because they are my covenanted. . . . No bishop will be expelled from his bishopric, no monk from his monastery, no priest from his place of worship, and no pilgrim will be detained in his pilgrimage. None of their churches and other places of worship will be desolated or destroyed or demolished. No material of their churches will be used for building mosques or houses for the Muslims, any Muslim so doing will be regarded as recalcitrant to God and His Prophet. . . . Every help shall be given them in the repair of their churches. They shall be absolved from wearing arms. They shall be protected by the Muslims. Let this document be not disobeyed till the Judgment Day.[46]

But Muhammad did not stop with the establishment of the Christians' right to practice their faith. He went even further by even permitting Christians to preach their faith. This may seem at odds with some Muslim-majority countries today that do not exhibit much tolerance for the open preaching of other religions, but history bears testimony to the fact that Muhammad allowed others to preach their faiths. While in Medina, a delegation of fourteen Christian leaders came to visit Muhammad from Najran in order to debate religious matters, especially concerning the divinity of Jesus. They met with Muhammad inside the mosque and discussed these matters for several hours. Not only were they allowed to come preach their religion and peacefully debate the Islamic views of Jesus, Muhammad even allowed them to use his mosque for worship when they asked to be excused in order to perform their religious services.

No further testament is required to validate that the protection of religious freedom is deeply rooted in Islamic teachings. Not only is compulsion in religion forbidden, but the freedom for all people to practice their religion is, in fact, protected in Islam. The Charter of Privileges will forever serve not only as a shining example of a true and practical application of religious freedom but also as a reason for Muslims to be appalled when they witness religious freedom attacked in the name of Islam.

6

DEMYSTIFYING ISLAM'S
VIEW OF FREE SPEECH

Along with the Islamic concepts of Jihad and Shariah, Islam's teachings regarding speech have been shrouded in much confusion and, thus, entirely misunderstood and misrepresented in mainstream discourse. Due to the severe reaction of some Muslims to derogatory videos, images, and writings in recent years, it has often been understood that Islam prohibits the freedom of speech, which is a cornerstone of a free society that grants every citizen the right to one's own opinion and expression, without fear of intimidation or persecution.

Those who claim that Islam is incompatible with modern Western ideals often cite free-speech issues to prove their case. They allege that Islam stifles free speech by punishing individuals who express views that are taken as insulting or contradictory to the teachings of Islam because what some view as expressions of free speech are viewed by others as blasphemy. It does not take long to create a list of cases where controversial or blasphemous forms of speech have resulted in backlash from various Muslims around the world.

In September of 2012, the amateur (and immature) YouTube film "Innocence of Muslims" was released, depicting the Prophet Muhammad in nefarious ways, which fueled a firestorm of protests, riots, and demonstrations around the world. Countries such as Yemen, Pakistan, and Egypt saw demonstrations turn violent, with one Pakistani government minister offering a $100,000 reward for anyone who killed the makers of this film.[1] He even went so far as to say that "if the government hands this person over to me, my heart says I will finish him with my own hands and then they can hang me."[2]

In November of 2011, the office of French satirical magazine, *Charlie Hebdo*, was destroyed by a firebomb after the magazine named the Prophet

Muhammad as the editor in chief of their next issue and highlighted a sarcastic caricature of the prophet on its cover page and more such caricatures inside.[3] This same magazine had been embroiled in controversy five years earlier when it reprinted the infamous twelve Danish cartoons of the Prophet Muhammad that had drawn condemnation from Muslims and non-Muslims around the world. While there were many peaceful responses from Muslims at the time of the Danish cartoon controversy, the publication sparked several attacks on embassies[4] and churches.[5] This bore striking resemblance to the publication of insulting cartoons by Swedish artist Lars Vilks, who depicted Prophet Muhammad with the body of a dog in 2007. This case resulted in not only countless peaceful demonstrations and condemnations but also death threats against Vilks, including a $100,000 reward offered to anyone who would kill him.[6]

Although all such incidents of "blasphemy" against Islam and the Prophet Muhammad are met with widespread peaceful disapproval from Muslims worldwide (including condemnation of violent reactions to such incidents), such rational voices are drowned out by extreme reactions and calls for violence made by the lunatic fringe within the Muslim world. Such extreme reactions, understandably, cause much angst in the minds of some non-Muslims, who then, unfortunately, conclude that Islam is not only intolerant and closed-minded but also incompatible with the Western ideals of freedom of speech.

In reality, Islam champions and protects freedom of speech while laying its focus on raising the standard of speech of its followers. It does not prescribe any punishment for those who use their speech to slander Allah or any of His prophets. Although accusations that Islam forcibly censors critics are due to the words and actions of some Muslim leaderships, their calls for punishing those who insult or deride Islam are an emotional response to criticisms that find no support in Islamic teachings.

Mirza Tahir Ahmad—the fourth Khalifa of the Ahmadiyya Muslim Community and world renowned scholar of Islam—made the same case after his extensive research on this topic. He wrote regarding Islam's view of blasphemy:

> Blasphemy is condemned on moral and ethical grounds, no doubt, but no physical punishment is prescribed for blasphemy in Islam despite the commonly held view in the contemporary world. Having studied the Holy Quran extensively and repeatedly with deep concentration, I have failed to find a single verse which declares blasphemy to be a crime punishable by man. Although the Holy Quran very strongly discourages

indecent behaviour and indecent talk, or the hurting of the sensitivity of others, with or without rhyme or reason, Islam does not advocate the punishment of blasphemy in this world nor vests such authority in anyone.[7]

PUNISHING BLASPHEMY

But, unfortunately, there are leaders within the Muslim world who call for extreme punishment of those who insult Islam in general or the Prophet Muhammad in particular. Several clerics, as well as governments of Muslim-majority countries, call for blasphemers to be punished through imprisonment, violence, or death. Pakistan's anti-blasphemy laws are among the most severe in the world, with Article 295-C of its constitution calling for harsh punishment not only of overt insults of the prophet but even indirect insinuations: "Whoever by words, either spoken or written, or by visible representation or by any imputation, innuendo, or insinuation, directly or indirectly, defiles the sacred name of the Holy Prophet Muhammad (peace be upon him) shall be punished with death, or imprisonment for life, and shall also be liable to fine."[8] Article 298-A goes a step further by prescribing imprisonment for anyone who directly or indirectly defiles the name of the Prophet Muhammad's wives, family members, righteous caliphs, or companions. Further to these laws, there are Muslim leaders around the world who also preach that anyone who insults the Prophet Muhammad or the religion of Islam must be executed.

Such claims of physical punishment for insulting speech have no basis in the teachings of the Quran and the life of the Prophet Muhammad. As discussed later in this chapter, such claims are in direct violation of the teachings of Islam and the example of the Prophet Muhammad. But still, some people quote verses from the Quran in a futile attempt to find Islamic justification for harsh punishments against insulting speech.

Those Maligning God and His Messenger

Some turn to the verse in the Quran that states, "Verily, those who malign Allah and His Messenger—Allah has cursed them in this world and in the Hereafter, and has prepared for them an abasing punishment."[9] This verse establishes that those who insult God—and, thus, put obstacles in the way of others seeing the truth—will not succeed in their plans to prevent others from believing. It establishes that God will curse their attempts and make their works vain. However, this verse is stretched and twisted by those arguing that Islam calls for punishing blasphemy. They claim that when the Quran says that God curses blasphemers in this world, He does so by allegedly permitting others to kill them. They put themselves at the same level of God by asserting that God's curse comes from their hands.

This is a blatant misrepresentation of God's words, which illustrate that God's curse comes from Him alone in the form of His displeasure—a curse that comes not only in this world but also in the afterlife. If one is to understand that God's curse means a violent death at the hands of Muslims, then how does that also apply to the hereafter? Will Muslims in the afterlife find this blasphemer and kill them once again? Such a nonsensical interpretation of this verse has no place in Islam's teachings. This verse only warns that defaming and slandering God or His prophet displeases God, Who will punish those who transgress to such a degree.

The Quran has a clear message when it states that God curses certain people. The Arabic word used for cursing people is لعنة (*la'anah*), which is derived from the root verb لعن, meaning "to drive away, execrate, deprive one of mercy and blessings, condemn."[10] It is used to speak of instances when God "disgraced him . . . excommunicated him" and "removed him from good."[11] So when the Quran speaks of God cursing someone, it means that God punishes that individual by driving him or her away from Himself or removing all good from his or her life by depriving him or her of His Divine mercy.

This can be evidenced by the multitude of verses in the Quran that use this same word to express the same meaning. For example, the Quran declares that those who make false or derogatory statements about innocent women are cursed. It states: "Verily, those, who calumniate chaste, unwary, believing women, are cursed in this world and the Hereafter. And for them is a grievous chastisement, on the day when their tongues and their hands and their feet will bear witness against them as to what they used to do."[12] If we are to twist the meaning of "curse" as some have done with the previous verse, then shall we take this present verse to mean that anyone who derides an innocent woman or maliciously injures her reputation should be killed? Of course not! This refers to the displeasure and disgrace such people will receive from God. Proof of that is this verse's statement about being held responsible for everything they have done in the afterlife.

For Muslims, the lesson here is to understand that if they truly believe in an all-powerful God, then they must have faith that He will reward and punish people fairly and appropriately. Many Muslims have made the mistake of thinking that they can take God's curse into their own hands, which is akin to losing faith in God's ability to give the offender the appropriate punishment. In no way can it be understood that God's curse means that another person should murder this individual. Thus, in this direct verse dealing with those people who use their speech for nefarious purposes, the only punishment mentioned is one that will be delivered by God; not by man.

Equating Blasphemy to Waging a War against God

Failing to find even one verse from the Quran that directly prescribes any earthly punishment for one who insults God or the Prophet Muhammad, some turn to verses that have nothing to do with this subject and twist its application in order to somehow "prove" that Islam sanctions death for blasphemy. The most common verse used in this context is where the Quran states: "The only reward of those, who wage war against Allah and His Messenger and strive to create disorder in the land, is that they be slain or crucified or their hands and feet be cut off on account of their enmity, or they be expelled from the land. That shall be a disgrace for them in this world, and in the Hereafter they shall have a great punishment; Except those who repent before you have them in your power. So know that Allah is Most Forgiving, Merciful."[13]

Thus, they conflate insulting forms of expression with waging a war against God. This type of gross misrepresentation of the Quran is more insulting than any immature or ridiculous cartoon ever produced about the Prophet Muhammad. This verse has been misused in order to justify a violent response toward not only those who have insulted Islamic teachings but also those who have changed their faith. As such, it has been analyzed in depth in chapter 5, "Demystifying Islam's View of Religious Freedom." This verse does not at all refer to one who either turns away from their faith in Islam or insults Islam or its prophet. Instead, the verse refers to those who actually wage a hostile war of aggression and violence and articulates what should be done to those who victimize innocent people by way of physical disorder, aggression, and war. The war this verse explicitly addresses has nothing to do with a change in belief or any form of expression.

This is a common strategy employed by hard-line clerics around the world to conflate blasphemy with apostasy. In order to prevent Muslims from uttering any words that they perceive as denigrating to Islam or the Prophet Muhammad, they advance the argument that such blasphemy committed by a Muslim makes them a disbeliever since a true Muslim can never say anything disparaging against Islam. If anyone perceives that a

Muslim has said anything blasphemous, that Muslim is labeled a disbeliever and, thus, no longer a Muslim. Then, by some twisted sense of justice, these hard-line clerics allege that this Muslim should be executed in accordance with their alleged punishment for apostasy. Thus, a person who firmly calls himself or herself a Muslim can be charged with the "crime" of apostasy simply if someone else claims they said something that Muslims can perceive as offensive.

Since many clerics incorrectly promote that Islam punishes apostasy with a death sentence, people begin calling for the execution of Muslims who are charged with blasphemy. As discussed in the previous chapter, the idea that apostasy is a punishable crime was manufactured several decades after the demise of the Prophet Muhammad, as a political tool used to exert control over people. This idea was then taken one step further when people began to allege that any Muslim making a remark perceived as critical of Islam had unwittingly recanted their faith in Islam and, thus, earned the death penalty.

This argument is ridden with issues. First, it must be made clear that nobody has the right to decide whether or not another person is a Muslim. Every individual has the God-given right to declare their belief in whatever religion one chooses (or even no religion). That is a matter between a person and God and must be left at that. Furthermore, irrespective of who decides whether a Muslim has recanted his or her faith, it remains a fact that Islam does not instruct anyone to be killed on account of apostasy. So it is simply erroneous to allege that insulting speech deserves death.

ISLAM'S STANCE REGARDING SPEECH

Now that it has been established what Islam does not say about speech, one must understand what Islam does say about speech. Islam's stance on free speech is just one piece of a much larger puzzle illustrating the essence of Islam and its mission on earth. As mentioned in chapter 1 of this book, the underlying spirit of Islam is the mission to establish peace (internally and externally) as well as foster love and concern for others. This mission was highlighted by the Prophet Muhammad when he said to his companions: "You will not enter Paradise until you believe, and you will not believe until you love one another, shall I tell you of something which if you do it, you will love each other? Spread peace among yourselves."[14]

Although some interpret this maxim of the Prophet Muhammad to simply indicate that one must go around saying "Asalaamo Alaikum"

("peace be to you") to everyone, many others understand the deep impli-
cation of the prophet's guidance. Although conveying a greeting of peace
was indeed in alignment with his example, what he meant was that the in-
trinsic mission given to Muslims by God is to cultivate a peaceful world by
establishing unity among all people. By equating one's own salvation (i.e.,
"Paradise") to peace, he powerfully illustrated that a Muslim's mission from
God is to unite with others through love and the manifestation of peace.
The Quran states that "Mankind were one community, then they differed
among themselves,"[15] which means that God created humankind in unity
with each other, but due to man-made differences, this unity has been
compromised. For this reason, the collection of Islam's commandments—to
believe in one God, to accept all previous prophets and all revealed books,
to enjoin good and forbid evil, to speak the truth, to vie with one another
in good works, to enjoin justice and forbid indecency, to avoid breaking
oaths after making them firm, to take care of the poor and the orphan, and
so on—are meant to reestablish a unity among people.

Islam's stance on free speech is deeply rooted in the same mission of
uniting humanity. Its teachings of speech contribute toward this mission by
instructing Muslims to use speech as a means not only to be truthful but also
to do good toward others and to be fair and respectful. With an emphasis
on truth and respect, the teachings of Islam attempt to preempt frictions
and misunderstandings by prescribing rules of conduct that guarantee for
all people not only freedom of speech but also fairness, absolute justice, and
the right of disagreement.

Speak the Truth

In order to achieve this goal of uniting mankind under a single banner
of peace, the approach taken in Islam is to both grant people the right to
express their views while also prescribing limits to speech so as to ensure
it is done in a proper manner. For this reason, the fundamental instruction
provided by Islam to its followers regarding speech is to seek and speak the
truth in all circumstances. This is emphasized in the Quran when it instructs:
"O ye who believe! fear Allah, and say the straightforward word."[16] This
verse sets the gold standard with regard to speech. It not only instructs Muslims to speak the truth but also goes a step forward by emphasizing that one
should only choose such words that do not even mislead others. Speaking
the straightforward word means to say only that which is completely true
and appropriate, with not even a hint of uselessness or misrepresentation.
Dishonesty is highly looked down upon in Islam, which is why Muslims are

commanded to adhere to honesty in all situations—no matter how easy or difficult it may be.

The commandment to speak the straight word, however, has deeper meanings as well. The standard set by Islam for speaking the straightforward word also includes speaking that which is appropriate and relevant. In this case, regardless of whether or not something is true, if uttering those words is inappropriate or irrelevant, Islam instructs its followers to refrain in order to give preference to the establishment and conservation of peace and unity. Likewise, overstating or exaggerating the truth is considered a violation of the principle of speaking the straightforward word. Therefore, this fundamental and central Islamic directive regarding speech is to say only that which is based on truth, wisdom, and fairness. Such high standards are put in place in order to fulfill the mission of Islam to unite humankind. The Prophet Muhammad emphasized this when he instructed his followers, saying, "Leave alone that which involves thee in doubt and adhere to that which is free from doubt, for truth is comforting, falsehood is disturbing."[17]

Speak in the Best Manner

Going further, the Quran contains the following words from God: "And say to My servants that they should always speak that which is best. Surely, Satan stirs up discord among them. Surely, Satan is an open enemy to man."[18] When instructing people to speak whatever is "best," the word used by God in the Quran is حسن (*husn*), which is defined as something that "was, or became, good, or goodly, beautiful, comely, or pleasing."[19] Therefore, this verse carries a heavy instruction for people to always use their speech for a good purpose. They must speak in a manner that is pleasing and comforting to others. It continues by warning that Satan will stir up conflict and friction among people, but the response should always be to "speak that which is best." Thus, even in the face of discord by evil forces, all believers of God are instructed to adopt a manner of speech that is best, offering wisdom and good counsel.

This same word (husn) is used elsewhere in the Quran, when believers are instructed to "speak to men kindly."[20] Hence, it is further established that Islam's teachings regarding speech draw people toward expressing themselves in a manner that is respectful and constructive. This makes it clear that Islam requires speech be used for only good purposes rather than destructive purposes. The objective remains to create an environment of peace, justice, and unity.

Speak Well in Public

So, with all the aforementioned Islamic guidance taken into consideration, it is clear that Islam guides believers to speak the truth, to speak clearly, to speak that which is appropriate, to speak that which is best and pleasing, and to speak kindly. Building upon this strong foundation, the Quran further speaks about the Islamic views regarding inappropriate and tasteless kinds of speech when it states: "Allah likes not the uttering of unseemly speech in public, except on the part of one who is being wronged. Verily, Allah is All-Hearing, All-Knowing."[21]

Here we are told to refrain from speaking ill of others publicly, as doing so creates ill will and bad blood, which can disturb public peace. The reasonable exception offered here is for people to speak aloud when they are being wronged so that others may come to their aid. But even in such a case, by saying that "Allah is All-Hearing and All-Knowing," assurance is given to those being wronged that it is better to remain patient instead of speaking ill against the one who wrongs them, as God is well aware of what everyone does.

Speech Is Allowed and Encouraged

This does not mean, however, that Islam only allows conformity. Muslims are instructed to indeed speak out again injustice, falsehood, crookedness, and wickedness. They are allowed to disagree and even argue but are instructed to do so in a dignified and appropriate manner. Muslims are reminded of the guidance from the Prophet Muhammad that all deeds are judged by their intentions. In that regard, Islam not only allows but also encourages all people to pursue free speech but cautions that the intention behind the speech should be to serve a good purpose, promote peace, and bring people closer to God and each other.

Islam even allows one to express disagreement in religious matters. In fact, the Quran encourages believers of God to share the message of truth with others who may be misled. Speaking from the standpoint of Islam, there is certainly significant disagreement with other faiths on particular topics and teachings. For example, Islam fundamentally disagrees with the deification of Jesus in the Christian faith, as the Quran is abundantly clear that Jesus was a noble prophet of God but neither God's partner nor son. Islam also clearly disagrees with the mainstream Christian view regarding the death of Jesus at the time of the crucifixion and what his second coming means for the world (see chapter 8, "Demystifying Islam's View of Jesus

Christ"). Expressing these disagreements or even having a debate on these topics is not a problem, as long as it is done with dignity and respect, as well as the good intention of helping people arrive at the truth. Thus, Islam teaches that speech should not only be truthful, dignified and conveyed in the manner that is best but should also be for a good purpose.

If, however, the speech is marred by the harmful intention to deliberately insult people or promote disorder or division, Islam instructs that one should refrain. The underlying principle that drives this call for human decency when speaking to or about others is Islam's mission to unite humankind together, which cannot happen if people seek to insult one another. Creating insulting or slanderous videos, cartoons, or advertisements serves no purpose other than degrading or demonizing a people.

This is the fundamental difference between Islam's guidance for free speech and the view that many in the West are beginning to adopt. One promotes unity, whereas the other promotes individualism. Islam's position regarding speech to be used for good purposes is a far cry from the path toward which the most vocal proponents of freedom of speech seem to advocate these days. Such activists argue that their freedom of speech grants them the right to say anything, even though in the United States, there are several examples of speech that is not protected by the law. For example, defamation, fighting words, child pornography, and any words that would result in imminent lawless action are not constitutionally protected speech. This is an ongoing debate, even within American courts that have shown disagreement over time regarding what type of speech is constitutionally protected. Despite this debate and the clear limitations to speech, many free-speech advocates still insist that this freedom entitles them the right to say anything and everything, with no regard for the impact it will have on segments of society. Such people even claim—rather boldly—that they have a legal right and privilege to insult others.

Imagine, for a moment, a world in which people are free to say literally anything and everything on their minds, no matter how negative, insulting, or meaningless it may be. With no restraint on the content or manner of speech at all, civility would wither away and be overcome by disrespect through offensive speech. Every form of provocation would not only exist but also be promoted through a treacherous retaliation game by those insulted by another person or party. Antagonism would become the order of the day, and people would become increasingly confrontational. Instead of being called toward decency, people would be called toward thickening their skin in order to take the abuse. This is the world for which these so-called "freedom advocates" fight. Such people ostensibly champion democracy and freedom of expression, but they play with people's sentiments; this is neither democracy nor freedom of expression. Unfettered speech leads to animosity, resentment, and disorder.

Now imagine a world in which people are free to speak but their moral codes helps them make the conscious decision to use their speech in a productive and dignified manner. They only utter words with good intentions of having a positive impact on people's lives or otherwise serving some good purpose. They speak in order to promote truth and justice. Even when speaking in opposition to an idea or critical of an ideology, they do so with grace and respect and without aggression—in order to enjoin good, forbid evil, and find the truth. This is the world that Islam seeks to create: a world where disagreements are certainly welcome but in a respectful and dignified manner. It seeks to create a world in which the moral fabric of society is raised to such a degree that one need not fear verbal (or physical) assault from one's neighbor.

CHOOSING PRINCIPLE OVER PRIVILEGE

Among those vigorously fighting for freedom to say anything, there are many who focus so highly on whether they can say whatever they like, that they seem not to pause and think whether they should. Islam draws a distinction between what may be lawful to say and what is good and appropriate to say, and it calls people toward the principle from the Quran to say that which is best. Regardless of whether or not insulting speech is protected by state law, Islam says to set a higher standard for our words and actions. This was precisely the point emphasized by the Prophet Muhammad not only by his own example but also by his instructions to his followers. One of his companions, Wabisa ibn Ma'bad, spoke of his experience when he asked Muhammad about the trait of righteousness. He states: "I went to the Holy Prophet [Muhammad] and he asked me: Have you come to inquire after virtue? I said: Indeed. He said: Ask your heart. Virtue is that which satisfies the soul and comforts the heart; and sin is that which perturbs the soul and troubles the heart, even if people should pronounce it lawful and should seek your views on such matters."[22]

With these words, the Prophet Muhammad makes it clear that one should refrain from any act that perturbs someone's soul and troubles someone's heart, even if that act has been declared lawful by society. He advised to consider such troubling acts to be a sin, which all believers of God should shun. In their stead, one should adopt virtue through piety by performing those acts that satisfy souls and provide comfort and solace to hearts. With regard to speech, the teachings of Islam, thus, call all people toward this higher principle of uniting mankind through truth, respect, and a good word rather than focusing on any privilege provided by man-made law to say anything one desires in any manner one so chooses.

During his first inaugural address in 1953, former president Dwight Eisenhower said: "A people that values its privileges above its principles soon loses both."[23] His words are just as profound today as they were sixty years ago and are in perfect harmony with the concept found in Islam. One should give higher value to the principle of avoiding those things that lead to separation and conflict instead of focusing on a privilege to say as one pleases. Humankind cannot be united if people continue to trouble the hearts of others through crude, uncivilized, or untamed forms of expression. One need not even sacrifice one's legal right to speak; rather, one simply should set higher standards for oneself regarding how to speak.

Islam does not contradict the fact that freedom of expression is absolutely necessary for the progress and development of any society. It simply prescribes a code of conduct with this freedom, which teaches humankind that all words and actions have consequences. Poorly chosen words have the potential of creating conflict not only between individuals but also between communities and even nations. Yet, staunch free-speech fighters encourage people to throw caution to the wind and hurl insults as they please, disregarding the discord that will surely ensue. Treating speech as supreme and uninhibited at the expense of peace and harmony is an incredibly flawed concept. This is precisely the point made by Mirza Masroor Ahmad—the worldwide spiritual leader (Khalifa) of the Ahmadiyya Muslim Community—in regard to the issue of insulting forms of speech when he responded to the "Innocence of Muslims" film that allegedly instigated worldwide chaos in September of 2012. Ahmad said, "Let it not be that in the name of freedom of speech the peace of the entire world be destroyed."[24] Since the cause of world peace and unity is paramount, it must trump any petty desire to offend or insult others.

HOW SHOULD MUSLIMS RESPOND?

Opponents of Islam often twist its teachings and claim that it denies freedom of speech and censors those who insult Islam. Their assertion is based on real-life events and reactions from Muslims around the world in the face of various forms of insulting expression. Whether it was Salman Rushdie's book in 1988, the Danish cartoons of Prophet Muhammad in 2005, the amateur film "Innocence of Muslims" in 2012, or the countless provocative statements, videos, cartoons, and writings in between; many Muslims have indeed taken the bait over the past few decades and have sought to censor, silence, imprison, or even kill those who insult Islam. The world has also witnessed a myriad of cases where Muslims themselves were punished or even killed based on allegations that they spoke insulting words about Islam or Prophet Muhammad.

Violent responses to provocative or offensive speech not only are clear threats to peace, justice, and liberty but are also violations of core Islamic principles. Islam's approach to dealing with speech does not come in the form of imprisonment or violence, as that is not in line with the teachings of Islam, which concentrate on guiding an individual's system of choice. Islam's doctrines focus on guiding people to make a conscious decision toward words and deeds that unite individuals, communities, and nations. It does not order anyone to punish people who have unseemly speech.

Certainly the Prophet Muhammad was the greatest of all adherents to the Shariah revealed to him, and one need look no further than his life for irrefutable evidence that no worldly punishment for speech is prescribed within Islam. As with all prophets before him, Muhammad was rejected by the people of his nation, which is verified by the numerous examples in which he was openly mocked and insulted. Far from censoring such people or responding with threats, Muhammad responded with restraint and self-control.

The Quran records disbelievers repeatedly ridiculing the Prophet Muhammad, saying to him, "Thou art surely a madman,"[25] a word bearing the accusation that he was smitten with insanity. They referred to him as "a man who is a victim of deception"[26] and "a man bewitched."[27] When speaking about the Quran and Muhammad, they said, "These are but confused dreams; nay, he has forged it himself: nay, he is but a poet"[28]—bearing an accusation of deception repeated in the Quran with the words "Thou art but a fabricator."[29] Some claimed, "It is only a man who teaches him,"[30] alleging that Muhammad was being taught by another person instead of receiving revelations from God. Some disbelievers used their speech to tell others, "Listen not to this Quran, but make noise during its recital."[31]

Through this all, the Prophet Muhammad never retaliated nor called for these people to be attacked, seized, or executed; rather, he courageously endured all of their verbal assaults. He did so because Allah did not prescribe any punishment at all for such verbal abuses. To the contrary, Allah instructed: "And follow not the disbelievers and hypocrites, and overlook their annoying talk and put thy trust in Allah; for Allah is sufficient as a guardian."[32] Thus, the Prophet Muhammad continued to overlook the unseemly and derogatory speech of his detractors instead of getting upset. This is the way of all prophets of the past, as indicated in the Quran: "And how many a Prophet did we send among the earlier peoples! But there never came to them a Prophet but they mocked at him."[33] Thus, all prophets have been the subject of mockery, but they remained focused on the completion of their mission. This was certainly not due to a fear of those who mocked. Rather, it was due to the undying conviction that being on the side of God's truth was sufficient and one need not lower their own standards to those of the ignorant.

The instruction for Muhammad to remain patient in the face of hurtful words by his enemies is further reinforced in two different places in the Quran, when God instructs to "Bear patiently what they say."[34] [35] This is a clear instruction for Muslims to remain patient in the face of negative speech. The most one can do is to avoid the company of those who continue their derogatory attacks against Islam. The Quran validates this teaching when it commands: "When you hear the Signs of God being denied and mocked at, sit not with those who indulge in such talk until they engage in some other talk."[36] Thus, the recourse of a Muslim is to walk away or even sever ties with those who persist in mocking their faith. There simply is no room in Islam for responding to mockery or blasphemy with violence.

The Quran continues by instructing Muslims to respond to insulting speech with words of peace. It says, "The true servants of the Gracious God are those who walk on the earth humbly and when the ignorant address them, they avoid them gracefully by saying, 'Peace!'"[37] Thus, true believers of God are told to respond to speech with speech, but their speech is to be higher, better, and more dignified. They are not to lower themselves to the level of those who use their speech for nefarious purposes, nor are they to respond with violence. Rather, they must have the same courage as the Prophet of Islam to face such insults in the eye and respond with forbearance and calm, righteous speech. They are required to use logic and reason to rationally respond to such depraved acts in order to convey the blessed model and teachings of Muhammad, who said differences of opinion are a blessing in society.

The violent reactions from various parts of the Muslim world to disparaging or inflammatory words are not only unsupported by Islamic teachings, they are also clear violations of Islam's commandments regarding how to respond to offensive speech. There simply is no justification for violence in response to speech. The overreaction by Muslims to cases of blasphemy is nothing short of appalling and is symptomatic of cowardice and a weakness of faith. Had those Muslims commanded a strong understanding of their faith, they would have known that protests, riots, and violence run counter to the doctrine of Islam.

Let us not forget the Quranic commandment: "O ye who believe! be steadfast in the cause of Allah, bearing witness in equity; and let not a people's enmity incite you to act otherwise than with justice."[38] God commands believers to remain steadfast and dedicated to the path of righteousness and to avoid taking the bait by allowing an enemy's provocation to trigger them to commit unjust acts. How sad that many Muslims have forsaken these words in the Quran. Yet, it is reassuring that the vast majority of Muslims around the world have faithfully held firm to Islam's commandment to respond to pejorative speech with patience and dignity. Irrespective of the actions of some violent madmen within the Muslim world, the fact remains that Islam calls for patience and dignity in the face of verbal abuse.

So when you hear lunatics such as the Australian cleric Imam Feiz Mohammad claim that people who mock Islam are required to be beheaded[39], tell him to go read the Quran and educate himself on the faith to which he claims allegiance but of which he remains ignorant. And when you hear free-speech fighters claim that the best thing for the world is for uninhibited speech to reign supreme—no matter how insulting or offensive it may be—tell them that Islam's stance on speech is a much better recipe for creating the healthy climate necessary for the survival of peace.

7

DEMYSTIFYING WOMEN'S
RIGHTS IN ISLAM

Many people are surprised to hear that Islam champions the empowerment of women and that the Prophet Muhammad actually came as a mercy for women and granted them rights that were not only denied to them in seventh-century Arabia but also would take more than one thousand years to gain through their own struggle. Karen Armstrong, renowned British author, historian, and scholar of religions, noted the change that Muhammad brought for women: "We must remember what life had been like for women in the pre-Islamic period when female infanticide was the norm and when women had no rights at all. Like slaves, women were treated as an inferior species, who had no legal existence. In such a primitive world, what Muhammad achieved for women was extraordinary. The very idea that a woman could be witness or could inherit anything at all in her own right was astonishing."[1]

Claims that Islam advocates oppression of women are not backed by fact, but such claims are made due to the reports heard about women in Muslim-majority countries, which paint a picture of men oppressing women. Some in the West impugn the religion of Islam for atrocities and injustices committed against women in Muslim-majority countries, claiming there is something deeply rooted in the faith itself that leads to misogyny, injustice, and oppression. Conversely, others in the West do not blame the religion of Islam for these injustices; rather, they blame the patriarchal, male-dominated cultures in those countries for trying to control women in their society. Irrespective of the conclusion drawn by these different people, the fact remains that they see, recognize, and take offense to the treatment meted out to Muslim women in various parts of the world.

As such, there is no denying that women are highly mistreated in many countries around the world, including countries governed by Muslim leaders. Certainly, this problem of injustice toward women is not confined to Muslims alone, as men of various religious identities have committed cruel, misogynistic acts that any just or compassionate person would loath. But Muslims must answer the question of why there is abuse and discrimination of women in states that people call "Muslim countries." This question must be confronted. It is far too easy for Muslims to simply say that their faith does not support it—that is a tacit dismissal of the problem that truly exists.

In different "Muslim countries" around the world, we hear and read about women who are forbidden from driving, forbidden from obtaining an education, forced into marriage against their will, prosecuted for being victims of rape, victims of honor killings, and often silenced by men in their family. In all honesty, anyone not repulsed and disgusted by such treatment of women must reassess their own humanity. When the above cruelties are committed repeatedly in cultures claiming adherence to Islam, it is no wonder that non-Muslims in the West begin to establish a perception that the religion of Islam considers women inferior to men, gives women fewer rights than men, or even calls for the oppression of women.

They do not know that Muhammad never forbade women from driving—or riding a horse or camel, for that matter. They do not know that Muhammad never forbade women from obtaining an education. They do not know that Muhammad never allowed a woman to be forced into marriage. They do not know that Muhammad came and gave rights to women they had not yet been given. In this state of ignorance about Muhammad's teachings, many have concluded that the aforementioned abusive treatment of women is somehow not only sanctioned by, but also advocated within, Islam. The truth, however, is that abusive men in positions of power have entrenched this cruel behavior into those cultures—not due to their knowledge of Islam but, rather, due to their blatant ignorance of and disregard for Islam.

But to assert that mistreatment of women exists only in Muslim countries is a blatant fabrication. In societies such as our own here in the United States, it is claimed that women are free, safe, and untroubled in comparison to what Islam would prescribe. Sadly, this is simply untrue. According to a report released in March 2013 by the U.S. Department of Justice, the United States witnesses 270,000 cases of women being sexually assaulted or raped per year—and this is among the best it has been for nearly twenty years.[2] This means that it is considered a marked improvement in this country that we now witness an average of 740 cases of women being sexually victimized every single day. This translates to a sexual assault in the United

States every two minutes throughout the year. Considering these statistics, can anyone reasonably say that women are truly safe in this country?

Although a very large number of Americans define the United States as a Christian nation, it would be unreasonable to impugn Christianity for this flagrant regularity of rape. There is some disease within a society that causes such a rate of rape, but a reasonable person would not blame religion. Rather, they would focus on the atmosphere that breeds such criminals who would violate a woman like that. This is similar to the wisdom of Dr. Martin Luther King Jr. During his eulogy for three young girls killed in the bombing of the Sixteenth Street Baptist Church in 1963, Dr. King profoundly stated: "We must be concerned not merely about who murdered them, but about the system, the way of life, the philosophy which produced the murderers."[3] This holistic view is equally pertinent and necessary when investigating the atrocious treatment of women in this country as well as other countries. This means we need to understand the mental problems of those committing these crimes as well as the cultural views, philosophies, norms, and systems that foster misogyny and disrespect for women.

There are cultural and societal deficiencies prevalent in the countries in which such brutalities transpire. Historically, countries that currently exhibit problematic treatment of women have had a history of female mistreatment that has spanned thousands of years. For example, the powerful and widespread Roman civilization established views and attitudes toward women that we would consider dangerous. According to historians, women were "always under the power of some [male] house-chief. Marriage, in the first stage, simply transferred her to a new joint-family, of which her husband was chief. Legally she was in the same relation to him as was her daughter. On the death of a house-father, the female members did not thereby gain their liberty. They simply passed under the control of the new house-father. Thereby the mother might come under subjection to her own son, sisters to their brother."[4]

Encyclopedia Britannica records,

> In Roman Law a woman was even in historic times completely dependent. If married she and her property passed into the power of her husband; if unmarried she was (unless a vestal virgin) under the perpetual tutelage of her father during his life, and after his death . . . of her kinsmen by blood or adoption who would have been under the power of the common ancestor had he lived. . . . The wife was the purchased property of her husband, and, like a slave, acquired only for his benefit. A woman could not exercise any civil or public office . . . could not be

a witness, surety, tutor, or curator; she could not adopt or be adopted, or make a will or contract.[5]

After deep study of such history, orientalists and historians have concluded that Muhammad came to save women from their state of mistreatment. Twentieth- and early-twenty-first-century Scottish historian William Montgomery Watt was a former Episcopal priest who went on to author many books about Islam and the Prophet Muhammad and become an emeritus professor of Islamic Studies and Arabic at University of Edinburgh for fifteen years. He said: "At the time Islam began, the conditions of women were terrible—they had no right to own property, were supposed to be the property of the man, and if the man died everything went to his sons. Muhammad improved things quite a lot. By instituting rights of property ownership, inheritance, education and divorce, he gave women certain basic safeguards. Set in such historical context the Prophet can be seen as a figure who testified on behalf of women's rights."[6]

CHOOSING A ROLE MODEL

Islam guides its followers with the underlying principle of worshipping and gaining nearness to God and understanding His attributes. In Islam, God is given many names or attributes in order to help humankind understand Him better. Upon studying these attributes, one can begin to see that there are some attributes that are more masculine in nature (e.g., "the Protector," "the All Powerful," "Possessor of All Strength," etc.), whereas there are other attributes that are more feminine in nature ("the Compassionate," "the Forgiver," "the Comforter," "the Loving One," etc.). Not only does this indicate that God is without gender—possessing (what humankind considers to be) masculine and feminine qualities—but this also indicates that the attainment of God's attributes is open to all, irrespective of their predispositions.

Islam instructs its followers to choose God as the role model and the standard of excellence that they should seek to emulate. In Islam, internal peace is defined as the extent to which one aligns one's own personal attributes with God's attributes. This means that in the pursuit to emulate Him, one must endeavor to become more forgiving, more compassionate, stronger, more honest (for God is called the Truth), and so on. This puts men and women on a level playing field by giving each the right, the expectation, and the ability to emulate God's attributes.

This is where many—not all—modern-day feminists and feminist movements fall short. In their pursuit of equality, some feminist groups ironically set manhood as the standard they seek to emulate, by arguing that they, as women, want to be able to do everything a man can do. They inadvertently have set manhood as the standard by demanding to be given the same rights, the same treatment, the same jobs, and, sometimes, the same appearance as men. This is what happens when God is taken out of the equation. Such groups have limited their own potential by seeking only that which has been granted to men. Instead, the message that Islam would have for a woman is to make God that single model by which she defines herself. She is not defined by any sort of rank vis-à-vis man; rather, she is defined as a servant of God just as a man must define himself as a servant of God.

As we know, men have historically been in the seats of power across various civilizations. The pursuit of empowerment, thus, spurred for some women the pursuit of becoming like a man. But should men and women be the same? Some indulge in vain efforts to make men and women the same, whereas Islam teaches that men and women, as made by God, are different. This does not mean that one is better than the other. Men and women are equally valued, loved, and judged by God but are not the same. A woman's honor is not defined by how similar she is to a man. God has honored women by making them distinctive from men.

This is the danger with using the word "equality," which, by definition, connotes the quality of being the same. Rather than being the same, men and women are complementary to one another. Islam preaches gender equity as opposed to gender equality, for "gender equity" signifies that the qualities of fairness, justice, and impartiality are guaranteed to men *and* women. Instead of desiring equality, we should desire a world in which womanhood is not treated less than manhood and manhood is not treated less than womanhood. They should be treated with equity and fairness. Men and women certainly are spiritually equal, as they are both honored by God based solely on their devotion to His teachings.

People should admire and seek to emulate only the One from Whom they came. Islam teaches that women, like men, came from God, which is why they should seek to emulate His attributes. What may be at the root of the subconscious emulation of manhood is the flawed view that a woman was created from a man, based on the story that Eve was created from the rib of Adam. Islam entirely disagrees with this view and, instead, argues that both a man and a woman were created together from God's miracle.

The Quran teaches that men and women are created from a single soul: "O ye people! fear your Lord Who created you from a single soul and of its kind created its mate, and from them twain spread many men and women; and fear Allah, in whose name you appeal to one another, and fear Him particularly respecting ties of kinship. Verily, Allah watches over you."[7] By stating that all humans are created from a single soul, the Quran speaks of both men and women together as one soul. There is no support offered in the Quran of the theory that Eve was created from the rib of Adam. Instead, the Quran puts men and women on an equal level as being from a common soul created by God, thereby validating the spiritual equality of the genders. The Prophet Muhammad used to recite this verse when delivering marriage sermons in order to guide the newlyweds in their responsibility of "respecting ties of kinship" and in treating each other well and with respect.

Elsewhere, when the Quran describes that God made this world for the sustenance of humans, it then states, "And We have created you in pairs,"[8] thereby advancing the teaching that God created man and woman together as partners in this world. In fact, this is part of God's design, as it is stated in the Quran, "And of everything have We created pairs that you may reflect."[9] This means that the normal design of God is to create things in pairs, and this is clearly seen in the manner in which He created humankind as well.

GENDER ROLES AND RELATIONSHIP

As partners who have been created complementary to one another, men and women should understand and respect their differences. The Quran even goes as far as to state: "Covet not that whereby Allah has made some of you excel others. Men shall have a share of that which they have earned, and women a share of that which they have earned."[10] Men and women have been given particular areas in which they excel one another. There should be no jealousy or envy in that regard. A man should not be jealous and desire to attain the nature that God has granted to women. Likewise, a woman should not be jealous and desire to attain the nature that God has granted to men. These differences do not set a superiority or inferiority over anyone. They simply impart on men and women areas of distinctiveness.

It is clear that men and women are different. Men and women have physical, physiological, biological, hormonal, and even genetic differences. The most obvious is the multitude of different physical and biological attributes given to women that grant them the ability to bear and nurture a child. Not only can a woman bear and deliver a child, but she can also single-handedly nourish a newborn with her body through nursing. If the child had no other access to food or drink at this sensitive stage of its life, he or she could survive exclusively due to the mother. A man simply cannot do that. On the other hand, physical and biological attributes have been given to men that generally grant them the capacity of greater physical strength. Of course, women can also possess great physical strength, but the biology of men allows for a greater capacity for strength and muscle mass.

As such, the general roles for women and men in Islam match these natural differences. With the higher capacity for physical strength, a man is obligated to work or labor in order to ensure his family is provided for, which means he is obligated to ensure the needs of the entire family (including his wife) are met. With the natural capacity for childbirth and nurturing of children, a woman is obligated to ensure the proper and healthy upbringing of the children. These are the general tasks for which each man and woman is held accountable. It does not mean, however, that women are forbidden from working and men are forbidden from taking care of their children. Women can indeed work and men can indeed help in the rearing of children, but they are still held accountable for ensuring that their primary responsibilities and obligations are fulfilled. This is how Islam establishes a fair and complementary partnership between men and women, in order to provide support and balance to one another.

The equity granted to men and women is repeated throughout the Quran, which goes to great lengths to establish that men have not been granted any favor in the sight of God. When defining the people who will be rewarded by God, the Quran states:

> Surely, men who submit themselves to God and women who submit themselves to Him, and believing men and believing women, and obedient men and obedient women, and truthful men and truthful women, and men steadfast in their faith and steadfast women, and men who are humble and women who are humble, and men who give alms and women who give alms, and men who fast and women who fast, and men who guard their chastity and women who guard their chastity and men who remember Allah much and women who remember Him— Allah has prepared for all of them forgiveness and a great reward.[11]

In this verse, we see the extent to which God has gone to establish equity and fair play among men and women. It could have been very easy for this verse to read: "Surely, people who submit themselves to God, believing people, obedient people, truthful people, those steadfast in their faith, those who fast, and so on." But a point was made to expressly state that each of these matters apply equally to men and women. This is meant to teach people that men *and* women have equal access and privileges in heaven. One is no more privileged than the other. In fact, equal protection is even guaranteed to men and women from God when it is said: "Those who persecute the believing men and the believing women and then repent not, for them is, surely, the punishment of Hell, and for them is the torment of heart-burning."[12] Men *and* women are protected by God, and Islam tells its followers that anyone—whether Muslim or not—who persecutes or oppresses a believing man or woman will be punished by God.

THE HEAD COVERING

The natural question people, then, raise is regarding the head covering. If men and women have the same responsibilities and privileges, they argue, then why does Islam command women to cover themselves? One must keep in mind that the head covering that Muslim women wear does not rob them of any privilege or access. Contrary to the accusation levied by many opponents of the Islamic head covering, it is not a form of oppression or repression—Muslim women from all academic and economic backgrounds still choose to cover their heads in Eastern and Western nations around the world. There are many incredibly accomplished Muslim women in various societies around the world—all of whom cover their head. Muslim women have been prime ministers of Muslim-majority nations (e.g., Benazir Bhutto in Pakistan and Sheikh Hasina in Bangladesh), Nobel Peace Prize winners (e.g., Yemini journalist and politician Tawakel Karman), and world-renowned activists (e.g., teenaged Pakistani Malala Yousafzai). Their head coverings clearly did not oppress or repress them.

It is also incorrect to claim that the head covering is purely a cultural tradition adopted by the early Muslims due to the prevailing form of female dress at that time. To the contrary, the head covering is a specific Islamic instruction that has its foundation in the Quran and the teachings of the Prophet Muhammad.

A woman's head covering can be understood within the greater context of Islam's commandments to be modest in dress and to protect one's chastity. Islam instructs both men and women to observe modesty and humility in the way they not only act and speak but also dress. This will certainly seem strange to those segments of society that admire immodest forms of dress and even put pressure on women to prove their liberation through immodest attire. But the stress on modesty cannot be mistaken for oppression or closed-mindedness. Rather, it should be seen as the act of remaining loyal to the guidance given by God.

The instruction about dress and head covering is mentioned twice in the Quran, with different words used in each verse to describe the types of covering. What seems to be the first of the two verses revealed is found in chapter 24, where it states:

> And say to the believing women that they restrain their looks and guard their private parts, and that they display not their beauty or their embellishment except that which is apparent thereof, and that they draw their head-coverings over their bosoms, and that they display not their beauty or embellishment save to their husbands, or to their fathers, or the fathers of their husbands, or their sons, or the sons of their husbands, or their brothers, or the sons of their brothers, or the sons of their sisters, or women who are their companions, or those that their right hands possess, or such of male attendants as have no desire for women, or young children who have not yet attained knowledge of the hidden parts of women.[13]

When describing the head coverings, this verse employs the phrase خُمُرِهِنَّ (*khu-mu-ri-hinna*), which is a plural form of the Arabic word خِمَارٌ (*khimaar*), which is translated by classical Arabic lexicons as "a woman's head-covering" or "a piece of cloth with which a woman covers her head."[14] The commandment given in this verse is for a woman to have a head covering that also covers her bosom. The word translated as "bosoms" actually has as its meaning "the opening at the neck and bosom of a shirt and the like,"[15] which describes the area of the body that this garment is meant to cover. Interestingly, this has the same application for the male use of the turban, which not only covers the head but also has a long end that hangs down, "because a man covers his head with it in the like manner as a woman covers her head with her خِمَارٌ (khimaar): when he disposes it in the Arab manner, he turns [the end of] it under the jaws [nearly in the same manner in which a woman disposes her خِمَارٌ (khimaar)]."[16]

By using this phrase, the Quran makes it clear the manner in which God calls upon women to cover their heads and the intimate area of the neck to the chest. This verse also makes clear the intention of this covering, which is to conceal their intimate beauty from those who have no right to see it. The verse makes clear that a woman is not called to cover herself at all times; rather, she is called to cover her head when in front of males who are not closely related, as a means of guarding and protecting herself.

Finally, this verse is a fitting response to the claim made by some Muslims that the instruction for head covering was only for the Prophet Muhammad's wives. This verse expresses very clearly that it is an instruction for all believing women.

The second verse revealed in the Quran on this topic is found in chapter 33, where it states: "O Prophet! tell thy wives and thy daughters, and the women of the believers, that they should draw close to them portions of their loose outer coverings. That is more likely that they may thus be distinguished and not molested. And Allah is Most Forgiving, Merciful."[17] The word used in this verse is جَلَا بِيْبِهِنَّ (*jalabi-bi-hinna*), which is the plural form of the singular Arabic word جلباب (*jilbab*), translated to mean "loose outer coverings" in this verse. This word carries the meaning of a "woman's outer wrapping garment . . . or one with which a woman covers over her other garments."[18] The verse also states the benefit derived from this outer covering—women covering themselves as such and concealing their beauty may, thus, be differentiated in society as Muslims who observe modesty and do not want men staring at, and commenting on, them. It also states that such a covering offers protection from being molested—translated from the Arabic word يُؤْذَيْنَ (*yu-thay-na*), which means to become "annoyed, molested, harmed, or hurt."[19] Thus, the modest dress is meant to save a woman from the annoyance and danger associated with men staring at her as she goes about her business.

It is important to note that the Quran does not give explicit instructions regarding the type of veil or head covering a woman should wear. This will differ from society to society based on the prevailing culture in that country. The underlying instruction in Islam is for women to dress modestly in a manner that does not attract attention to them, thereby distinguishing themselves from others and providing themselves with a safeguard against harassment and other dangers.

But a discourse about the head covering would be incomplete if the Quran's verse isn't taken in further context. As discussed earlier, there is wisdom with not only the words used in the Quran but also the sequence of the words. As already discussed, the verse in chapter 24 contains instructions for women to restrain their eyes and dress modestly by guarding their private parts. But in the verse that precedes it, God first focuses on men—thereby indicating a greater burden on men—by stating: "Say to the believing men that they restrain their looks and guard their private parts. That is purer for them. Surely, Allah is Well-Aware of what they do."[20] There is deep wisdom to be found in the fact that God first addresses men before addressing women regarding the instruction about modesty.

The sequence of the verses helps us understand that the instruction for women to cover themselves as a form of protection is a safety measure, but the real obligation and expectation is put upon the man in this verse to restrain his eyes when in front of a woman. As with most things, Islam does not deal with matters superficially nor attempt to simply cover problems with bandages. Instead, Islam goes to the root of issues—in this case, the root of moral issues within a society. With regard to women, of course, it is still an instruction from God for them to conceal their beauty from those who are not intimate relatives as a form of moral and physical protection, and they are commanded to protect their own morals by restraining their eyes from staring at men. But the primary responsibility of protecting the honor and comfort of women—as well as protecting their own morals, which, in turn, affects the morals of society—is put on men, with the instruction to restrain their eyes when in the presence of women.

PROTECTING THE MORAL FABRIC OF SOCIETY

Restraining one's eyes has deep significance and builds the basis of Islam's moral code for society. Men and women are both instructed to dress modestly and refrain from staring at each other in order to protect the moral values of society from eroding. Therefore, to "restrain one's eyes" means that one should restrain oneself from impure and immoral thoughts about others.

This is a far cry from what we have become accustomed to in Western societies. There really is no protection from impure and immoral thoughts about members of the opposite sex. In fact, impure thoughts are provoked and promoted. We are surrounded by a society that implicitly (and sometimes explicitly) teaches women and girls that their value lies in the shape and size of their body or how pretty they are. Women are used as sexual objects in order to sell cars, alcohol, and even food. Cover photos emphasize how a woman should present her body in a manner that is attractive to others. Even when highlighting female sports figures, instead of honoring their skills and achievements, magazines highlight their body and sex appeal. Lust is, sadly, promoted—mostly for commercial gain, but it ends up affecting popular views toward sexuality.

As a result, some women starve themselves, get plastic surgery, and go to great lengths and expense to fit this "standard" set by modern society. While writing about the rising epidemic of eating disorders, Courtney E. Martin argues that we are now faced with "a generation of girls obsessed with the shape of their bodies, the number of calories they consume, and their fitness regimens. I challenge you to find a female between the ages of nine and twenty-nine who doesn't think about these issues more than she would like to, who doesn't feel racked by guilt and unsatisfied with her body a lot of the time."[21] Such is the effect when women no longer remain women; rather, they become objects of desire, physical perfection, and lust.

This is also the basis for the separation of men and women in Islam. Often it is asked why there is segregation in Islam. In truth, there is no segregation—for, "to segregate" means "to exclude or isolate one group from the rest." Women are not segregated from men; Islam does not teach to segregate or exclude women. Rather, there is separation in Islam—that is, men and women are instructed to generally remain separate from one another. It does not generate a subculture for women; rather, it generates a parallel culture. Of course, this is not an absolute separation—men and women are not forbidden from interacting with one another. Rather, it is a general principle to safeguard oneself by refraining from openly and uninhibitedly intermingling with members of the opposite sex who are not close relatives.

It is a natural, innate tendency for men and women to seek privacy and comfort by separating from the opposite sex. This why there are separate men's and women's bathrooms all over the world; not simply for privacy but also for comfort. For, if privacy was the only concern, there would be no need for separate bathrooms since the individual stalls within the bathroom would provide enough privacy. Yet, the wide acceptance to maintain completely separate bathrooms showcases the innate comfort of women among other women and of men among other men. This would perhaps explain the data that show that boys and girls in single-sex education facilities perform considerably higher than those who attend coed facilities. For example, an analysis in the UK of more than 700,000 girls showed "that those at girls' schools consistently made more progress than those in co-ed secondaries."[22] This is an instinct that God has installed within humans to maintain some wall of separation as a protection of our own morality and decency; a separation that had always been understood and honored even in the United States.

It is only in modern times that this wall has slowly withered away and, thus, slowly damaged society's views of morality. Not too long ago in this country, a man and woman would not even touch or shake hands when they first met. This was the instinctive wall of separation to maintain their sexual morality and chastity. Now, in the twenty-first century, men and women who are complete strangers often enter a full embrace—and, depending on the country, perhaps a kiss on the cheek—the very first time they meet. This free intermingling and constant physical contact has clouded modern-day judgment of decency, resulting in great social ills. This explains not only the skyrocketing rate of extramarital affairs and, thus, broken families, but also the disturbingly lucrative pornography industry—estimated to generate roughly $13 billion a year in revenue in the United States alone.[23] This is more than the market value (also called "gross domestic product") of more than a third of the world's nations.[24] Considering so much adult entertainment is available for free online, prevalence of pornography is even higher than this revenue figure would indicate. This perpetuates not only the moral degradation of society but also the objectification of women, who are made into objects of lust.

Islam's instructions are meant to save women from becoming subjected to this perverse view. It teaches that women are to be honored and cherished, for their honor has been granted to them by God; not by man or any other person. This is the same instruction brought by other prophets for the people of various times and cultures. Thus, not only Muslim women but also women of other faiths were given this instruction to dress modestly.

For example, in the New Testament, it is written: "Likewise, I want women to adorn themselves with proper clothing, modestly and discreetly, not with braided hair and gold or pearls or costly garments."[25] Modesty in dress is often associated in such texts with chastity and piety, which is why the head covering had been a normative practice for millennia. It wasn't until 1976 that this view was changed when the Catholic Church issued a document, which included the statement that "these ordinances, probably inspired by the customs of the period, concern scarcely more than disciplinary practices of minor importance, such as the obligation imposed upon women to wear a veil on their head (1 Cor. 11:2–16); such requirements no longer have a normative value."[26] In 1983, a new code of the Canon Law was issued as the system of laws for the church, and it was the first such code of Canon Law to not include the canon of the head coverings or veils. Until then, even reform-minded Christian theologians accepted the head covering of women, especially during public worship service.

Thus, it was modernization—not the decree of God—that led people to abandon the original teaching of modesty concerning head covering. The principle of head covering in Islam is driven by the desire to obey divine commandments due to one's love for God. To call the Islamic head covering a form of oppression is not only incorrect but also an example of one's forgetfulness of similar principles found in other faiths. It cannot be considered oppression if sincere Muslims are the ones who remain loyal to God's instructions.

It is absolutely true that too many Muslim women are compelled by men or governments to cover their heads, but this is not the spirit of Islam. As with all other commandments and instructions from God in Islam, the burden is on the individual to obey the law. They cannot be made to follow the law by force. A man has every right to admonish his wife, daughter, or sister to obey the commandments of God, but he cannot forcibly compel her to do so. Muslim men who do so are disobeying the guidance of Islam.

In all fairness, the only scripture that disagrees with this is the Bible, which gives men the authority to govern and enforce a woman's head covering. Whereas the directive for head covering in the Quran is given to women, the Bible speaks to those around the woman, instructing them to enforce her head covering. After stating that a man should not cover his head, it declares that "every woman who has her head uncovered while praying or prophesying disgraces her head, for she is one and the same as the woman whose head is shaved. For if a woman does not cover her head, let her also have her hair cut off; but if it is disgraceful for a woman to have her hair cut off or her head shaved, let her cover her head."[27] So whereas the Bible calls for a woman's head to be shaved if she refuses to cover her hair, the Quran leaves the matter in God's realm.

This is where Islam takes a divergent view from that of Christianity. Both agree that women should conceal their beauty, but they seem to disagree as to the motivation for women to do so. The Bible states: "For a man ought not to have his head covered, since he is the image and glory of God; but the woman is the glory of man. For man does not originate from woman, but woman from man; for indeed man was not created for the woman's sake, but woman for the man's sake. Therefore the woman ought to have a symbol of authority on her head, because of the angels."[28] Islam fundamentally disagrees with this and does not claim that woman is the glory of man. Islam advocates that she is the glory of God, just like a man is the glory of God. According to Islam, man cannot be the glory of God because God creates everything in pairs. So the glory of God's creation of humans lies in both man and woman equally, according to the Quran. Additionally, as stated earlier, Islam disagrees with the claim that woman originated from man. Just like man, she originated from God only. This is why the Quran declares that man and woman were created from a single soul, together from God. This is the equality established by Islam—in the sight of God, men and women are on an equal level.

ISLAM'S TREATMENT OF WOMEN

Considering the equity that Islam grants to women, as well as the spiritual equality that is guaranteed for women, it is tragic to witness the brutal treatment women face in countries professing to follow the teachings of Islam. Muhammad brought rights that were not previously granted to women by divine order. Islam is the first religion to grant women the right to inheritance. It is the first to afford women the right to own property. Regardless of economic position, Islam requires a man to provide a dowry to his wife, which becomes her wealth and which he is not allowed to take from her. Islam grants both men and women the right to divorce. Islam granted women the same access to heaven as it granted men, with the aforementioned verses delineating the equal requirements for a man or a woman to be granted "forgiveness and a great reward." After God established this harmonizing relationship between man and woman, it is appalling to witness the inequity delivered to women by Muslim men in many countries around the globe. Such men abandon the high level of honor they are required to give to women.

Motherhood

Islam lays great stress on the commandment to honor and respect one's parents, with particular emphasis made on a greater honor to be reserved for the mother. The Quran records a commandment that shows just how significant it is to behave compassionately toward parents: "Thy Lord has commanded, that ye worship none but Him, and that ye show kindness to parents. If one or both of them attain old age with thee, never say to them as much as *ugh* [an expression of disgust] nor reproach them, but always address them with kindly speech. And lower to them the wing of humility out of tenderness."[29] Respecting parents and behaving benevolently toward them is given so much value that this instruction is presented immediately after the commandment to maintain an unwavering belief in the One God. Far from allowing callous actions toward parents, this verse even prohibits the utterance of harsh words to them.

After establishing the respect and honor due to parents, Islam then begins to lay further emphasis particularly on the mother. It begins by highlighting the greater role the mother plays in bringing a child into the world: "And We have enjoined on man to be good to his parents. His mother bears him with pain, and brings him forth with pain."[30] A great deal of appreciation is taught to Muslims for the pain and effort that the mother must endure during pregnancy and childbirth, as well as the sacrifice, love, and education she provides to the child. It is recorded in the books of Hadith that "someone went to Muhammad and asked him, 'Who has the first priority to be well treated?' Prophet Muhammad answered him, 'Your mother.' He asked, 'Then who?' He answered 'Your mother.' Asked again, 'Then who?' 'Your mother,' answered the Prophet. Asked 'Then who?' The Prophet answered, 'Your father.'"[31] The fact that he emphasized the mother three times before mentioning the father was meant to teach his followers the high degree of care and respect owed to women because of the distinction God has given to them of being able to be mothers. Muslims are taught that motherhood is a noble role of high distinction and one that a man can never obtain.

Due to the critical role that the mother specifically maintains in the life of her children, a great level of respect and adoration is given to her. This took the Arabs at that time by surprise. Considering the popular view of women in Arabia at the time when Muhammad brought these teachings, one can imagine why this was originally considered an absurd thought by the male-dominated society. But Muhammad pushed further by telling the people "Paradise lies at the feet of your mothers."[32] Since every woman is a potential mother, he effectively stated that paradise lies at the feet of women—meaning one can attain paradise based on how one treats women. This statement by the Prophet Muhammad indicates the high level of honor and status of women in Islam. Thus, the depraved seventh-century Arab society was commanded that women are to be protected, respected, honored, treated equitably, and allowed to own property, obtain education, and seek divorce for any reason. The Arabs at that time laughed at and ridiculed these teachings, which became a big hindrance for them to accept Islam. This is why Muhammad was considered a revolutionary.

Wives

This respect for women is not simply confined to one's mother. As mentioned, Islam prescribes a loving relationship between a husband and wife, calling for them to be partners and friends to one another.

The Quran states, "And the believers, men and women, are friends one of another. They enjoin good and forbid evil and observe Prayer and pay the Zakat and obey Allah and His Messenger. It is these on whom Allah will have mercy. Surely, Allah is Mighty and Wise. Allah has promised to believers, men and women, Gardens underneath which rivers flow, wherein they will abide, and delightful dwelling-places in Gardens of Eternity."³³ This verse refers to men and women as being friends of one another. The Arabic word used for friends is اوْلِيَاء (*awliya*)—the plural form of ولِي (*wali*), which means not only a friend but also a helper, protector, and ally. It refers to one we can rely on for support, help, and protection. This is the guidance Islam provides to its followers regarding the type of relationship that men and women are to establish with each other.

In light of this verse, it is not only shocking but also shameful to know that there are some so-called "Muslim" men who abuse their wives. Not only does Islam teach that his wife is a friend and ally for him, but it also teaches that a husband and wife are required to protect one another. Elsewhere, the Quran refers to a husband and wife as a garment for one another, expressing that husbands and wives are at an equal level and are meant to provide comfort and protection to one another. How can such a man who abuses his wife ever consider that he is living up to the expectation that Islam has put upon him?

Beating Wives?

Some Muslim men reference a particular verse from the Quran in defense of their so-called "right" to abuse their wife. As expected, this is the same argument used by opponents of Islam to contend that the Quran promotes the physical abuse of women. Far from promoting domestic abuse, the Quran confronts the reality of the male weakness that allows a man's anger to be incited to the point that he would strike his wife, and thus presents a path of anger management. The verse in question reads as follows:

> Men are guardians over women because Allah has made some of them excel others, and because men spend on them of their wealth. So virtuous women are obedient, and guard the secrets of their husbands with Allah's protection. And as for those on whose part you fear disobedience, admonish them and keep away from them in their beds and chastise them. Then if they obey you, seek not a way against them. Surely, Allah is High and Great.³⁴

The verse should be considered in its entirety. The fact of the matter is that this verse of the Quran imposes a restriction on men rather than providing them with permission to spank or strike their wives. Here in the United States, there are laws that punish domestic violence, but this only comes *after* the fact and has not curbed the rate of domestic abuse, which remains rampant. The U.S. Department of Justice published a report in

2000 that states that nearly one in four women experience at least one physical assault by a spouse or partner during adulthood. It estimates that about 1.5 million women are assaulted by their partner every single year in this country, and women who are physically assaulted by an intimate partner average nearly seven physical assaults by that same partner.[35] So, there is clearly a problem that even strict laws cannot curtail.

Islam describes a process that endeavors to prevent the abuse of women *before* it happens. The above verse begins by defining a family unit. To set its appropriate context, it appears shortly after the verse quoted earlier that tells men and women not to covet what the other has because each excels the other in particular ways: "Covet not that whereby Allah has made some of you excel others. Men shall have a share of that which they have earned, and women a share of that which they have earned."[36] The present verse continues by stating that it is a man's responsibility and obligation to provide for and protect the family and, thus, appoints him the guardian of his wife and family. This authority implies that the man must be noble, as a guardian must behave in a manner that is worthy of this responsibility.

This authority does not give any man the right to resort to violence to resolve family disputes. As stated previously, men and women are instructed to support one another and treat each other kindly. So the man's responsibilities as a guardian do not give him license to mistreat his wife. By guarding, loving, and providing for his wife, he can earn her love, affection, and willingness to follow his lead. That is what it means when the verse tells the wife to be obedient and protect her husband by cooperating with and listening to him in all good things.

The Quran takes the much-needed approach of teaching men how to curb their anger when it is aroused. This is an absolute necessity. Professor James Q. Wilson explained the significance of this approach in his summary of the extensive research of Dr. Louann Brizendine—a neuropsychiatrist at the University of California, San Francisco, and founder of the first clinic in the country to study gender differences in brain, behavior, and hormones. Professor Wilson reported that according to Dr. Brizendine's research:

> The part of the brain that stimulates our anger and aggression (the amygdala) is much larger in men than in women, while the part of the brain that restrains anger (the prefrontal cortex) is smaller in men than in women. The areas of the brain that influence aggression are also much larger in men than in women . . . and the testosterone in boys' brains makes them much more aggressive and less interested in talking or in social connections than (largely) testosteronefree girls. All the evidence

points in one direction: Men, by no choice of their own, are far more prone to violence and far less capable of self-restraint than women.[37]

Of course, this does not absolve men of blame if they resort to violence; rather, it indicates that men must take conscious measures to curb their tendency toward violence. This is why the Quran presents a process for reducing environmental triggers and curbing biological urges. Instead of dealing with the matter of domestic abuse *after* the fact, the wisdom of Islam is to address the anger that leads men to abuse their wives.

Women are instructed to reduce these triggers, and men are instructed to curb the urge to resort to violence if their wives display gross disobedience or rebellion. The Arabic word translated as disobedience in this verse is نشوز (*nushooz*), which does not refer to a simple disagreement. Rather, its root verb signifies to rise up in general or, more specifically, to rise up against someone "for the purpose of contention [or] altercation."[38] It, thus, describes a situation in which the wife—far from being a partner and companion to the husband—has rebelled against her husband, "exalted herself against him . . . deserted him, or she disliked him or hated him, and was an evil companion to him."[39] Thus, the Quran deals with a crisis in which the wife has compromised the very security of the family and its structure.

The process then prescribed is for anger management, reformation, and reconciliation. The first step prescribed to the man is to verbally admonish his wife. This means to verbally express his unhappiness with her behavior. After doing so, if the behavior persists over time, the second step is to separate beds. What this indicates is for the man to separate from his wife for some time not only to further express the gravity of the situation with the hopes of changing her behavior and reconciling but also to calm himself down and control his anger. Again, the purpose behind this act is to seek reconciliation. Regarding this separation from one's wife, the Quran states, "The maximum period of waiting is four months; then if they go back to their normal relationship, surely, Allah is Most Forgiving, Merciful."[40] So this separation can last from one night to as many as four months, during which time both the man and woman are expected to reform themselves and seek reconciliation. As American Islamic scholar, professor, and author Ms. Amina Wadud explained, "It is a cooling-off period which would allow both the man and the woman, separately, to reflect on the problem at hand. As such, this measure also has equally mutual implications."[41]

More often than not, the time elapsed during these two steps cools tempers, and the urge to resort to violence is diminished. After such a lengthy period, however, if the gross behavior continues, a third step is offered if the urge still persists to employ stricter measures. It is described in the Quran as اضْرِبُوهُنَّ (*idribu-huna*), which is derived from the root Arabic verb ضرب (*daraba*) and has a wide variety of meanings according to all comprehensive Arabic lexicons. This word has been used throughout the Quran to mean the act of striking, splitting apart, or moving or traveling away. Many believe this means permission to beat your wife, while others believe this means a further separation between the two parties. The Prophet Muhammad explained the meaning of this verse and word (daraba) by his example. It is recorded in history that he never beat any of his wives. As the Prophet Muhammad is an example for all believers to follow, this profound display of restraint is a lesson for all Muslim men on how to handle themselves in this situation.

If the process fails, the next verse describes a process of arbitration. Islam introduces many steps for reconciliation before considering divorce. Although divorce is allowed for both men and women, Islam prescribes many steps for the husband and wife to resolve their issues together and, thus, avoid divorce. Professor Wadud explains that in light of the excessive violence prevalent among the Arabs and early Muslims at that time, "this verse should be taken as prohibiting unchecked violence against females. Thus, this is not permission, but a severe restriction of existing practices."[42]

Contrast with Some "Muslim" Countries

This is a far cry from the popular view today about women in Muslim societies. The manner in which women are treated in many of these countries—where they are beaten, prohibited from obtaining education, become victims of senseless honor killings, are prosecuted and persecuted for being victims of rape, suffer torture through female genital mutilation (FGM), or are forced to become child brides—are travesties of the highest degree and absolutely unjustifiable according to the teachings of Islam. One cannot deny that these atrocities are indeed committed in countries that call themselves a "Muslim nation."

Considering the aforementioned Islamic commandments about revering women and treating them with fairness, the only logical conclusion is that all such atrocities are truly sins according to Islam. The criminals enacting these brutalities are not doing so due to religion. After all, honor killings are committed not only by some Muslims but also by some Arab Christians, as well as some Hindus and Sikhs from India. This is why *Time Magazine* published an article in 2010 asking why there is such a rise in honor killings among Hindus in India.[43] This is a cultural and personal disease that must be eradicated. Of course, some Muslim perpetrators claim their crimes are justified by harsh Islamic penalties, including death for adultery. But as already proven in chapter 4, "Demystifying Shariah," death is not the Islamic punishment for adultery. So honor killings are truly antithetical to Islam.

Likewise is the case for FGM, also known as "female circumcision." This is an ancient, barbaric practice that predates Islam. First century BCE historian and geographer Strabo recorded ancient practices of female circumcision among Egyptians, stating: "circumcision and excision of girls is also customary among them, as among the Judaeans, for the latter also are, in origin, Egyptians."[44] And although there are ignorant Muslims who practice this ancient tradition under the false notion that it is an Islamic injunction, the fact is that neither the Quran nor Muhammad called for female circumcision. The founding director of the International Program at the Center for Reproductive Rights, Ms. Anika Rahman, even wrote: "The practice predates the arrival of Christianity and Islam in Africa and is not a requirement of either religion. In fact, FC/FGM is practiced by Jews, Christians, Muslims and indigenous religious groups in Africa."[45]

Sheikh Ali Gomaa—Grand Mufti of Egypt from 2003 to 2013—made a clear statement in 2007 that female circumcision "was not just 'un-Islamic' but forbidden"[46] and also stated that "the traditional form of excision is a practice totally banned by Islam because of the compelling evidence of the extensive damage it causes to women's bodies and minds."[47] Likewise, the Ghana News Agency quoted Dr. Ahmed Talib—dean of the Faculty of Sharia at Al Azhar University in Cairo—as saying: "All practices of female circumcision and mutilation are crimes and have no relationship with Islam. Whether it involves the removal of the skin or the cutting of the flesh of the female genital organs . . . it is not an obligation in Islam."[48]

The barbarians who perpetrate these cruelties should be punished here in this world, but even if they aren't, they will have their punishment from God. Men and women who claim allegiance to the Islamic faith must take it as their duty to challenge the misogyny that is explicitly and implicitly engrained in both Eastern and Western cultures. Women are victimized, subjected, and objectified in Western countries as well, but Muslims must look at the treatment of women in countries dominated by Muslims. When fellow Muslims brutalize and victimize women in their societies, it must be the Muslim men and women who take the first and most bold step to speak out and find ways to bring such behavior to an end.

Polygamy

A common source of angst in the minds of non-Muslims is the concept of polygamy within Islam—or more specifically, polygyny, which is the practice of a man having more than one wife. Some have called this oppressive and some see it as misogynistic. Thus, it is an area requiring clarification. First and foremost, there is no commandment within Islam for men to marry more than one woman. Muslim men are not required, nor even encouraged, to marry multiple women. If that were the case, the vast majority of Muslim men in the world would be committing a sin, since this practice is so rare.

The verse in question from the Quran was revealed in order to reform and improve the conditions prevalent at that time, but its wisdom is still applicable today. As mentioned before, women were treated as objects in the seventh century, and Arabs in particular would maintain dozens—some say even a hundred—relationships with women. With this verse, Islam then became unique in its clear instruction to marry only one woman. The New Testament does contain an instruction in First Timothy and Titus about marrying one woman, but it is clear that this instruction applies only to bishops and deacons—considered elders of the church.

The Quran states: "If you fear that you will not be just in dealing with the orphans, then marry of other women as may be agreeable to you, two, or three, or four; and if you fear you will not be able to do justice, then marry only one."[49] Thus, the instruction is to marry only one, with exceptions permissible to those who meet certain requirements. The first and foremost requirement is expressly stated in this verse, which is that the man must be able to do justice with his wives if he were to marry more than one. This is more significant than it may sound. It means equitable treatment, love, care, and time. Many Muslim men in various parts of the world today who have multiple wives do not live up to this standard set by the Quran and, thus, are committing a gross injustice to their wives and children.

Even in cases where the man is able to do justice between wives, this verse is far from a promotion for multiple wives. To the contrary, it imposed a limit to men due to the consideration of justice. The wisdom offered by Islam is that it is a very exceptional person who could do justice to two wives, and even more rare and exceptional is one who can be just and fair to three wives. But what Islam would consider absolutely impossible is for a man to be able to balance and, thus, be fair to more than four wives.

As discussed earlier, the obligation of the husband is to provide for the needs of his wife and children. This brings physical and financial obligations on the husband. So an additional wife should not be seen as a pursuit of carnal pleasures. Far from it, an additional wife meant responsibility for the care and needs of another person. This was the true intention of marriage for a man—to gain a friend and partner whom he is responsible to take care of.

Karen Armstrong contextualizes the circumstances in which polygyny was introduced in Islam when she writes about the wars and battles at that time, thus leading to "a shortage of men in Arabia, which left a surplus of unmarried women, who were often badly exploited. The Quran is most concerned about this problem and resorted to polygamy as a way of dealing with it. This would enable all the girls who had been orphaned to be married, but it insisted that a man could take more than one wife only if he promised to administer their property equitably. It also stipulates that no orphan girl should be married to her guardian against her will, as though she were simply a moveable property."[50]

Revolutionary Rights for Women

Lord Headley was an early twentieth-century British convert to Islam who wrote the following with regard to the manner in which the Prophet Muhammad dealt with women and their rights:

> In Arabia woman was a mere chattel. When a husband died the son inherited, among other things, his father's wives and did exactly as he liked with them. He could marry one or more of them or take them as his concubines, or sell them, or make a present of them. In Arabia daughters were buried alive; and every year in Egypt a young virgin was drowned in the Nile. . . . At that time Muhammad startled the world by declaring that "Paradise was under the feet of the mother"; that a Muslim should not speak evil of women; that in the sight of God man and woman were the same; that Islam bound man and woman by a spirit of union, love, and brotherhood; that education was obligatory on woman as well as man. And he assigned to woman her rights as daughter, wife, mother, and a member of society. The rights which these Muslim women had all these centuries ago have only lately been given to European women—for example, through the Married Women's Property Act in England.[51]

Lord Headley made the point that Muhammad commanded rights to be given to women more than one thousand years before Western societies agreed. The constitution of Medina was declared in the year 622 CE and outlined the improved legal status for women. It is recorded that Muhammad not only allowed but also required both men and women to obtain education and increase their knowledge, stating that obtaining "knowledge is the duty of every Muslim man and woman."[52] In fact, his own wife Aishah not only obtained knowledge but was also an educator, and Muhammad had instructed his followers that they can learn half of their faith from her. Today, Malala Yousafzai's selfless persistence toward education for girls in Pakistan is deeply rooted in this Islamic philosophy granting both men and women equal access to education. She expressed this as her basis when she spoke at the United Nations, saying: "Islam says that it is not only each child's right to get education, rather it is their duty and responsibility."[53]

In the United States, however, it was not until 1833 that a college allowed admission of women. Oberlin College became the first four-year college in the United States to accept both male and female students, even though initially the "women admitted were limited to 'ladies' courses,' and they were also required to perform domestic tasks to support the school and the male student population. Over time, both requirements were phased out. Within four years, women and men took the same curriculum."[54] Not only was education granted to women by Muhammad more than 1,200 years earlier, he did not limit the education to "ladies' courses." So Muslim extremists (who forbid or impede access to school for girls) and secular extremists (who have forbidden Muslim girls and women in their schools if they cover their heads) should consider this point carefully before obstructing a Muslim woman from obtaining an education.

Prophet Muhammad had also explicitly forbidden the repulsive Arab custom at that time of murdering female infants. This barbaric practice was not forbidden in British India until the year 1870, despite the fact that it had been raised as a major issue in Britain's House of Commons nearly 50 years earlier, after years of philanthropic attempts failed to resolve the issue. As recorded by Baptist missionary James Peggs in 1830, "The Parliamentary Papers on Hindoo Infanticide, printed by order of the Honourable House of Commons June 1824, and July 1828, fully substantiate the fact, that, notwithstanding the philanthropic and successful efforts of Colonel Walker and Governor Duncan to abolish this unnatural custom, it has revived; and that the most decisive measures are requisite to effect its entire and speedy abolition."[55] It wasn't until 1870, however, that the Female Infanticide Prevention Act was passed. And still, it hasn't worked. Even today, baby girls in India are killed or aborted. In 2006, a government minister admitted that over the course of 20 years, parents in India had killed ten million of their baby girls either after detecting the sex through ultrasound or immediately after birth.[56] So these measures have not worked, whereas this rampant custom was successfully abolished by Muhammad nearly 1,250 years earlier when he revealed it to be a grievous sin.

Prophet Muhammad granted permission for divorced women to obtain custody of their children. This right was not granted to women in the great Western civilization of Great Britain until 1839. Until then, mothers had no rights to custody of their children in the case of a divorce, but English law was challenged by a divorced mother who simply refused to give up on pursuing custody of her sons after divorcing a violent husband. "Faced with the fact that she had no rights to her children in law and could get no redress in the courts, she used her talents and connections to fight back and change the law. The results of her efforts was the Custody of Infants Act 1839. For the first time in English law, a mother was given the right to apply to the courts with respect to her children. It was a modest step forward and her rights were limited, but it did represent the first crucial recognition of mothers."[57] Whereas the current rights afforded to mothers after a divorce are a result of brave women fighting for justice against the prevailing law, Muslim women were given this right through the religion of Islam nearly 1,400 years ago.

Likewise, it was nearly 1,400 years ago that Muhammad declared that women had the right to own and inherit property. Before his declaration, a woman herself was property, and the idea of women having the right to own and inherit property was unthinkable. Despite the prevailing views at that time, Islam was adamant about this right for women. As stated by Mirza Masroor Ahmad, the worldwide spiritual leader (Khalifa) of the Ahmadiyya Muslim Community, "In the Holy Quran daughters are given rights of inheritance from their parents, wives have a right on husbands' inheritance; mothers have rights on their children's inheritance, if they happen to die before her. Similarly in some situations daughters and sisters are heirs of their brothers. No other religion established women's rights like this before Islam. Husbands have no rights on their wives' money, or her earnings; this is strictly forbidden."[58] Even 1,200 years later, this right was not given to women in the Western nation of Canada. Women in Canada were forced to wait until 1859 for the "statute giving all married women in Canada West ownership of their property independent of their husbands' control. . . . But these powers were subject to telling limitations: for example, women still could not sell their property without their husband's consent, and husbands retained their claim over their wives' earnings."[59] If there are Muslim men today who try to lay claim over their wives' earnings, they are in gross violation of Islam.

Thus, when discussing women's issues in Islam, it is critical to distinguish between the teachings of Islam and the behavior and subculture of some Muslim people. There is no denying the fact that there are indeed Muslims who mistreat, abuse, and oppress women in their families, cities, and countries. It must be remembered, however, that such mistreatment and oppression is not in consonance with the teachings of Islam. In fact, they are gross violations of Islamic teachings. Any time Muslims witness injustices anywhere—whether at the hands of Muslims or non-Muslims—they must be vocal in helping the victims. And when these injustices are perpetrated by those claiming allegiance to Islam, Muslims must not only condemn but also make efforts to remedy the situation.

Far from being the problem, Islam is indeed the solution to these problems. The dictates of fairness demand not only the study and understanding of a faith based on its teachings but also clarification about what is advocated by a religion versus what is a product of moral and/or spiritual decay of people. Islam presents commandments from God on the equitable rights and treatment of women, as well as guidance regarding the manner in which women and men are complementary partners of one another and how to maintain a civil and safe society. If these commandments were to be followed, there would be no subjugation, oppression, or misogyny, and nothing would be forced upon women.

8

DEMYSTIFYING ISLAM'S
VIEW OF JESUS CHRIST

What comes as a surprise to many non-Muslims is the realization of the importance given to Jesus Christ within Islam. Some have assumed that the advent of the Prophet Muhammad indicates that Jesus plays no role in Islam, but this is absolutely not true, as Jesus is accepted as a true prophet sent by God and the Messiah for whom the Israelites had been awaiting. As mentioned in the first chapter of this book, one of the core tenets of Islam is the acceptance of all prophets before Muhammad. Thus, a Muslim cannot be a Muslim if he or she does not accept and believe in Jesus Christ as a true, noble prophet of God. This belief in Jesus, however, requires a deeper look, as it encompasses many agreements with that of modern-day Christians, as well as some fundamental disagreements.

Some ignorant people find it "offensive" for Muslims to believe in Jesus Christ, calling it "a delegitimization of Christianity."[1] Such people, amazingly, take exception with Islam's acceptance of the prophethood of Jesus instead of seeing this common belief as a means of building bridges of kinship between Christians and Muslims. Their argument is based on the false premise that Christians somehow have a monopoly over the man known as "Jesus of Nazareth." This ignorance can only be cured by looking within the faith of Islam to understand the respect and honor it gives to him and his mother, Mary.

In July of 2013, *NY Times* bestselling author and professor of creative writing and religious studies Reza Aslan released a book about Jesus, which provided an uncommon historic perspective of Jesus of Nazareth. Although the book received a wide range of reactions among the great attention it attracted, some objected to the idea that a Muslim could write a book about Jesus. This viewpoint is based entirely on the ignorant view that Jesus is exclusively a Christian figure. The Quran mentions Jesus by name twenty-five times across eleven different chapters. The Arabic rendition of Jesus is "Isa" (pronounced ee-sa), which is very similar to the Greek rendition "Iesou" and not very different from the Aramaic rendition "Eashoa" or the Hebrew "Yeshua." Thus, the modern English rendition, "Jesus," is the most divergent from what can be understood to be the true original manner in which his name was pronounced. Even the original edition of the King James English translation of the Bible in 1611 renders his name as "Iesus."

In Islam, Jesus is considered not only a prophet but the last prophet of Israel and the Messiah of the Israelites as had been prophesied by the Prophet Moses. According to the Quran and Hadith, Jesus lived a pious life in the humble service of God and did not die on the cross. The different interpretations of the events of the crucifixion are explored later in this chapter, but all Muslims around the world are united in the belief that Jesus was not killed on the cross. Islam also teaches its followers that the Messiah will return some time in the latter days.

MARY AND HER VIRGIN BIRTH

The Quran asserts that Jesus was born to a virgin, Mary, and rejects the accusation levied against her at that time that she had not been pious and that her pregnancy was illegitimate. In fact, Mary is held in such high esteem as an incredibly pious and dedicated person of God that chapter 19 of the Quran is given her name ("al-Maryam"). Mary's story in the Quran begins with an account of her own mother's pregnancy, attesting Mary's mother as being very pious and dedicated to God. When Mary's mother was pregnant, the Quran records that she turned to God and said, "My Lord, I have vowed to Thee what is in my womb to be dedicated to Thy service. So do Thou accept it of me; verily, Thou alone art All-Hearing, All-Knowing."[2] Thus, even before her birth, Mary had been dedicated by her mother to be a humble servant of God.

What becomes clear in the very next verse is that Mary's mother had expected or hoped that she was pregnant with a boy but still decided to dedicate her new daughter to the service of God: "But when she was delivered of it, she said, 'My Lord, I am delivered of a female,'—and Allah knew best of what she was delivered and the male she desired to have was not like the female she was delivered of—'and I have named her Mary, and I commit her and her offspring to Thy protection from Satan, the rejected.'"[3] So it is recorded that not only did Mary's pious mother continue with her wishes to dedicate her child to God but also God's words are interjected here to indicate that the female child she had given birth to was superior to the male child she had desired to have. The prayer of Mary's mother for Mary and her own offspring was fulfilled in a manner she likely never expected.

The teachings of Islam testify that Mary lived a very pious life—even from a very young age—and that God had exalted her to a very high station. The Quran states, "And remember when the angels said, 'O Mary, Allah has chosen thee and purified thee and chosen thee above all women of the time.'"[4] Thus, in Islam, Mary is considered to have a very high status, which is why all Muslims—men and women—are told to look at Mary's example as a lesson in obedience to God and righteousness.[5]

The Quran then confirms the account of the virgin birth of Jesus by describing the moment when Mary was visited by an angel sent by God to deliver the message that she would give birth to a blessed son:

> And relate the story of Mary as mentioned in the Book, when she with-drew from her people to an eastern place; and screened herself off from them. Then We sent Our angel to her and he appeared to her in the form of a well-proportioned man. She said, "I seek refuge with the Gracious God from thee if indeed thou dost fear Him." The angel said, "I am only a messenger of thy Lord, that I may give thee glad tidings of a righteous son." She said, "How can I have a son when no man has touched me, neither have I been unchaste?" The angel said, "Thus it shall be." But says thy Lord, "It is easy for Me; and We shall do so that We may make him a Sign unto men, and a mercy from Us, and it is a thing decreed."[6]

Thus, the story within Islam of Mary's revelation begins while she was praying to God in seclusion. Suddenly, an angel appeared in front of her in the form of a very handsome man who conveyed to her the divine message that she would be blessed with a son. This vision of the appearance of an angel was so lifelike and realistic that Mary, being a chaste and moral woman, became frightened that a young man was in front of her. For this reason, she addressed him saying that she seeks God's protection from him. The angel responded that he is only a messenger from God with this very important message that although a virgin, God will grant her a son whose virgin birth will be a great sign for the Israelites and whose humility and modesty toward the Jews will be a great mercy for them. Referring to her son as a sign for his people and a mercy from God indicates his prophet-hood, as the Quran also records other prophets who had been called a sign and a mercy from God. For example, the Prophet Ezekiel was called "a

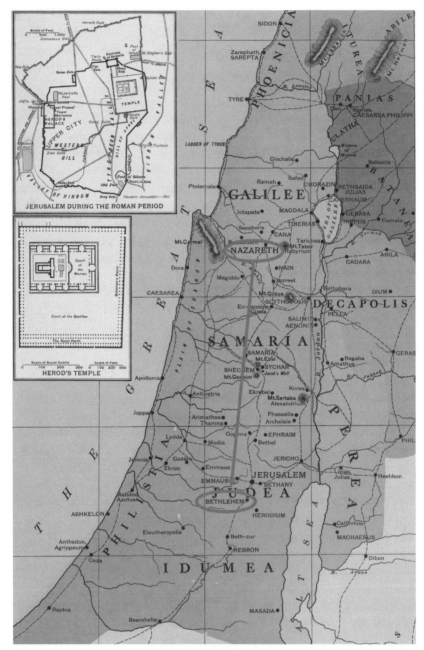

Figure 8.1.   Distance traveled by Mary from Nazareth to Bethlehem, illustrated in this map of Palestine in the time of Jesus (4 BC–30 AD)

Sign unto men,"[7] and the Prophet Muhammad was referred to as "a mercy for all peoples."[8]

This revelation from God to Mary through an angel is also recorded elsewhere in the Quran when it states: "When the angels said, 'O Mary, Allah gives thee glad tidings of a son through a Word from Him; his name shall be the Messiah, Jesus, son of Mary, honoured in this world and in the next, and of those who are granted nearness to God.'"[9] This establishes without a shadow of any doubt that Muslims recognize Jesus (1) as having been born of the Virgin Mary, (2) as a true prophet from God, and (3) as the Messiah foretold to come among the Israelites. The Quran even recounts the birth itself when it states that the pregnant Mary relocated to a remote place that we now understand to be Bethlehem: "So she conceived him, and withdrew with him to a remote place."[10] This means that Mary traveled with Joseph about seventy miles south from Nazareth to the hills around Bethlehem.

The narration in the Quran, coupled with the narration in the Bible, leads us to believe that Jesus was born sometime during the summer, which is another reason Christmas does not have any meaning within Islam. The Quran details that at the time of Mary's child labor, when she was in pain and exhausted, God informed her to leverage a nearby stream of water to quench her thirst and to shake the date–palm tree under which she was in labor in order to eat some dates and replenish her energy. The Quran states, "Then the angel called her from beneath her, saying, 'Grieve not. They Lord has placed a rivulet below thee; And shake towards thyself the trunk of the palm-tree; it will drop upon thee fresh ripe dates; So, eat and drink and cool thine eye.'"[11] The Quran paints a picture of a summer day since palm trees in Bethlehem would not contain fresh ripe dates at the end of December. The Bible corroborates the Quran's indication of a summer day when it says that at the time of Jesus' birth, "there were in the same country shepherds abiding in the field, keeping watch over their flock by night."[12] A shepherd watching over his flock in a freezing field in the middle of a winter night is highly unlikely. Thus, Muslims do not accept December 25 as the birth date of Jesus Christ, just like a growing number of Christian theologians and historians.

LIFE OF JESUS

Early Life

The Quran describes Jesus as intelligent from a very young age. When the angel gave Mary the news that she would become a mother, he shared the following words from God about her son: "He shall speak to the people in the cradle and when of middle age, and he shall be of the righteous."[13] This promise from God is that Jesus will possess extraordinary wisdom and knowledge when he speaks during his youth and during his middle age. Thus, Islam asserts that Jesus spoke words of exceptional wisdom both as a child and as an adult.

The Quran records the mission with which God sent Jesus:

> And [God] will teach him the Book and the Wisdom and the Torah and the Gospel; and will send him as a Messenger to the Children of Israel with the Message, "I come to you with a Sign from your Lord, which is, that I will fashion out for you a creation out of clay after the manner of a bird; then I will breathe into it a new spirit and it will become a soaring being by the command of Allah; and I will heal the night-blind and the leprous, and I will quicken the dead, by the command of Allah; and I will announce to you what you will eat and what you will store up in your houses. Surely, therein is a Sign for you, if you are believers."[14]

The Bible records all miracles that Jesus is reported to have performed. And since the Bible records no miracle in which Jesus physically created birds from clay, it is clear that the above verse speaks in metaphorical terms. The ability to fashion clay after the style of birds is a metaphor illustrating the ability of Jesus to spiritually transform immovable and passive people into souls soaring like birds into higher levels of spirituality. This is why the verse states that Jesus would transform such people "after the manner of a bird" referring to the method or way of the bird as opposed to the literal shape of it. This signifies that he would shape people to take some property of the bird (i.e., the ability to soar instead of sitting still like clay). The word used for clay in this verse is طين (*teen*), which relates to "the natural, or native, constitution or disposition"[15] of a person. Thus, it refers to such people who possess the natural character, like clay, that can be molded into something greater. After reforming people so they possessed the ability to soar, the verse states that purely "by the command of Allah," these people received a new life of spiritual joy and, thus, truly began to soar. We see this in the example of his disciples—simple and humble fishermen in Galilee who were transformed by the message Jesus brought them. After their transformation into spiritual people, they then began bravely preaching to the people of Israel and enduring all kinds of hardships with a zeal that can only be a gift from God.

The healing powers mentioned in this verse must also be understood in the spiritual sense in that Jesus restored sight to those who were spiritually blind and gave life to those who were spiritually dead. Jesus specifically referred to the Pharisees of his day as being blind because, among other ills, they were hypocritical in nature. The Quran repeatedly refers to those who refuse to believe as being blind. It states, "Proofs have indeed come to you from your Lord; so whoever sees, it is for his own good; and whoever becomes blind, it is to his own loss."[16] Thus, the Quran states that those who are blind are those who close their eyes to the clear proofs and signs that God has sent. This refers not to a problem with one's eyes but, rather, with one's heart, as this is a malady of one's unwillingness to hear or understand. This is made clear by the Quran itself when it states, "Surely, it is not the eyes that are blind, but blind are the hearts which are in the breasts."[17] So the miracle of Jesus to heal the blind is much more significant than the incorrect interpretation of a literal healing of someone's eyes. He was able to cure the hearts of those who before refused to understand. This is the way of the prophets. The Quran states that even the Prophet Muhammad gave life to the dead when it states, "O ye who believe! respond to Allah, and the Messenger when he calls you that he may give you life."[18] But we understand that the life that Muhammad gave to people was a spiritual life. He revived those who were, before, spiritually dead.

Mission of Jesus

The verse from the Quran stating the mission of Jesus also contains an important passage, which clarifies the scope of his mission even further. It states that God sent Jesus "as a Messenger to the Children of Israel," which is a critical elucidation of why Jesus was sent by God to earth. He was not the universal prophet that present-day Christians claim; rather, he was a prophet sent for a particular people—the Children of Israel (i.e., the Israelites). The term "Children of Israel" refers to the twelve tribes of Israel (the twelve descendants of the Prophet Jacob, who was later renamed "Israel"). Biblical and historical records narrate the story of the twelve tribes and how they were united as one Kingdom of Israel until a schism among the tribes caused much fighting that led to their split into two kingdoms: the Kingdom of Israel (comprised of ten of the tribes; also called the Northern Kingdom) and the Kingdom of Judah (comprised of the tribes of Judah and Benjamin). Eventually, more than seven hundred years before the birth of Jesus, multiple sieges by the Assyrians overtook the Northern Kingdom of Israel, and the Assyrians took the ten tribes of that land captive to the east and northeast. The people of those ten tribes were scattered across the vast lands occupied by the Assyrians and have become known in history as the "lost tribes of Israel" (or the "lost sheep of the house of Israel") because historians do not exactly know what happened to them. The Kingdom of Judah was eventually overtaken by the Babylonians almost six hundred years before the advent of Jesus and deported to Babylon.

The difference, however, between the captivity and deportation of the two kingdoms is that the two tribes of the Kingdom of Judah (called "Jews") remained together and were able to maintain their identity in Babylon, and they eventually returned to Jerusalem after the fall of Babylon a few decades later. The ten lost tribes of the Kingdom of Israel, however, never returned. A prophecy then emerged that these lost tribes would eventually be found, even though they had been scattered, which would have prevented them from maintaining their community identity. The Hebrew Bible foretells of this gathering of the lost ten tribes when it states, "Those who were perishing in the land of Assyria and who were scattered in the land of Egypt will come and worship the Lord in the holy mountain at Jerusalem."[19] It then goes further by prophesying, "Then it will happen on that day that the Lord Will again recover the second time with His hand The remnant of His people, who will remain, From Assyria, Egypt, Pathros, Cush, Elam, Shinar, Hamath, And from the islands of the sea. And He will lift up a standard for the nations And assemble the banished ones of Israel, And will gather the dispersed of Judah from the four corners of the earth."[20] In another place within the Hebrew Bible, it states, "For thus says the Lord God, 'Behold, I Myself will search for My sheep and seek them out. As a shepherd cares for his herd in the day when he is among his scattered sheep, so I will care for My sheep and will deliver them from all the places to which they were scattered on a cloudy and gloomy day. I will bring them out from the peoples and gather them from the countries and bring them to their own land; and I will feed them on the mountains of Israel, by the streams, and in all the inhabited places of the land.'"[21]

Thus, as the Messiah sent exclusively for the Israelites, Jesus was commissioned by God not only to revive the true spirit and clarify misunderstandings of Mosaic Law in the hearts of the Children of Israel but also to gather the scattered lost tribes of Israel. He could not confine his ministry to the two tribes of Israel that still inhabited Judea. God required him to present himself to all of the tribes of Israel and revive the spirit of God within them all.

The New Testament confirms this to be the mission of Jesus. The Book of Matthew records that when asked to help a Canaanite woman, Jesus himself responded, "I was sent only to the lost sheep of the house of Israel."[22] Jesus repeatedly instructed his disciples to not waste their time with other people. He was so focused on finding and preaching to the tribes of Israel that the New Testament states, "These twelve Jesus sent out after instructing them: 'Do not go in the way of the Gentiles, and do not enter any city of the Samaritans; but rather go to the lost sheep of the house of Israel.'"[23] Here, Jesus expressly ordered his disciples not to preach to anyone except the Israelites. We also read Jesus saying, "I have other sheep, which are not of this fold; I must bring them also, and they will hear My voice; and they will become one flock with one shepherd."[24] These are the words of one who is fully convinced of his mission to reach the other sheep of the house of Israel. He makes this abundantly clear when he says to his disciples, "Truly I say to you, that you who have followed Me, in the regeneration when the Son of Man will sit on His glorious throne, you also shall sit upon twelve thrones, judging the twelve tribes of Israel."[25] Here, Jesus specifically states that when he speaks of the sheep of Israel or Children of Israel, he is referring to all twelve tribes of Israel. Let us not forget that Jesus also stated, "For the Son of Man has come to seek and to save that which was lost."[26]

SON OF GOD

Islam clearly states that Jesus was a noble prophet sent by God but was no different from any other prophet in that he was nothing more than human. Islam presents Jesus as a human being whom God chose for the reformation of His people. This is a point of major disagreement with the majority of the Christian world, as Islam takes a very firm stance against the view that Jesus was the son of God or in any way (even partly) divine himself. It also holds the view that Jesus himself never preached this doctrine, which was a future addition or modification made to the teachings that were later referred to as "Christianity."

The Quran quotes Jesus on two different occasions as having said, "Surely, Allah is my Lord and your Lord; so worship Him; this is the right path."[27] This forms the basis for the Islamic view that Jesus himself never declared himself to be a partner or son of God. According to Islam, the lesson he imparted upon his followers was to believe in and worship only the One God, who is the same One God who Jesus himself worshipped. Muslims, thus, see Jesus regarding himself as a human and subservient to God, just like all other humans. The Quran establishes Jesus' firm belief and submission to the One God when it quotes Jesus as saying, "I am a servant of Allah. He has given me the Book, and has made me a Prophet."[28] These are the words of a humble messenger of God who did not call people to worship anyone but the One God.

Islam is a monotheistic religion in its purest sense in that it preaches the absolute unity and oneness of God, Who has neither a partner nor helper. Its doctrine of unity is absolute, with no room offered for another form of God. He has neither a parent nor spouse. When such a perfect ideal of the oneness of God is accepted, the very suggestion for Him to give birth to a child is unthinkable. The Quran contains a permanent command for its followers to repeatedly say and remind themselves: "He is Allah, the One! Allah the Independent and Besought of all. He begets not, nor is He begotten. And there is none like unto Him."[29] So, whereas there are Christians who call Jesus "the only begotten son of God," the scripture of Islam fundamentally disagrees by stating that God is neither the creation of some other god, nor will He ever create another entity like Himself. Since God cannot be created, there is no way for us to accept that a god could have been created through the womb of Mary, for that would indicate that such a god was not eternal and was, rather, created. On the other hand, if we are to assume that this other god was indeed eternal, then what need has it to be born through a human womb for it to finally manifest? This belief violates the fundamental teaching within Islam of the perfect and eternal unity of God.

After establishing the unshakable belief in the absolute unity of God, the Quran goes a step further by addressing those who claim that God has had a son. By the time that the Quran was revealed to Muhammad, Christians had already taken to this belief in Jesus as the son of God. So it seems appropriate for God to reveal such words to His messenger: "And they say, 'The Gracious God has taken unto Himself a son.' Assuredly, you have indeed uttered a most hideous thing. The heavens might well-nigh burst thereat, and the earth cleave asunder, and the mountains fall down in pieces because they ascribe a son to the Gracious God. It becomes not the Gracious God that He should take unto Himself a son."[30] It is considered an enormous and grievous sin in Islam to claim that our one Lord has any associate or son.

This is a concept upon which there is agreement within the New Testament as well. It records the incident when a scribe came to Jesus and asked him for the foremost and primary of all commandments. Jesus responded that the foremost of all commandments is the following: "Hear, O Israel! The Lord our God is one Lord; and you shall love the Lord your God with all your heart, and with all your soul, and with all your mind, and with all your strength."[31] Upon hearing this, the scribe answered Jesus, saying "Right, Teacher; You have truly stated that He is One, and there is no one else besides Him."[32] Thus do we see captured in the New Testament the words of Jesus himself advocating that God is alone the Lord of all the worlds and has no associate.

Jesus continued to draw a line of distinction between himself and God. The New Testament records the following story about Jesus: "And, behold, one came and said unto him, Good Master, what good thing shall I do, that I may have eternal life? And he said unto him, Why callest thou me good? there is none good but one, that is, God: but if thou wilt enter into life, keep the commandments."[33] Here, Jesus stopped someone from referring to him as good, stating that only God is good. He made a point to indicate his dissimilarity with God, furthering his repeated calls for people to worship only the One God.

Upon full study of the Hebrew Bible and New Testament, Muslims understand the term "son of God" to be entirely metaphorical—a belief based on the teachings of Jesus himself, who openly stated that he is the son of God only in a metaphorical context. The New Testament records:

> Then the Jews took up stones again to stone him. Jesus answered them, Many good works have I shewed you from my Father; for which of those works do ye stone me? The Jews answered him, saying, For a good work we stone thee not; but for blasphemy; and because that thou, being a man, makest thyself God. Jesus answered them, Is it not written in your law, I said, Ye are gods? If he called them gods, unto whom the word of God came, and the scripture cannot be broken; Say ye of him, whom the Father hath sanctified, and sent into the world, Thou blasphemest; because I said, I am the Son of God?[34]

This is such a critical moment in the ministry of Jesus, as the crucial question about Godhead was directly asked of him. He was confronted with the question of whether or not claimed to be God or the second person in the Trinity. It is an absolute necessity for his answer to be understood and accepted by anyone claiming to believe in him.

Knowing that Jesus was a courageous man of conviction, if he was truly God in the form of man, he would have courageously proclaimed that indeed this was the case. But how profound it is to read Jesus state that he is the son of God in the same context as when the Hebrew Bible states, "Ye are gods." Jesus was referring to when the Judges of Israel are called children of God, according to the Book of Psalms, when it states, "I have said, Ye are gods; and all of you are children of the most High."[35] Thus, when the expression "son of God" is applied to Jesus, by himself or others, it has the same significance as the application of such an expression to others in scripture.

So who else has been referred to as the son of God?

1. Adam
   - "Adam, which was the son of God"[36]
2. Israel (Jacob)
   - "And thou shalt say unto Pharaoh, Thus saith the Lord, Israel is my son, even my firstborn"[37]
   - "When Israel was a child, then I loved him, and called my son out of Egypt"[38]
3. Judges of Israel
   - "Ye are gods; and all of you are children of the most High"[39]
4. Ephraim
   - "They shall come with weeping, and with supplications will I lead them: I will cause them to walk by the rivers of waters in a straight way, wherein they shall not stumble: for I am a father to Israel, and Ephraim is my firstborn."[40]
5. David
   - "Also I will make him my firstborn, higher than the kings of the earth"[41]
   - "I will proclaim the decree of the LORD: He said to me, 'You are my Son; today I have begotten you'"[42]
6. Solomon
   - "Behold, a son shall be born to thee, who shall be a man of rest; and I will give him rest from all his enemies round about: for his name shall be Solomon, and I will give peace and quietness unto Israel in his days. He shall build an house for my name; and he shall be my son, and I will be his father; and I will establish the throne of his kingdom over Israel for ever."[43]
   - "He shall build an house for my name, and I will establish the throne of his kingdom for ever. I will be his father, and he shall be my son."[44]
7. All righteous people
   - "For as many as are led by the Spirit of God, they are the sons of God"[45]
8. Peacemakers
   - "Blessed are the peacemakers: for they shall be called the children of God"[46]

Thus does the Bible record many people who are called "the son of God," "the only begotten son of God," and even "God's firstborn." Therefore, if Jesus was called the son of God during his time, the title was only employed metaphorically in like manner to all other instances of people referred to as sons of God in the Bible. It also cannot be forgotten that Jesus was referred to—by himself and others—as "son of man" more than eighty times in the New Testament.

CRUCIFIXION

Across Judaism, Christianity, and Islam, the events of the crucifixion are of grave importance. Perhaps for this reason, discourse about crucifixion often generates not only emotion and sensitivity but also varying opinions. From an Islamic perspective, although all Muslims are united in the belief of Jesus as a very noble and important prophet sent by God as the Messiah for the Israelites—and agree that the Quran defends the honor of Jesus and his mother throughout its recorded accounts of their lives—there is difference of opinion with regard to what happened at the crucifixion. The Quran declares that Jesus did not die by crucifixion. The difference between Muslim views on this matter lies in the interpretation of the Quran's declaration that Jesus escaped death by crucifixion, but all Muslims agree that Jesus was saved from this accursed death.

According to the Hebrew Bible, death on the cross was considered to be an accursed death—one to which no true prophet of God could ever succumb. It is stated, "He that is hanged is accursed of God."[47] Death by crucifixion on the cross would, thus, prove Jesus to be a false Messiah. So Muslims are united in rejecting the belief that Jesus died while hanging on the cross.

The Quran states the following about the crucifixion: "And for their saying, 'We did slay the Messiah, Jesus, son of Mary, the Messenger of Allah;' whereas they slew him not, nor did they bring about his death on the cross, but he was made to appear to them like one crucified; and those who differ therein are certainly in a state doubt about it; they have no certain knowledge thereof, but only pursue a conjecture; and they did not arrive at a certainty concerning it."[48] So what can be agreed upon here is that the Quran clearly states that the plan of those Jews who sought to kill Jesus inevitably failed, as they were not able to bring about his death on the cross. The disagreement among Muslims lies in the interpretation of Jesus appearing to have died by crucifixion.

Substitution Theory

Mainstream Muslims believe that this verse from the Quran asserts that Jesus himself was never put on the cross and that someone else was hung on the cross instead. There are some translators who translate this verse from the Quran as "but they killed him not, nor crucified him, but so it was made to appear to them"[49] or "They slew him not nor crucified, but it appeared so unto them."[50] Since the phrase is taken to mean "nor crucified him," many Muslims have interpreted this to mean that Jesus himself was never hung on the cross. In his place, they believe that either a companion or an enemy experienced a miraculous transformation in appearance that caused him to be mistaken for Jesus, and that man was hung on the cross instead.

With someone else destined to be crucified in his place, they believe Jesus himself ascended bodily into heaven. Muslims who believe in this substitution theory also rely on the very next verse from the one cited above, which states, "On the contrary, Allah exalted him to Himself. And Allah is Mighty, Wise."[51] Again, different English translations of the Quran present this verse as "Nay, Allah raised him up unto Himself; and Allah is Exalted in Power, Wise"[52] and "But Allah took him up unto Himself. Allah was ever Mighty, Wise."[53] When Muslims read this verse stating that God "raised" Jesus or "took him up" unto Himself, they interpret this to mean that Jesus physically ascended into the clouds, leaving another man to be hung on the cross in his stead.

Some Muslims believe that it was Judas—the one who betrayed Jesus—whose face was miraculously transformed to look like Jesus and was, thus, crucified in his place. As Professor Saiyed Jafar Reza argues, "According to Islamic sources, it was Judas, known as Tatyanus in Arabic history, who faced death on the Cross and not Jesus, whom God had 'raised unto himself' because, when the Rabbis could no longer bear Prophet Jesus' preaching, they hatched a conspiracy to eliminate him with the help of Judas, one of his disciple."[54]

Some Muslims believe that one of Jesus' own companions volunteered to be crucified in his place. According to this view,

> When Allah wanted to raise Jesus to heaven, Jesus went out to meet his followers at a house where all his twelve disciples assembled. He went out to them from a well in the house and his hair was dripping with water. He said, "Among you are those who will disbelieve in me twelve times even after having believed in me." Then he added, "Which one of you agrees to look like me and be killed in my place and enjoy the

status reserved for me with my Lord?" Their youngest stood up, but Jesus told him to sit down. He repeated the question to them, and the same young man stood up again, whereupon Jesus said, "Then you shall be the one." He immediately was made to look just like Jesus, then Jesus was raised to heaven. The Jews came and took the disciple who looked just like Jesus, killed him, then crucified him.[55]

Irrespective of the disagreement regarding who was crucified in Jesus' place (and whether they were crucified willingly or unwillingly), such Muslims believe that "Jesus was not crucified but was raised to heaven and is still alive. He will come back near the end of life on this planet to fight those who distorted his message."[56] His return, thus, would bring about the slaughter of those who disbelieved and distorted his original message.

Other Muslims Disagree

On the other hand, there are other Muslims who find the substitution theory not only irrational but also against fundamental teachings of Islam. They do not believe that Jesus, a human, could be alive right now in heaven. For one, heaven is not a material location that Jesus could have physically ascended into. Within Islam, heaven is accepted as a spiritual world completely separate from this world in which we live. Second, the verse from the Quran does not state that God lifted Jesus into heaven (for such a concept would contradict the separation of this world from the spiritual afterlife where only dead souls can enter). The verse reads as follows, in response to the plans of the Pharisees to kill Jesus through crucifixion: "Remember the time when Allah said, 'O Jesus, I will cause thee to die a natural death and will raise thee to Myself, and will clear thee of the charges of those who disbelieve, and will exalt those who follow thee above those who disbelieve, until the Day of Resurrection; then to Me shall be your return, and I will judge between you concerning that wherein you differed.'"[57]

As with all verses in the Quran, the structure and order of its words are meaningful rather than inconsequential. In this verse, God tells Jesus that a time will come when He will cause Jesus to die and then raise him. This means that God will first bring about death by causing Jesus to die before he is raised. The Arabic phrase متوفيك (*mutawaffi-ka*)—translated as "cause thee to die a natural death"—is derived from the root word (*waffa*), which has been used twenty-five times in the Quran in relation to something coming from God and has, thus, been taken to mean "death" or "to take away one's soul." When God is the subject, this word always means "He takes away one's soul."

Mahmud ibn Umar al-Zamakhshari—most commonly known as "al-Zamakhshari"—was a twelfth-century Arab scholar and linguist who wrote a well-known commentary of the Quran entitled *al-Kashshaf*. Some have referred to it as "one of the best-known Qur'an commentaries . . . the *Kashshaf* has known at least twenty editions and reprints over the last one hundred and fifty years."[58] In this commentary, al-Zamakhshari wrote about the Arabic phrase *mutawaffi-ka* by stating that "*Mutawaffi-ka* means, I will protect thee from being killed by the people and will grant thee full lease of life ordained for thee, and will cause thee to die a natural death, not being killed." So this verse is understood to mean that Jesus has been promised by God that he would die a natural death first.

Following that, the verse states that he would be raised to God. Within Islam, we know that God does not exist in material form and, thus, does not live in the sky or atmosphere. So this cannot mean that Jesus was raised or lifted physically. Rather, it signifies the raising in status, honor, or rank. This speaks of a spiritual ascension, for it is impossible for any human to physically ascend to God. This was God's rebuttal to the claim by many Jews at the time that they were able to bring about the accursed death on the cross to Jesus. God promises Jesus here that He will save Jesus from such disgrace and, instead, raise not only his own rank and honor but also that of his followers.

This view finds justification in the fact that others in the Quran are also said to be raised, and the meaning is always understood to be a spiritual exaltation or raise in rank and honor. For example, the same word is used in the following verse: "And relate the story of Idris as mentioned in the Book. He was a truthful man, and a Prophet. And We exalted him to a lofty station." This speaks of a prophet (most commonly understood to be the Biblical Prophet Enoch) who God claims to have raised or exalted to a high station. This certainly does not refer to a physical ascension to a high location or heaven. It has a spiritual meaning instead.

It is regrettable that some English translators have parted from the linguistic meaning of this phrase and mistranslated this verse as "Remember, when Allah said: 'O Isa (Jesus)! I am going to recall you (from your mission) and raise you up to Myself."[59] This is a wholly incorrect translation, and it is shocking that the translator would assert that instead of honoring Jesus, God would decide that he is not suitable to complete his mission. Another translation states, "(And remember) when Allah said: O Jesus! Lo! I am gathering thee and causing thee to ascend unto Me."[60] This is starkly incorrect for several reasons. First, the tense is incorrect—it uses present tense language of "I am" and "causing" whereas the Arabic refers to something in the future. Secondly, this translator decided to add the word "Lo," which does not exist in the original Arabic nor is it implied. Finally—and most important—there is no version of the phrase "Mutawaffi-ka" that can even come close to meaning "I am gathering."

Hence, the substitution theory becomes implausible considering that a physical ascension is not grounded in the language of the Quran. Also, the idea that God would deceptively change one man's face to resemble Jesus is seen by many as bereft of sound logic and beneath the dignity of God. This is why millions of Muslims around the world understand that Jesus was indeed hung on the cross, and the sign of his truth was that he survived.

Survival Theory

These Muslims deny the death of Jesus on the cross, as opposed to denying the crucifixion altogether. They reject the claim that God would cause someone else to be unjustly arrested and punished in the place of Jesus. Thus, even if the aforementioned verse is understood to say, "They killed him not, nor crucified him, but so it was made to appear to them," a failure to crucify Jesus indeed means a failure to kill him through crucifixion. They argue that "the crucifixion of Jesus was an attempt made on his life, like any attempted murder. Crucifixion was only the weapon used in that murderous attempt. However, the attempt to crucify him failed in inflicting death. This is tantamount to saying that they failed to crucify him. When we say this, we express ourselves exactly as we would in any other case of attempted murder. If an attempt is made on someone's life and the attempt fails, it cannot be said that the intended victim was murdered. For instance, if such an attempt is made with a sword, and the attempt fails, no one can say that the intended victim was put to the sword."[61]

So when the Quran states that Jesus "was made to appear to them like one crucified," it means that to one who was witnessing his agonizing torture and nailing on the cross, it could have appeared that he had died. But the same verse makes it clear that the Jews were not able to "bring about his death on the cross." So how did he survive? This requires closer examination.

First, it must be established that the Bible depicts Jesus as very unwilling to be caught and put to the cross. Knowing he was about to be betrayed, Jesus was restless and told his disciples to stay in prayer while he went ahead, fell on his knees, and began to pray humbly, crying and weeping in the following words: "Father, if thou be willing, remove this cup from me: nevertheless not my will, but thine, be done."[62] Jesus was in such agony that the Bible states his perspiration fell from him like "great drops of blood falling down to the ground."[63] He told his disciples, "My soul is exceeding sorrowful even unto death."[64] Three times that night, he reprimanded his disciples and told them to pray. So we see Jesus very concerned and restless about what he knew was about to happen. It was with this thought that he turned to God to ask Him to remove this bitter punishment from him.

It is inconceivable to think his prayer could have possibly remained unanswered, for Jesus claimed that God heard his prayers. He told his disciples, "Therefore I say unto you, What things soever ye desire, when ye pray, believe that ye receive them, and ye shall have them."[65] Jesus acknowledged that his prayers were heard, as it is written, "And Jesus lifted up his eyes, and said, Father, I thank thee that thou hast heard me. And I knew that thou hearest me always."[66] The Bible furnishes evidence that his prayer was heard and God saved him from death upon the cross, as is written in Paul's words to the Hebrews, "In the days of His flesh, He offered up both prayers and supplications with loud crying and tears to the One able to save Him from death, and He was heard because of His piety."[67]

The chief priests of the people took Jesus before the governor of Judea, Pontius Pilate, to lobby to put Jesus to death. But Pilate's wife sent word to him, as she had a terrible dream the night before. She warned, "Have nothing to do with that righteous Man; for last night I suffered greatly in a dream because of Him."[68] This appears to be a warning administered by God to Pilate, as he took his place on the judgment seat, to inform Pilate that it was not God's design to let Jesus die.

The Bible paints Pilate as being very reluctant to sentence Jesus to death, quoting him as saying, "I have found no guilt in this man regarding the charges which you make against Him . . . behold, nothing deserving death has been done by Him."[69] Since the Jews threatened Pilate that they would complain against him to Caesar, he reluctantly handed Jesus over for crucifixion.

It is important to note the purpose of crucifixion versus any other death penalty. Crucifixion was not meant to cause immediate death; rather, it was meant to serve as a torture that continued for three or four days. This is because people put to the cross would not die of their wounds; rather, they would die from suffocation over time as more pressure mounted on their chest after weakness prevented them from holding themselves up with their legs. After a few hours or even the day after the crucifixion, if it was considered that the criminal had suffered enough on the cross and he was taken down, he could survive. If a crucified man was taken down in time and given careful treatment, he could recover.

The Jewish historian, Flavius Josephus, described a story in which one of his own friends survived a crucifixion in the first century. While traveling, he noticed three of his friends hanging on crosses and requested Titus (the Roman general) to allow them to be brought down. Upon receiving permission, the three were brought down immediately and given medical care. Two of them died, but the third did survive.[70]

Far from three to four days, the Gospels testify that Jesus was on the cross for three to six hours. He spent such short time on the cross because Pilate appointed the crucifixion for Friday, and Sabbath would begin at sunset that very same day. Since the holy day of Sabbath is not allowed to be tarnished by the hanging of an accursed man, Jesus had to be taken off the cross prior to Sunset—thus, he was on the cross for three to six hours.

Jesus was hung on the cross at the same time as the two bandits were put on their crosses on either side of him. In order to prevent these bodies from remaining on the cross on the Sabbath, the Jews requested for the implementation of the only way to quicken the process of death on the cross: "Then the Jews, because it was the day of preparation, so that the bodies would not remain on the cross on the Sabbath (for that Sabbath was a high day), asked Pilate that their legs might be broken, and that they might be taken away. So the soldiers came, and broke the legs of the first man and of the other who was crucified with Him; but coming to Jesus, when they saw that He was already dead, they did not break His legs."[71]

There are two points of significance in the above verse. First, the demand of the Jews to break the legs of those nailed to the cross clearly illustrates that they did not consider their time spent on the cross sufficient to induce death. Additionally, the decision on the part of the soldiers to refrain from breaking the legs of Jesus prevented the hastening of his death. Breaking the legs of the two men hanging around Jesus hastened their death by instigating suffocation, blood volume depletion, and its consequences. This did not happen to Jesus.

Instead, the soldiers poked Jesus with a spear to see if he was alive—presumably, the stabbing would prompt him to stir if he were alive. The Bible records that "one of the soldiers pierced His side with a spear, and immediately blood and water came out."[72] This indicates that Jesus was only unconscious at the time and not dead. If a corpse is stabbed, blood does not immediately gush forth like it did in the case of Jesus. In a dead body, the heart ceases entirely and circulation of blood discontinues, making it impossible for blood to flow out with force. The sudden flow of blood indicates that the heart was still beating and there was still blood pressure in his body. The only declaration of death was by a bystander who had no confirmation that Jesus had indeed died.

Another abnormal act was performed shortly thereafter. In violation of Roman law, Pilate directed the body of Jesus to be given to Jesus' disciples: "When it was evening, there came a rich man from Arimathea, named Joseph, who himself had also become a disciple of Jesus. This man went to Pilate and asked for the body of Jesus. Then Pilate ordered it to be given to him. And Joseph took the body and wrapped it in a clean linen cloth, and laid it in his own new tomb, which he had hewn out in the rock; and he rolled a large stone against the entrance of the tomb and went away."[73]

Haim Hermann Cohn, a renowned lawyer who was CEO of Israel's Ministry of Justice and attorney general of Israel before eventually being appointed to the Supreme Court of Israel, studied Roman law extensively, thus exposing the puzzling behavior of Pilate: "The Roman law was that a convict after execution, might not be buried. We have seen that the crucified, in particular, were left on the cross until beasts and birds of prey devoured them. Guards were mounted on duty to prevent kinsfolk or friends from taking down a corpse and burying it; unauthorized burial of a crucified convict was a criminal offense."[74] Against all odds, the body of Jesus was handed over to his own disciples.

After Jesus' body had been placed in Joseph's tomb, the Pharisees rushed to Pilate and asked him: "Command therefore that the sepulchre be made sure until the third day, lest his disciples come by night, and steal him away, and say unto the people, He is risen from the dead: so the last error shall be worse than the first."[75] What was this "first error" that they regretted? The first error could be none other than that Jesus had been taken off the cross much earlier than was necessary, that his bones had not been broken, and that he had been given over to his own disciples. Now, they feared, if they did not secure the tomb, an even greater error would occur.

What happened next is further testimony to Jesus' survival of the crucifixion. After being taken to the tomb—which was really a room large enough to accommodate more than one person—the physician Nicodemus applied to the wounds of Jesus an ointment that had been prepared in advance. The nearly one hundred pounds of ointment contained rare ingredients (such as aloe and myrrh),[76] which have properties of healing wounds and subduing pain. The only justifiable reason for going through the rigorous and intense process of collecting rare ingredients to prepare about one hundred pounds of ointment is that the disciples had strong reasons to believe that Jesus would be delivered alive from the cross. The ointment applied by Nicodemus to Jesus is recorded in many Greek and Latin medical journals and books, many of which claim that it was the ointment applied to the wounds of Jesus when he was taken down from the cross.[77]

As final evidence that Jesus survived this attempt on his life, we must turn to the words of Jesus himself, who foretold that he would survive this ordeal. Long before the crucifixion, when the Jews demanded a sign from Jesus, his answer was, "An evil and adulterous generation craves for a sign; and yet no sign will be given to it but the sign of Jonah the prophet; for just as Jonah was three days and three nights in the belly of the sea monster, so will the Son of Man be three days and three nights in the heart of the earth."[78] Clearly, Jonah did not die in the belly of the whale—at most, we can accept that he may have become temporarily unconscious. The Bible bears witness that Jonah remained alive throughout the time he was in the belly of the whale and came out alive, and his people ultimately accepted him. Jonah spent three days and nights in extremely precarious circumstances and experienced a miraculous revival from near death—not a return back to life from the dead. If, then, Jesus had died in the belly of his proverbial "whale," what resemblance could there be between a dead man and one who was alive? As Jesus was a true prophet who knew God would save him from an accursed death, he hinted that he would not die on the cross. Like Jonah, he would only pass through a state of unconsciousness.

So when Jesus emerged after three days of recovering—and shocked those disciples who thought he must have died—his behavior is befitting a man who narrowly escaped death. Had he indeed died and miraculously been sent back through resurrection as a sign from God, the true sign would have been for him to have returned unscathed and perfect. That would be a true miracle. But, instead, Jesus emerged battered, bruised, physically scarred, and hungry for food. Far from a resurrected body, he had the body of a recovering patient. The Bible records that Jesus showed his disciples his own wounds, thereby illustrating that he did not die. Instead, God saved him from the torment, just as He had saved Jonah.

As would be expected from a man who narrowly survived death at the hands of the ruling government and priestly class, Jesus kept a very low profile. This wasn't a man making a triumphant return from the dead; rather, it was a man who secretly met with his followers and planned to escape from Judea, telling them: "Go and take word to My brethren to leave for Galilee, and there they will see Me."[79] Hence, Jesus survived and traveled out of Judea in order to finally complete his mission to seek and find the lost tribes of Israel, who had been scattered to the east. His ministry continued until he fulfilled his mission, found the lost tribes, and eventually died a natural death.

MUSLIMS ACCEPTING THE SURVIVAL THEORY

In his landmark book, *Jesus in India*—first written in the Urdu language in 1908—Mirza Ghulam Ahmad brought groundbreaking evidence and arguments to argue that Jesus continued to the east and found descendants of the lost ten tribes of Israel. Ahmad even maps the course Jesus likely traveled and furnishes evidences of Jesus' presence from Jerusalem through modern-day Iran, Afghanistan, and Pakistan before settling in modern-day Kashmir.[80]

Professor Mahmud Shaltut of the renowned Al-Azhar University in Cairo issued a fatwa (religious edict) in the May 11, 1942, edition of the weekly *Al-Risalah* in Cairo. In this fatwa, he argued on the basis of the Quran that Jesus Christ had indeed been hung on the cross but had survived the crucifixion. He rejected the claim that Jesus had ascended into heaven, where he still sits today.[81]

Twentieth-century renowned Muslim scholar and speaker Ahmad Deedat also accepted and preached the survival theory of Jesus' crucifixion. He published a book entitled *Crucifixion Or CRUCIFICTION?* in 1984 in which he vigorously made the case that Jesus had survived the brutal attempt on his life at the crucifixion and had not ascended bodily into heaven. He relies on verses from the Quran and Bible to conclude that God protected His messenger.

Thus, Islam honors Jesus by exonerating him from the claims that he is the son of God and that he sits at the right hand of God. It aims to remedy the distortion of his teachings that have spread over the past two thousand years and protects him from allegations that he claimed to be divine in any way. Far from claiming that Jesus sits bodily in heaven, Islam came with a message in the Quran that "Muhammad is but a Messenger. Verily all Messengers have passed away before him."[82] Thus, it has made it clear that all prophets before Muhammad (including Jesus) have already passed away. As such, there is no room in Islam for the belief that Jesus is sitting alive in heaven.

9

DEMYSTIFYING
THE SECTS OF ISLAM

A common mistake made by pundits in the media, as well as lay people around the world, is to speak of the worldwide Muslim population as a monolithic group or society. Such people present Muslims as a singular group who share one ideology and worldview. This could not be any further from the truth. Certainly, there are many matters that unite the entire world's Muslim population—such as the belief in one God, and the belief that Muhammad is the last prophet of God to bring a law—but the diversity of thought, identity, and culture are just as rich among Muslims as they would be among any other body of people who happen to believe in the same faith. Understandably, much of the diversity among Muslims relates to their cultural and ethnic diversity. It is estimated that only 15 percent of the worldwide Muslim population is of Arab descent,[1] with large populations of Muslims from Central and East Asia to Africa, Europe, and South America. The differences, however, go beyond simple ethnic or geographic diversity. There are a large number of different sects (or denominations) within the Muslim world, as Muslims have differed on various historical and doctrinal matters over time.

People have generally heard of the terms "Sunni" and "Shia," but these two terms do not accurately illustrate the extent to which differences of opinion have surfaced among Muslims and their scholars for more than one thousand years. Yet, the distinction between Sunni and Shia is significant, as it shaped the ongoing disunity among Muslims for centuries to come. At its root, the split of the hitherto united Muslim community had to do with the issue of leadership and succession to the Prophet Muhammad. Shia and Sunni scholars will invariably have different views about historical events, but the core of the disagreement has to do with the question of rightful leadership within Islam. This takes a little explaining but is not too complicated.

THE QUESTION OF LEADERSHIP

After the Prophet Muhammad passed away in the year 632 CE, the question arose as to who should be appointed the leader of Muslims in order to keep them united. There were differing opinions even at that time as to who was the right person for that role, but the matter was decided based on the instruction and guidance of Muhammad himself. During the lifetime of the Prophet Muhammad, he had spoken about the role of the Khalifa (also known as "caliph"), defined as a successor. The role of a Khalifa (pronounced kha-lee-fa) is to be the successor after the prophet's demise and continue the prophet's mission of education and reformation of his followers, as well as the ongoing spread of his teachings. Whereas the prophet had planted the seed of Islam, the elected Khalifa was tasked to help it nourish and grow. The Khalifa would, thus, hold both a temporal and spiritual significance for Muslims at that time.

The word خَلِيْفَة (Khalifa) derives from the Arabic root word خلف (kha-la-fa), which is defined as a verb meaning "to succeed" or "to come after" and refers to one who "came after, followed, succeeded or remained after, another"[2] person. It, thus, refers to a person who succeeds or comes after someone else. In the religious context, the Khalifa is a person who succeeds, follows, or comes after a prophet. The word "Khilafat" (also called "caliphate") refers to the institution or system by which each individual Khalifa is elected in succession. According to the words of the Prophet Muhammad, all prophets were succeeded by someone (a Khalifa) who was charged with carrying forward the prophet's message and keeping the people united. He is quoted as having said: "There has been no Prophet who has not been followed by Khilafat."[3] Thus did Muhammad foretell of the coming of the system of Khilafat, whereby a Khalifa would be elected after his demise.

The Quran also speaks of the appearance of a Khalifa (successor). After several consecutive verses reminding Muslims to obey God and the Prophet Muhammad—who it states is there to deliver the message to them—the Quran then states: "Allah has promised to those among you who believe and do good works that He will, surely, make them Successors in the earth, as He made Successors from among those who were before them; and that He will, surely, establish for them their religion which He has chosen for them; and that He will, surely, give them in exchange security and peace after their fear; They will worship Me, and they will not associate anything with Me. Then whoso disbelieves after that, they will be the rebellious."[4] This verse captures God's promise that, at a moment of fear for the people,

He will grant them security and peace through the establishment of a successor. By following the verses about the importance of obeying the prophet with this verse about a successor, the Quran foretells of the great fear and anxiety that would overtake the Muslims upon the sad demise of the Prophet Muhammad, which would be remedied by the appointment of his successor.

When Muhammad passed away, a great sadness and fear took over the Muslim world, the population of which had already grown significantly during his life. As news spread through the land, many were in disbelief that the man they loved so dearly could possibly be gone. There was a very large group of people who had only recently become Muslim as Islam expanded. As such, they had not yet been educated about all of the teachings of Islam. For this reason, Muhammad's passing shook the faith of many people. In concert, several false claimants to prophethood began to attract those of weak faith and grow a large following. Immediately, a council of Muslim leaders came together to elect the Khalifa, who would be charged not only with continuing Muhammad's role as head of the state but also with maintaining unity among the Muslims through spiritual leadership.

As would be expected with a diverse group of people and tribes who had accepted the prophet's message over the years, there were differing opinions regarding who should be elected. However, consensus was then reached to elect Abu Bakr as Islam's first Khalifa. Abu Bakr was the first man to convert to Islam early in Muhammad's ministry and was a very close friend of the prophet. During Abu Bakr's short two-and-a-half years as Khalifa, he showcased his tremendous strength as a rightly guided leader for the Muslims. Faced with a large number of tribes who had renounced Islam after the prophet's death, the rise of several people falsely claiming to be prophets, a refusal from many people to pay the Zakat (which was needed in the operation of the state and for the care of the poor), as well as brewing incursions from the Roman and Persian empires, the leadership Abu Bakr provided was instrumental in preventing the entire Muslim nation and belief system from falling apart.

After the demise of Abu Bakr, Umar bin Khattab was elected the second Khalifa. Umar remained Khalifa for ten years, during which time the Muslim empire expanded considerably, as the Muslim army continued to fend off repeated attacks from the Roman and Persian empires and their vassal states, such as Egypt and Syria. Muslims remained united as they continued to fight these aggressors, with each victory on the battlefield resulting in more land coming under Muslim rule. The people in these new territories were allowed to maintain their religion, culture, language, and way of life. Since they were now part of the state, they were required to pay only the tax of the state. Through preaching, however, a large number of people accepted Islam, though they were not forced to do so. As a result of the rapid expansion, a great variety of customs and cultures were introduced into the Muslim empire. Through this all, Umar's incredible strength and leadership (especially in matters of administration) were crucial in maintaining the unity of the Muslims. Eventually, Umar was fatally wounded by a Persian slave who stabbed him while he was offering prayers in the mosque.

After Umar's demise, Uthman bin Affan was elected as the third Khalifa. During the election, there were originally six candidates being considered for this position, but it was narrowed down to two: Uthman and Ali (the Prophet Muhammad's younger cousin who had married Muhammad's daughter, Fatima). In the end, Uthman was elected, and everyone swore allegiance to him as Khalifa—including Ali. Uthman proved to be the rightly guided man for this role, as his twelve years as Khalifa were full of much progress for Islam. As Khalifa, he established one standard copy of the Holy Quran, which was then sent to each of the provinces of the great state. He was an exceptionally tenderhearted person who took great pains to ensure the unity of Muslims. After six years of successful unity during his Khilafat, however, dissent began to surface among Muslims. Thus began the initial stages of disagreement among Muslims that would eventually culminate in a split down the road.

With the rapid expansion of Islam—especially during the time that Uthman was Khalifa—and great diversity of education, language, culture, and practices among the Muslims, many younger new converts failed to understand that Islam was not a worldly enterprise. Thus, they began to desire important roles in running the state and were jealous that most of those roles were held by older companions of the Prophet Muhammad. It is recorded in history that such "people who were not complete in their faith became envious upon witnessing the honour, status, success and authority of the companions. As has been a practice since time immemorial, they began to desire that these companions resign from all their responsibilities of government and hand over positions to them so that others are given the opportunity to exhibit their skill as well."[5]

They began to object to the appointments of various governors around the state, alleging there was nepotism involved in the appointments. The mixture of ambition and ignorance led them to spread rumors about governors and even the Khalifa himself, and they began saying that Ali should have been elected instead of Uthman. These rebels grew so strong in number that they laid siege to Medina, where Uthman lived, and demanded him to abdicate his position as Khalifa. After refusing, the insurgents eventually attacked Uthman's house and murdered the eighty-two-year-old while he was reading the Quran. The true intentions of these rebels were exposed when, after Uthman's murder, their first act was to loot the state's treasury of whatever money it had. There was no religious motivation behind his murder; rather, the Khalifa was killed by those seeking temporal power. Yet, Uthman became the first Muslim to be callously murdered at the hands of another Muslim. The irony is that when Uthman was urged to strike down the rebels, he refused to allow Muslims to be killed at the hands of other Muslims.

One can only imagine the complete state of disorder and chaos created by the brutal murder of the presiding Khalifa by a large faction of Muslims. Ali bin Abu Talib was chosen as the fourth Khalifa and gained acceptance not only by the Muslim masses but also by the rebels, who assumed Ali would oppose whatever Uthman had done. Many also supported Ali because of his blood relation to the Prophet Muhammad, being not only the prophet's much younger first cousin but also his son-in-law, due to his marriage with the prophet's daughter, Fatima. There grew, however, growing opposition to Ali by others demanding he seek and kill Uthman's murderers. Ali refused to spill more Muslim blood and, instead, announced his top priority would be to restore law and order around the Muslim empire—in light of the growing rebellion and sedition spurred by those seeking power. Under the influence of the mischievous rebels who initiated the conflict, noted members of the Muslim community raised an army to seek revenge for the murder of Uthman, resulting in a battle with Ali's army after his attempts to dissuade them from taking the law into their own hands and creating disorder did not succeed. This was the first battle between two Muslim armies, but the matter was inevitably settled.

This was a pivotal time in the history of Islam. Islamic scholar and historian Muhammad Ali addressed Ali's reign as Khalifa as follows: "This period of four years and a half was a period of domestic dissensions within the house of Islam. In the internecine warfare that ensued great and prominent figures were involved. This exactly was the warning Uthman had repeatedly given to the insurgents: 'Once you draw the sword against me' he had told them, 'you will be opening among Muslims a door of dissension that will never be closed.' The warning turned out to be true. Till the reign of Uthman, there was practically no division in Islam."[6] Things began to unravel due to the death of Uthman at the hand of the mischief makers, as calls for retribution came from the corners of the empire. But in his wisdom, Ali knew that to arrest and punish those responsible meant to deal with a very large number of people from various provinces of the empire, which would result in disruption of the great empire.

In order to remove the charge of nepotism with regard to the governors of the provinces, Ali replaced each and every governor. One governor, however, refused to yield to this commandment from the new Khalifa. Muawiyah was the long-standing governor of Syria who had been appointed by the second Khalifa, Umar. He was among the most vocal about avenging the death of Uthman, and since Ali refused to do so in favor of peace and order of society, Muawiyah and others began to accuse Ali of having a part in Uthman's death. Due to his hitherto valiant service to the empire and his position at the top of Syria, Muawiyah was very highly regarded and followed. He had even sent warning to Ali that sixty thousand men in Damascus were ready to avenge the death of Uthman.[7] Because Muawiyah, a governor, refused to submit to the Khalifa, who was the head of the state, Ali was forced to advance his army to Syria in 567 CE for a battle against Muawiyah's army. After several days of battle, Ali and Muawiyah decided to settle the matter through arbitration, with two parties appointed to meet and determine what should be done about Utham's murderers. Ali and Muawiyah returned to their respective cities awaiting a decision.

Although Ali set out with fifty thousand troops, twelve thousand abandoned him on the way back due to their extreme objection to the arbitration. The main reason was that they were among the original insurgents whose complaints and siege led to the murder of Uthman. Even though they were not the ones who slayed the Khalifa, they feared what would become of them if the arbiters decided to punish all those involved in the insurrection. These insurgents were the very people who favored Ali to become Khalifa, but due to Ali's observance of justice and peace making, they turned on him. They favored neither Muawiyah nor Ali. They have become known in history as the "Khawarijites," a term meaning the outsiders or the ones who seceded, for they had separated and formed their own faction.

In the end, arbitration between Ali and Muawiyah failed, the Khawarijites gained numbers, and Ali slowly lost supporters. This led to a battle against the Khawarijites in 658 CE when they initiated a revolt against Ali. Many Khawarijites surrendered, but the rest perished. Muawiyah increased his own empire by invading and taking over Egypt, thereby maintaining Egypt and Syria in his control. When years of peace-making efforts failed, Ali agreed to a treaty, recognizing Egypt and Syria as being under Muawiyah's rule, separate from the rest of Arabia, which was under Ali's rule. This, once again, upset the Khawarijites, whose goal it was to see the two Muslim parties at continual war. They eventually conspired to kill both Ali and Muawiyah on the same day. Their attempt against Muawiyah failed, only resulting in an injury, whereas they successfully attacked Ali on his way to the morning prayer, and he succumbed to his injuries two days later. Years of his valiant and commendable affection for Muslims and attempts to reconcile the various groups came to an end when the sixty-three-year-old was murdered in the year 661 CE.

THE OFFICIAL SPLIT AMONG MUSLIMS

With the assassination of Ali, his eldest son Hasan (the Prophet Muhammad's grandson) was selected as Khalifa, but this resulted in hostilities between him and Muawiyah, who called for Hasan to renounce his role as Khalifa. After battle between the two sides, Hasan decided to abdicate his position of Khalifa in the better interest of peace and reconciliation among Muslims and avoid further bloodshed. Therefore, Hasan never fully assumed the role as Khalifa. This debate over leadership is what resulted in the major split of Muslims into three branches:

1. Sunnis: those who believe in all four of the rightly guided Khalifas and argue that whoever was elected was done so in accordance with the teachings of Islam and instructions of the Prophet Muhammad;
2. Shias: those who believe that Ali was the rightful heir to Muhammad from the beginning since he was his blood relative. They reject the first three Khalifas and accept Ali as the first Imam of Islam;
3. Khawarijites: those who believe in the first two Khalifas but reject the third and fourth as sinners who had to be either killed or replaced, and generally believe any Muslim who sins, by default, renounces his or her faith (i.e., commits apostasy).

Although the seeds of dissension had been sown at the occasion of each election for Khalifa, peace still remained within the Muslim community until the open rebellion by a surprisingly large group of defectors. The death of Ali and the abdication of his son Hasan as Khalifa were the final nails that ended what is called the reign of the rightly guided Khalifas. Thus, within thirty years of the death of the prophet, the misgivings of Muslims caused the separation of the house of Islam into three factions. Some Sunnis claim that the system of Khilafat continued because Muawiyah claimed to be the Khalifa and then passed it on to his son, Yazid, upon his death. But, in reality, with Ali's death, the era of Khilafat ended and was replaced by a long line of dynastic monarchies. Each monarch that inherited this kingship was still referred to as a "Khalifa" for hundreds of years to come, but these despotic rulers of the Muslim empire were regarded as secular kings and did not have the religious position of the first four pious Khalifas.

Thus, the entire unity of Muslims was compromised over the critical issue of leadership. Khilafat is, thus, a very important aspect of Islam. The divisions that were created within the Muslim world are due to Muslims ignoring its significance and rebelling against this institution, which led to the despotic rule of monarchs. What is most striking is that this had been foretold by the Prophet of Islam himself. In a Hadith, a close companion of the Prophet Muhammad, Hudhayfa ibn al-Yaman, testified that Muhammad said:

> Prophethood shall remain with you for as long as Allah wills. He will then cause it to end. Then Khilafat will be established on the precepts of Prophethood, which will last for as long as Allah wills. He will then cause it to end. Oppressive kingship will then follow and its rule will last for as long as Allah wills. He will then cause it to end. After this, tyrannical monarchies will follow, and their rule will last for as long as Allah wills. Allah will then cause it to end. Khilafat will then be re-established on the precepts of Prophethood.[8]

Hudhayfa then stated that upon saying these words, Muhammad became silent.

It is amazing indeed to see the prophecy of the Prophet Muhammad come into play with such precise accuracy. This prophecy also hints at the idea that, due to the question of leadership, the Muslim population will face great difficulties and tyranny, but through leadership and Khilafat the Muslim community would be reunited in the future.

After the death of the fourth Khalifa, Ali, a long history of bloody violence ensued between Sunnis (those who accepted all four of the elected Khalifas) and the Shias (those who were supporters of Ali and argued that he, as the blood relative of Muhammad, was the only one entitled to be Khalifa from the beginning). When Ali's eldest son, Hasan, agreed to relinquish his title of Khalifa to Muawiyah in order to establish some semblance of unity, he did so on the condition that upon Muawiyah's death, the Khalifa role should be given back to him, if he were alive, or be given to his younger brother, Hussein, if he were not alive. To this, Muawiyah agreed but reneged at the end of his life by appointing his own son, Yazid, to be the next "Khalifa." This betrayal was enough to further enrage the followers of the family of Ali. But what made matters worse was the tyrannical style of leadership Yazid implemented—he eventually had Hussein, Ali's younger son and the Prophet Muhammad's grandson, killed and beheaded at the Battle of Karbala. This bloody phase of Islam's early history set the tone for centuries of continual violence between Shias and Sunnis all around the world.

Irrespective of their differences, Sunni and Shia Muslims agree on the prophecy of Muhammad concerning the renaissance of Islam in the latter days. Muhammad had foretold of the second advent of the Messiah as well as the arrival of a reformer he called "the Imam Mahdi." Many Muslims understand this to mean that Jesus Christ will descend from the sky in the latter days as a Muslim, thereby fulfilling the coming of the Promised Messiah, and he will join forces with another figure who will fulfill the role of the Promised Mahdi. Other Muslims, however, understand the prophecies of the Promised Messiah to refer to the same person as the prophecies of the Promised Mahdi (i.e., one person will come as a reformer in the latter days who will unite Muslims and all mankind and usher in an era of peace, justice, and prosperity).

SUNNIS

Sunnis are the main body of Muslims around the world. It is estimated that up to 87–90 percent of the Muslim world is Sunni.[9] The word "Sunni" is short for the Arabic term "*ahl-e-Sunnah*," which means "the people of the tradition" of the Prophet Muhammad and implies that those who call themselves "Sunni" are those who follow the traditions of the Prophet Muhammad. They are also the body of Muslims who accept the authenticity and authority of the first four elected Khalifas of Islam.

As would be expected, there is great diversity in this large body of Muslims. As such, the word "Sunni" is an umbrella term that refers to many sects or denominations of Muslims who are all considered Sunni because they accept the authority of the four pious Khalifas. Sunni Muslims also recognize four distinct orthodox schools of jurisprudence, which are similar in many regards but disagree on several matters relating to interpretation of Shariah, practices, and rituals. Generally, many Sunni sects claim allegiance to one of these four schools of law:

1. Hanafi school: Based on the interpretation of Islamic law by Imam Abu Hanifa (699–767 CE), it was founded in Baghdad and is considered to be the most open to modern ideas, since it relies not only on religious text but also on reason. It is the oldest and largest of the four schools, with estimates that 30 percent of the worldwide Muslim population follows this school. Populations of this school are scattered among various countries, including Turkey, Iraq, India, Pakistan, Afghanistan, Russia, Syria, and Jordan.

2. Maliki school: Based on the interpretation of Islamic law by Imam Malik bin Anas (711–795 CE) and relying mostly on religious text, Maliki is a stricter interpretation of law compared to the Hanafi school. It is most dominant in North and West Africa, with some population of followers in Middle East nations such as Kuwait and Bahrain as well.

3. Shafi school: Based on the interpretation of Islamic law by Imam Muhammad bin Idris al Shafi (767–820 CE), who had spent time studying with Imam Malik, this school understandably has many similarities with the Maliki school, but the Shafi school is considered more liberalized. It is found mostly in Southeast Asian countries such as Indonesia, Malaysia, and the Philippines, but its followers are also quite scattered across Saudi Arabia, Yemen, Jordan, Egypt, and other Middle East countries.

4. Hanbali school: Based on the interpretation of Islamic law by Imam Ahmad bin Hanbal (780–855 CE), who was once a student of Imam al Shafi, it is known to be the most strict and conservative, as well as the smallest, of the four Sunni schools. This interpretation relies more heavily on the text of the Quran and Hadith, with less room for reason and consensus. Followers of this school are often characterized as "less tolerant" and "more literal" in their approach to religion. It is predominant in Saudi Arabia, with followers in Qatar as well.

These four jurists or theologians interpreted religious law according to their own scholarship of Islam, and they likely did not intend to publish interpretations that would further divide Sunni Muslims. Today, the popularity of various interpretations can be seen. The majority of Sunnis give importance to not only the Quran but also the recorded traditions and maxims of the Prophet Muhammad. Disagreements with regard to the authenticity of various Hadith attributed to the Prophet Muhammad have given rise to many sects within the Sunni world.

SHIAS

Shias comprise a relatively small percentage of the Muslim population, estimated at approximately 10–13 percent of the global Muslim community.[10] Whereas Sunni Muslims can be understood to be those Muslims who believe in the election of the four Khalifas, Shia Muslims are those Muslims who reject the election of the Khalifas, arguing that Ali should have been the one and only leader (Imam) selected after the Prophet Muhammad passed away. The word "Shia" is an Arabic word, which literally translates as "a follower" and is short for the Arabic term "Shiatu Ali," which means "the followers of Ali" or "the partisans of Ali."

Shias believe that a Muslim leader cannot be elected. Instead, they believe that the leader comes from the lineage of the Prophet Muhammad, arguing that the holy bloodline of the prophet's family grants them unique spiritual and political authority. Although the origin of the Shia belief dates back to the time of the third Khalifa, Uthman, it is believed that the death and decapitation of Ali's youngest son, Hussein, severed all ties between the supporters of Ali's family and the rest of the Muslims.

Instead of Khalifas, Shia Muslims recognize Imams, who they believe are divinely appointed spiritual leaders. All Shia Muslims recognize Ali as the first Imam of Islam and greatly revere him with the title "Commander of the Faithful." His eldest son, Hasan, is recognized by Shia Muslims as their second Imam, and Ali's younger son, Hussein, is recognized as their third Imam. Like "Sunni," "Shia" is an umbrella term, referring to a body of many different groups, not just one body of Muslims. There are many sects and branches of Shias who disagree on different matters, most important of which is the succession of Imams after the first three listed above.

It is commonly accepted that all of the world's Shia Muslim population falls into one of the following groups:

1. The Twelvers: The largest body of Shias is called "Ithna ashariyyah" but is commonly referred to as "The Twelvers," for they accept the appearance of twelve Imams, beginning from Ali. It is estimated that about 85 percent of the world's Shia population belongs to The Twelvers sect. They believe that their twelfth and final Imam, Muhammad ibn al-Hassan, disappeared in 873 CE and will eventually return in the latter days as the long-awaited Promised Mahdi, for whom the entire Muslim world is waiting. Twelvers are found mostly in Iran and Iraq, with populations in Bahrain and Lebanon

and smaller numbers in Pakistan, Afghanistan, and Saudi Arabia, among other countries.

2. The Seveners: Another well-known body of Shias is called "al-Ismailiyya" (also called "Ismailis"), which derives from the belief in Ismail bin Jafar as the seventh Imam in the hereditary line of Imams after Ali. This was the first of many splits and disagreements within the Shia community regarding the legitimacy of different Imams. The Ismailis are often referred to as "The Seveners," because they disagree with other Shia Muslims concerning the legitimacy of the seventh Imam. They believe Ismail bin Jafar is the seventh Imam. Although all Ismailis differ from The Twelvers on the matter of the seventh Imam, the term "The Seveners" is not completely accurate for all Ismailis, since there is at least one sub-sect of Ismailis who believe that the hereditary chain of Imams has continued to today, with the current Imam being the forty-ninth in this continual chain. The remainder, however, believe that one of the Imams disappeared and will return in the latter days as the much anticipated Promised Mahdi. However, there is disagreement about which of their accepted Imams is the one who disappeared and, thus, which will reappear.

3. The Zaydis: Perhaps the most unique group of Shia Muslims is known as "Zaydiyya," which derives from the belief in Zayd ibn Ali, who was the son of the fourth Imam accepted by all Shia Muslims, as well as the grandson of Hussein and great-great-grandson of the Prophet Muhammad. Although other Shias accepted Zayd's half-brother as the fifth Imam, the followers of Zayd preferred a bolder Imam who would be willing to fight against their oppressors. Zayd rejected his half-brother as Imam and claimed himself to be a real Imam, since he was willing to revolt against unjust rulers.[11] Consequently, Zaydis are known to be more conservative, with a desire for Imams that will fight oppressors. What is unique about the Zaydis as compared to other Shias is their similarity to Sunni Muslims in the sense that they accept the first three Khalifas of Islam.[12] Today, Zaydis are mostly found in Yemen.

With each group, there are a wide variety of sub-sects. For instance, the Alawites are a small mystical sub-sect of The Twelvers, even though they possess clear differences of opinion. They were founded in the latter half of the 800s CE by Abu Shuayb Muhammad ibn Nusayr, who claimed not only to have special contact with both the tenth and eleventh Imams but also to be a representative of the hidden twelfth Imam whom The Twelvers expect to return one day as the Promised Mahdi.[13] Although the vast majority of the Syrian population is Sunni, the Alawites are the next largest religious group, comprising 13 percent of the population.[14] Bashar Al-Assad—Syria's controversial president—is an Alawite.

Although at the heart of the split between Shias and Sunnis was the issue of leadership through Khilafat, invariably further differences in practices, rituals, and beliefs have emerged in the 1,300 years that these two sects have maintained separate identities. Much of this has to do with the intense persecution the Shias have faced at the hands of more-powerful Sunni empires, which caused the Shias to become more insular. Some are relatively minor differences such as the manner in which prayers are performed, whereas other differences are more significant—such as the practice of praying to Imams and saints at shrines.

Shias "revered their imams as specially blessed by God and immaculate from sin. . . . They invoke these sanctified figures in prayer and commemorate the days of their births and deaths. . . . Shias believe that their shrines are locations of spiritual grace, where God is present in a special way and most likely to answer cries for help. They seek blessings from these shrines and pray to saints to heal them and grant them their wishes. They believe that the shrines will imbue them with divine blessings and cleanse their souls."[15] Some Shias have claimed that these deceased Imams have the power to heal them and that praying to them is really a means of praying through an intercessor in order for prayers to be heard and answered more quickly by Allah. Sunni Muslims find this practice of praying to deceased people to be a grave violation of the commandment to worship only the One God. It is akin to the grievous sin of associating partners with God, often called "the only unforgivable sin."

KHAWARIJ

The Khawarijites are those who believed in only the first two Khalifas and rejected the third and fourth as sinners. They are mostly known as the group of Muslims who took the life of the fourth Khalifa, Ali. Like Sunni and Shia, the formation of the Khawarij group was due to the question of leadership. Regardless of whether a leader was an elected Khalifa or an appointed Imam, the Khawarajites believed that Muslims can (and should) rebel against any leader through an open revolt if they deemed that leader to be straying from Islam. They are a completely distinct group from the

Sunni and Shia, and their numbers did not survive very long over time. Considered more strict and extreme in their view compared to other Muslims, they became known for their habit of declaring people "non-Muslim" for not behaving in a manner they considered Islamic.

It is claimed that there is one modern-day spin-off of the Khawarij interpretation of Islam in a group of Muslims called the "Ibadiyya," a group that originated as part of the same Khawarijite secession in 657 CE. Though its followers do not consider themselves to be part of the original Khawarij group, "Ibadis maintain a special interest in Kharijism, and even if they are interested in distinguishing themselves from the Khawarij, they feel compelled to defend the Khawarij on a number of points."[16] In fact, the Ibadis' first Imam is the man whom Khawarajites had selected as their leader after they abandoned Ali. Today, Ibadi Muslims consider themselves distinct from Sunni and Shia, with their own line of Ibadi Imams through history. They are the predominant majority of Muslims in Oman today, with 75 percent of the population in Oman being Ibadi Muslim.

THE DIVERSITY OF
TWENTY-FIRST-CENTURY MUSLIMS

As can be seen, it is a mistake to consider Muslims a monolithic group with no diversity of thought or history. There are many differences between Muslims that go deep into the early history of Islam. The biggest mistake of ignorance one can make is to simply refer to Muslims as "they." Today in the twenty-first century, Muslims run the full spectrum, from ultraliberal to ultraconservative, from ultratraditional to modern-day reformist movements.

Sufism

One of the common areas of interest, confusion, and debate is a mystical and contemplative form of Islamic practice known as "Sufism." Some call it a sect of Islam, some call it a form of Muslim practice, and some completely divorce Sufism from Islam all together. In reality, there are both Sunnis and Shias who identify themselves as being "Sufi." So this Sufi philosophy transcends sectarian differences with regard to leadership in Islam.

"Sufism" is the practice of Muslims that focuses squarely on the development of a direct approach and communication with God. The original point of focus within this practice was on the idea of giving preference to the underlying spirit of religion over and above the form of religion. There are varying degrees among Sufi practices of adhering to the religious teachings, practices, and forms of Islam, but common among them is the desire to pursue a direct communion and love with God. The pursuit of a relationship and communion with God finds its basis within the life and teachings of the Prophet Muhammad, who would not only spend time in this endeavor but would also advocate it among his followers. After all, as mentioned in the opening chapter of this book, the underlying objective of this faith is to love and worship the one and only God, as well as to love and serve His creation. It is recorded as a Hadith that the Prophet Muhammad would recite the prayer of the Prophet David by saying: "Allah, I beg of Thee [for] Thy love, and the love of those who love Thee, and such conduct as should lead me to Thy love. Allah, make Thy love dearer to me than my [own] soul and my family and dearer than cold water."[17]

So the mystic search for one's Creator is a quality that is inherent to Islam and is deeply grounded in profound wisdom. Where some Sufi practices stray, however, is the overemphasis on this mystic custom to the extent that they consider adherence to the form of Islam not required. As such, although there are many Sufis who adhere firmly to the five pillars of Islam and other practices of Islam, there are some Sufis who do not do so. Some have concentrated their efforts on yogic practices that find similarities in Hinduism, believing it possible to find eternal truth through deep inner contemplation and prayer.

Sufi practices among Muslims are often credited for keeping the spirit of Islam alive in different nations throughout history. They provided the much-needed balance vis-à-vis such Muslims who would take a staunch and rigid approach to religion. Some notable Sufi Muslim personalities from whom current Sufis continue to glean guidance are Muhiyudeen ibn al-Arabi (known more commonly as simply "ibn al-Arabi") and Abu Hamid Muhammad ibn Muhammad al-Ghazali (known more commonly as simply "Imam al-Ghazali"). Their philosophies were based on the teachings of Islam.

This is a point that some Western Sufis today seem to forget when they search for inner truth and guidance through the teachings of Sufi saints while claiming these teachings have nothing to do with Islam. The thirteenth-century Persian poet Jalaluddin Rumi (otherwise commonly known simply as "Rumi") is considered the most popular poet in America[18] and is often quoted and cited by people who may not truly understand his philosophy. Rumi himself wrote that his works are based entirely on the Quran and Islam, and he strongly rebuked anyone who would claim otherwise. He once wrote: "I am the slave of the Quran while I still have life, I am dust on the path of Muhammad, The Chosen One. If anyone interprets my words in any other way, I deplore that person and I deplore his words."[19]

One must keep in mind that Rumi was a theologian who wrote his poetry at a time when the Quran remained primarily in Arabic, since many considered it taboo to translate its words. His poetry, thus, was a mechanism to introduce Islamic and Quranic concepts to those who could not understand Arabic. For this reason, fifteenth-century Sufi poet, Abdul Rahman Jami, referred to Rumi's most acclaimed writing, *Masnavi*, as nothing more than the Persian translation of the Quran.[20]

As would be expected, there are many differences of opinion within the Sufi movement, and there are different groups of Sufis. There are known to be a multitude of Sufi orders (or brotherhoods) that were founded by various Sufi saints or theologians throughout history. Just a few of the major orders are Naqshbandiyya, Chishtiyya, Soharverdiyya, and Qadiriyya—each then consisting of multiple off-shoot schools or further orders. The emphasis on mysticism is a fairly common attribute among them.

Wahhabi (Salafist) Movement

Known by the name "Wahhabiyya," the Wahhabi movement is an ultraconservative Sunni sect of Islam. Often seen as synonymous with the Salafi or Salafist movement, the Wahhabi group takes its name from eighteenth-century Arab scholar Muhammad ibn Abdul Wahhab, who taught a very strict and puritanical interpretation of Islam. Citing the noble desire to rid the Muslim world of unnecessary rituals and traditions that had been invented over time, al-Wahhab went to extreme lengths to prevent all such inventions, such as the practice of some Muslims to over-revere religious relics and historically significant locations. Wanting to rid Muslims of what he perceived as polytheism, ibn Abdul Wahhab took it upon himself to physically destroy the sites that he felt were causing Muslims to stray from Islam.

What garnered momentum for ibn Abdul Wahhab's reformation philosophy was an alliance he established with Muhammad bin Saud—ruler of the Arabian town of Dariiyyah—after ibn Abdul Wahhab was expelled from his village of Uyayna due to his rigid interpretation and enforcement of Islamic law. The ruler—considered the founder of today's Saudi royal family (also called the "Saudi Dynasty")—invited ibn Abdul Wahhab to continue his mission as an Islamic reformer in Dariiyyah, where they formed an alliance. Muhammad ibn Saud granted not only protection but also a platform to ibn Abdul Wahhab. In turn, the reformer's rigidity would grant ibn Saud stricter control and acceptance of the people who looked to him for religious guidance.

According to Dr. Madawi Al-Rasheed, professor of Anthropology of Religion at King's College in London and author of several books about Saudi Arabia,

> The Saudi ruler agreed to support the reformer's demand for *jihad*, a war against non-Muslims and those Muslims whose Islam did not conform to the reformer's teachings. In return the Saudi amir [ruler] was acknowledged as political leader of the Muslim community. Muhammad ibn Abdul Wahhab was guaranteed control over religious interpretation. The reformer started teaching his religious message in a mosque, specially built for him. He insisted on the attendance of men and children. Men who did not attend his special *dars* (teaching sessions) were required to pay a fine or shave their beards.[21]

In 1744, ibn Saud established the first Saudi state and legalized this strict interpretation preached by ibn Abdul Wahhab. That is how the rigid Wahhabi tradition and interpretation became the official interpretation of the Saudi Kingdom, which it still maintains today.

Followers of this tradition prefer not to be called "Wahhabi." They consider it a derogatory word, since they claim not to be following just Muhammad ibn Abdul Wahhab but, rather, to be following the original teachings of Islam. Thus, they prefer to call themselves "Salafis," because the word "Salaf"—literally meaning "ancestors" or "predecessors"—was used in history to describe the early pious followers of the Prophet Muhammad. As such, they see themselves as the reformist movement that brings Muslims back to the practices of the early Muslims.

Ahmadiyya Muslim Community

Juxtaposed to the movement of ibn Abdul Wahhab is the reformist movement founded in 1889 called the "Ahmadiyya Muslim Community." As mentioned earlier, nearly all Muslims are awaiting the appearance of the Promised Messiah and the Promised Mahdi. The Ahmadiyya Muslim Community consists of those Muslims who believe that this appearance took place in the latter part of the 1800s in the person of Mirza Ghulam Ahmad of Qadian, India, whom they believe fulfilled the prophecies made by the Prophet Muhammad about the second coming of the Messiah and the advent of the Promised Mahdi. Ahmad's followers believe that all of these prophecies referred to the coming of one person, whom Muhammad referred to as both "the Messiah" and "the Mahdi."

Ahmad sparked an unprecedented era of revival within Islam by focusing on the moral and spiritual reformation of Muslims. In fulfillment of the Prophet Muhammad's prophecy about the degraded state of Muslims in the future, as the Messiah, Ahmad declared his mission to bring Muslims back to the true, original teachings of Islam. Although this sounds very similar to the intentions expressed by the founder of the Wahhabi movement, Ahmad's focus was on rational discourse as the means to reform Muslims, as opposed to the rigid compulsion employed by the founder of the Wahhabi movement.

In concert with his calls for a peaceful, rational discourse to call people to the way of Islam, Ahmad penned more than eighty books and tens of thousands of letters, and engaged in scores of public debates in order to rigorously and logically defend the teachings of Islam. He recognized that many Muslims (including ibn Abdul Wahhab) had been misusing the term "Jihad" for nefarious purposes and, therefore, wrote: "Muslims violated human rights by unjustly raising the sword and calling it *jihad*."[22] The coming of the Messiah was meant to bring about an end to religious wars. As such, Ahmad said that with his arrival, "those who now raise the sword on religion's behalf have no excuse before God Almighty. Those who possess sight, read the *ahadith* [written accounts of the Prophet Muhammad's words] and ponder over the Holy Quran should understand well that the kind of jihad practiced by many of today's barbaric people is not Islamic jihad."[23] He then advanced his bold claim, saying: "I have come to you with an order: jihad with the sword has ended from this time forward, but the jihad of purifying your souls must continue. I do not say this of my own accord. This is indeed the will of God."[24]

Thus, Ahmad argued that Muslims then lived in a time where they were no longer being physically attacked due to their faith—a precondition for Jihad-e-Asghar (i.e., "the lesser Jihad"). So, he drew Muslims back to their higher obligation of Jihad-e-Akbar (i.e., "the greatest Jihad"), of purifying themselves and developing themselves morally and spiritually. But he also recognized that Islam continued to be the target of assault by way of accusations and allegations. Instead of a physical defense of Islam, then, he recalled the spirit of Jihad-e-Kabeer by calling Muslims toward what he called "Jihad bil Qalam" (i.e., "Jihad by the pen"). Although the word "*qalam*" literally translates to pen, it also symbolizes knowledge and wisdom. Thus, he called Muslims to defend their faith by way of wisdom and intellect. He wrote: "In the present age, the pen has been raised against us (Muslims), and it was through the pen that Muslims had been caused so much pain and suffering. Therefore, the pen should be the weapon of the Muslims. . . . In this age, God wants us (Muslims) to defeat critics by using the pen as our weapon to refute their allegations. Therefore allegation by pen against Islam should not be responded by sword, but pen."[25]

In addition to the belief that the long-awaited Messiah and Mahdi has already appeared, what differentiates members of the Ahmadiyya Muslim Community (called "Ahmadi Muslims") is that they have reestablished the system of Khilafat. In accordance with the aforementioned Hadith, Muhammad had foretold not only that the early Khilafat would end but that it would re-emerge as a solution to the problems facing the Muslim world. Again, Muhammad had said: "Prophethood shall remain with you for as long as Allah wills. He will then cause it to end. Then Khilafat will be established on the precepts of Prophethood, which will last for as long as Allah wills. He will then cause it to end. Oppressive kingship will then follow and its rule will last for as long as Allah wills. He will then cause it to end. After this, tyrannical monarchies will follow, and their rule will last for as long as Allah wills. Allah will then cause it to end. Khilafat will then be re-established on the precepts of Prophethood."

There have been failed attempts in history by Muslims to reestablish Khilafat in the world as a means to reunite Muslims and usher in an era of prosperity within the Islamic world. Based on this quote of Prophet Muhammad, however, all such efforts will invariably fail because he said that Khilafat would only be reestablished following prophethood, which is controlled only by God. This refers to the coming of the Messiah, after whom Khilafat would be reestablished, for the Messiah is the only prophet whose advent had been foretold by Muhammad.

In fulfillment of this prophecy—built on the belief that Mirza Ghulam Ahmad is indeed that long-awaited Messiah and Mahdi—the Ahmadiyya Muslim Community reestablished Khilafat in the world upon Ahmad's demise in 1908. Just as the original Khilafat after the demise of Prophet Muhammad, the Ahmadiyya Muslim Community's Khilafat has seen a line of elected successors to the Promised Messiah. The fifth and current Khalifa, Mirza Masroor Ahmad, resides in London, UK, with members of this sect of Islam residing in more than two hundred countries around the world.

In conclusion, not only has there been wide diversity of thought within the Muslim world since the early history of Islam, but there is even wide diversity of thought among those groups established more recently with the aim of reforming Muslims and reviving the original, pure teachings of Islam. It is up to the individual to study and pray in order to follow the path toward which one's heart leads one.

NOTES

CHAPTER 1

1. Malik Ghulam Farid, ed., *The Holy Quran: Arabic Text with English Translation and Short Commentary* (Islam International Publications Ltd, 2010), 5:4, p. 235.

2. Muhammad Zafrulla Khan, *Muhammad: Seal of the Prophets* (Routledge & Kegan Paul, 1980), p. 262.

3. Ibid.

4. Avril Ann Powell, *Scottish Orientalists and India: The Muir Brothers, Religion, Education and Empire* (The Boydell Press, 2010), pp. 261–62.

5. Sir William Muir, *The Life of Mahomet: From Original Sources* (Smith, Elder & Company, 1878), p. 525.

6. Malik Ghulam Farid, ed., *The Holy Quran: Arabic Text with English Translation and Short Commentary* (Islam International Publications Ltd, 2010), 2:3, p. 12.

7. Dr. Ahmad Lidan and Dina Lidan, *Mokhtaser Sahih Muslim: Text and Translation*, vol. 1 (Islamic Inc. Publishing & Distribution, 2000), p. 30.

8. Malcolm X and Alex Haley, *The Autobiography of Malcolm X* (Ballantine Books, 1992), pp. 390–391.

9. Malik Ghulam Farid, ed., *The Holy Quran: Arabic Text with English Translation and Short Commentary* (Islam International Publications Ltd, 2010), 112:2–5, pp. 1322–23.

10. Ibid., 2:187, p. 76.

11. Ibid., 17:25, p. 554.

12. Ibid., 16:37, p. 526.

13. Ibid., 35:25, p. 885.

14. Ibid., 20:116, p. 641.

15. Ibid., 2:287, p. 116.

16. Ibid., 2:29, p. 22.

17. Ibid., 2:63, p. 36.

CHAPTER 2

1. Malik Ghulam Farid, ed., *The Holy Quran: Arabic Text with English Translation and Short Commentary* (Islam International Publications Ltd, 2010), 3:85, p. 148.
2. The Holy Bible (King James Version) (American Bible Society, 1987), Gen. 25:16, p. 20.
3. Ibid., Deut. 18:18, p. 171.
4. Ibid., Matt. 5:17–18, p. 4.
5. Malik Ghulam Farid, ed., *The Holy Quran: Arabic Text with English Translation and Short Commentary* (Islam International Publications Ltd, 2010), 73:16, p. 1193.
6. Ibid., 46:11, p. 1011.
7. Deborah Abecassis, "Reconstructing Rashi's Commentary on Genesis from Citations in the Torah Commentaries of the Tosafot," March 1999, McGill University, p. i.
8. The Holy Bible: King James Version (American Bible Society, 1987), Sol. 5:16, p. 576.
9. Ibid., John 14:15–16, p. 104.
10. Ibid., John 16:7–13, pp. 105–6.
11. Malik Ghulam Farid, ed., *The Holy Quran: Arabic Text with English Translation and Short Commentary* (Islam International Publications Ltd, 2010), 21:108, p. 666.
12. Ibid., 53:4–5, p. 1067.
13. The Holy Bible: King James Version (American Bible Society, 1987), Luke 1:13–15, p. 54.
14. Ibid., Matt. 3:16, p. 3.
15. Ibid., Matt. 4:1, p. 3.
16. Ibid., Luke 1:35, p. 55.
17. Ibid., John 1:19–25, p. 88.
18. Malik Ghulam Farid, ed., *The Holy Quran: Arabic Text with English Translation and Short Commentary* (Islam International Publications Ltd, 2010), 2:214, p. 85.
19. Ibid., 22:79, p. 688.
20. The Holy Bible: King James Version (American Bible Society, 1987), Isa. 62:2, p. 619.

CHAPTER 3

1. Malik Ghulam Farid, ed., *The Holy Quran: Arabic Text with English Translation and Short Commentary* (Islam International Publications Ltd, 2010), 7:57, p. 322.
2. Ibid., 11:86, p. 449.
3. Edward William Lane, *An Arabic-English Lexicon*, part 2, (Librairie Du Liban, 1968), p. 473.

4. Edward William Lane, *An Arabic-English Lexicon*, part 7, (Librairie Du Liban, 1968), p. 2587.

5. Malik Ghulam Farid, ed., *The Holy Quran: Arabic Text with English Translation and Short Commentary* (Islam International Publications Ltd, 2010), 29:7–8, pp. 804–5.

6. Ibid., 91:8–11, p. 1270.

7. Ibid., 30:42, pp. 825–26.

8. Ibid., 62:3, p. 1136.

9. Ibid., 75:3, p. 1203.

10. Edward William Lane, *An Arabic-English Lexicon*, part 7, (Librairie Du Liban, 1968), p. 2586.

11. Malik Ghulam Farid, ed., *The Holy Quran: Arabic Text with English Translation and Short Commentary* (Islam International Publications Ltd, 2010), 25:53, p. 739.

12. Ibid., 4:96, p. 211.

13. Ibid., 2:3, p. 12.

14. Ibid., 16:126, p. 543.

15. Edward William Lane, *An Arabic-English Lexicon*, part 2, (Librairie Du Liban, 1968), p. 617.

16. Malik Ghulam Farid, ed., *The Holy Quran: Arabic Text with English Translation and Short Commentary* (Islam International Publications Ltd, 2010), 2:257, p. 104.

17. Mirza Ghulam Ahmad, *Malfoozat*, vol. 1 (al-Shirkatul Islamiyyah Limited, 1984), pp. 44, 59.

18. Mirza Ghulam Ahmad, *The British Government and Jihad* (Islam International Publications Ltd, 2006), p. 20.

19. Edward William Lane, *An Arabic-English Lexicon*, part 4, (Librairie Du Liban, 1968), p. 1692.

20. Malik Ghulam Farid, ed., *The Holy Quran: Arabic Text with English Translation and Short Commentary* (Islam International Publications Ltd, 2010), 22:40–41, pp. 680–81.

21. Ibid., 2:252, p. 102.

22. Ibid., 5:65, p. 253.

23. Ibid., 2:191, p. 78.

24. Ibid., 2:194, pp. 78–79.

25. Ibid., 8:40, p. 366.

26. Ibid., 9:5, pp. 377–78.

27. Ibid., 8:62, pp. 371–72.

28. Ibid., 8:63, p. 372.

29. Ibid., 9:4, p. 377.

30. Ibid., 9:6, p. 378.

31. Ibid., 2:196, p. 79.

32. *The Holy Quran with English Translation and Commentary*, vol. 2 (Islam International Publications Limited, 1988), 4:30, p. 516.

33. "Majlis Khuddamul Ahmadiyya UK 38th National Ijtema," Selected Compilation of Pictorial Reports from 2009 to 2010 (Ahmadiyya Muslim Youth Association UK, 2010).

34. Fazlur Rahman, *Islam and Modernity—Transformation of an Intellectual Tradition* (University of Chicago Press, 1982), p. 116.

35. Raj K. Pruthi, *Encylopaedia of Jihad*, vol. 2 (Anmol Publications Pvt. Ltd, 2002), p. 335.

36. Maulana Abu Ala Maududi, *Al-Jihad fil Islam*, 15th ed., translated from original Urdu language (Adara Tarjman Al-Quran Pvt. Ltd., Pakistan, 1996), p. 171.

37. Ibid., pp. 173–74.

38. Malik Ghulam Farid, ed., *The Holy Quran: Arabic Text with English Translation and Short Commentary* (Islam International Publications Ltd, 2010), 88:23, p. 2815.

39. Mirza Tahir Ahmad, *Murder in the Name of Allah* (Islam International Publications, 1989), p. 15.

40. Ibid., p. 16.

41. Karen Armstrong, Islam: *A Short History* (Modern Library, 2002), p. 168.

42. Maulana Abu Ala Maududi, *Jihad in Islam* (The Holy Koran Publishing House, 2006), p. 6.

43. Raj K. Pruthi, *Encylopaedia of Jihad*, vol. 2 (Anmol Publications Pvt. Ltd, 2002), pp. 328–29.

44. Ibid., p. 536.

45. Philip Jenkins, "Clerical Terror," *The New Republic*, December 24, 2008, http://www.newrepublic.com/article/clerical-terror, accessed February 26, 2013.

46. Sayyid Qutb, "al-Damir—al-Amrikanit . . .! wa-qadiyat Filastin," *al-Risalah* no. 694 (October 21, 1946), p. 1155.

47. Yvonne Y. Haddad, "Sayyid Qutb: Ideologue of Islamic Revival," in *Voices of Resurgent Islam*, ed. John L. Esposito (Oxford University Press, 1983), p. 69.

48. Sayyid Qutb, *Milestones* (International Islamic Federation of Student Organizations, 1978), p. 96.

49. Ibid., p. 104.

50. Sayyid Qutb, *Milestones* (Maktabah Booksellers and Publishers, 2006) p. 67.

51. Sayyid Qutb, *Milestones* (International Islamic Federation of Student Organizations, 1978) p. 109.

52. Malik Ghulam Farid, ed., *The Holy Quran: Arabic Text with English Translation and Short Commentary* (Islam International Publications Ltd, 2010), 12:41, p. 1156.

53. Sayyid Qutb, *Milestones* (International Islamic Federation of Student Organizations, 1978), p. 113.

54. Ibid., pp. 114–15.

55. Khaled M. Abou El Fadl, *The Great Theft: Wrestling Islam from the Extremists* (HarperCollins Publishers, 2005), p. 82.

56. Ibid., pp. 82–83.

57. Karen Armstrong, *The Battle for God: A History of Fundamentalism* (Random House Publishing Group, 2000), p. 243.

58. Sayyid Qutb, *Milestones* (International Islamic Federation of Student Organizations, 1978), pp. 110–12.

59. Lawrence Wright, *The Looming Tower: Al-Qaeda and the Road to 9/11* (Random House, 2006), p. 37.

60. Ibid., p. 80.

61. Ibid., p. 79.

62. Karen Armstrong, *Islam: A Short History* (Modern Library, 2002), p. 170.

63. Scott Shane and Souad Mekhennet, "Imam's Path from Condemning Terror to Preaching Jihad," *New York Times*, May 8 2010, http://www.nytimes.com/2010/05/09/world/09awlaki.html, accessed February 26, 2013.

CHAPTER 4

1. "Pakistani Soldier Stoned to Death for Love Affair, Tribesmen Say," Reuters, March 13, 2013), http://www.reuters.com/article/2013/03/13/us-pakistan-stoning-idUSBRE92C0BK20130313, accessed March 25, 2013.

2. "'Don't Kill Me,' She Screamed. Then They Stoned Her to Death," *The Independent*, November 9, 2008, http://www.independent.co.uk/news/world/africa/dont-kill-me-she-screamed-then-they-stoned-her-to-death-1003462.html, accessed March 25, 2013.

3. "IRAQ: 'Honour Killings' Persist in Kurdish North," IRIN News, December 6, 2007, http://www.irinnews.org/Report/75714/IRAQ-Honour-killings-persist-in-Kurdish-north, accessed March 25, 2013.

4. "Saudi Police 'Stopped' Fire Rescue," BBC News, March 15, 2002, http://news.bbc.co.uk/2/hi/1874471.stm, accessed March 25, 2013.

5. "Rape Victim Sentenced to 200 Lashes and Six Months in Jail," *The Guardian*, November 16, 2007, http://www.guardian.co.uk/world/2007/nov/17/saudiarabia.international, accessed March 25, 2013.

6. "America at Risk: Camus, National Security and Afghanistan," an address by Newt Gingrich, American Enterprise Institute for Public Policy Research, July 29, 2010, http://www.aei.org/files/2010/07/29/Address%20by%20Newt%20Gingrich07292010.pdf, accessed April 2, 2013.

7. "Bans on Court Use of Sharia/International Law," "Gavel to Gavel," the newsletter of the National Center for State Courts, May 29, 2012, http://gaveltogavel.us/site/2012/05/29/bans-on-court-use-of-shariainternational-law-signed-into-law-in-kansas-sent-to-study-committee-in-new-hampshire-still-technically-alive-in-mi-nc-pa-sc/, accessed April 2, 2013.

8. "Law Expert Explains Sharia and Islam," CNN.com, April 2, 2011, http://religion.blogs.cnn.com/2011/04/02/law-expert-explains-sharia-and-islam/, accessed March 30, 2013.

9. Edward William Lane, *An Arabic-English Lexicon*, part 4 (Librairie Du Liban, 1968), pp. 1534–36.

10. 'Abd ar-Rahman I. Doi and 'Abdassamad Clarke, *Shariah: Islamic Law* (Ta-Ha Publishers Ltd, 2008), p. 23.

11. Imam Raghib Asfahani, *Mufridatul-Qur'an*, 4th ed., translated from original Arabic (At-Tab'atur-Rabi'ah, 2009, distributed in Damascus through Darul-Qalam and in Beirut through Ad-Darush-Shamiyyah), pp. 450–51.

12. Dr. Abdullah Abbas al-Nadwi, *Vocabulary of the Holy Quran* (IQRA' International Educational Foundation, 1986), p. 303.

13. Edward William Lane, *An Arabic-English Lexicon*, part 4 (Librairie Du Liban, 1968), p. 1535.

14. Ibid.

15. Malik Ghulam Farid, *The Holy Quran: Arabic Text with English Translation and Short Commentary* (Islam International Publications Ltd, 2010), 45:19, p. 1005.

16. Rabbi Michael Lotker, *A Christian's Guide to Judaism* (A Stimulus Book, Paulist Press, 2004), pp. 26, 87.

17. Edward William Lane, *An Arabic-English Lexicon*, part 5, (Librairie Du Liban, 1968), p. 1974.

18. Abdul Mannan Omar, *Dictionary of the Holy Quran* (Noor Foundation, 2003), p. 362.

19. Edward William Lane, *An Arabic-English Lexicon*, part 5 (Librairie Du Liban, 1968), pp. 2522–23.

20. Abdul Mannan Omar, *Dictionary of the Holy Quran* (Noor Foundation, 2003), p. 454.

21. Malik Ghulam Farid, *The Holy Quran: Arabic Text with English Translation and Short Commentary* (Islam International Publications Ltd, 2010), 4:59, p. 201.

22. Ibid., 5:43, p. 247.

23. Ibid., 4:136, p. 220.

24. Ibid., 2:43, p. 29.

25. Ibid., 5:9, p. 238.

26. Ibid., 4:59, p. 201.

27. Muhammad Zafrulla Khan, *Muhammad: Seal of the Prophets* (Routledge & Kegan Paul, 1980), p. 191.

28. Malik Ghulam Farid, *The Holy Quran: Arabic Text with English Translation and Short Commentary* (Islam International Publications Ltd, 2010), 42:39, p. 980.

29. Ibid., 3:160, p. 168.

30. Ibid., 2:257, p. 104.

31. Brian Duignan, *Modern Philosophy: From 1500 CE to the Present* (Britannica Educational Publishing, 2011), p. 86.

32. "Is Islam for Germany?," *The Review of Religions* 106, no. 7 (July 2011) (Al Shirkatul Islamiyyah Ltd.), pp. 48–49.

33. Malik Ghulam Farid, *The Holy Quran: Arabic Text with English Translation and Short Commentary* (Islam International Publications Ltd, 2010), 5:49, p. 249.

34. Jan Michiel Otto, *Sharia Incorporated: A Comparative Overview of the Legal Systems of Twelve Muslim Countries in Past and Present* (Leiden University Press, 2010), p. 31.

35. The Holy Bible (King James Version) (American Bible Society, 1987), Deut. 22:20–21, p.174.

36. Ibid., 22:23–24, p. 174.

37. Malik Ghulam Farid, *The Holy Quran: Arabic Text with English Translation and Short Commentary* (Islam International Publications Ltd, 2010), 24:3, p. 709.

38. 'Abd ar-Rahman I. Doi and 'Abdassamad Clarke, *Shariah: Islamic Law* (Ta-Ha Publishers Ltd, 2008), p. 366.

39. Edward William Lane, *An Arabic-English Lexicon*, part 3 (Librairie Du Liban, 1968), p. 1260.

40. Ibid.

41. Malik Ghulam Farid, *The Holy Quran: Arabic Text with English Translation and Short Commentary* (Islam International Publications Ltd, 2010), 5:39, p. 245.

42. Edward William Lane, *An Arabic-English Lexicon*, part 4 (Librairie Du Liban, 1968), p. 1352.

43. Abdul Mannan Omar, *Dictionary of the Holy Quran* (Noor Foundation, 2003), p. 257.

44. Malik Ghulam Farid, *The Holy Quran: Arabic Text with English Translation and Short Commentary* (Islam International Publications Ltd, 2010), 2:189, p. 77.

45. "Crime in the United States 2011," FBI: Uniform Crime Reports, http://www.fbi.gov/about-us/cjis/ucr/crime-in-the-u.s/2011/crime-in-the-u.s.-2011, retrieved April 9, 2013.

46. John Deigh and David Dolinko, *The Oxford Handbook of Philosophy of Criminal Law* (Oxford University Press, 2011), p. 287.

47. Maulana Abu Ala Maududi, *Jihad in Islam* (The Holy Koran Publishing House, 2006), p. 6.

48. Ibid., pp. 19–20.

49. Mark Graham, *How Islam Created the Modern World* (Amana Publications, 2006), p. 21.

50. 'Abd ar-Rahman I. Doi and 'Abdassamad Clarke, *Shariah: Islamic Law* (Ta-Ha Publishers Ltd, 2008), p. 7.

CHAPTER 5

1. Edward Lawson, *Encyclopedia of Human Rights*, 2nd ed. (Taylor & Francis, 1996), p. 551.

2. "Afghan Judge in Convert Case Vows to Resist Foreign Pressure," *New York Times*, March 23, 2006, http://www.nytimes.com/2006/03/23/international/asia/23cnd-convert.html, accessed May 2, 2013.

3. "Egyptian Islamic Lawyers Urge Death Sentence for Convert," Assyrian International News Agency, February 26, 2009, http://www.aina.org/news/20090226172430.htm, accessed May 2, 2013.

4. "State Dept: Release Pastor Jailed for 1,000 Days, Sentenced to Death in Iran," CNN.com, July 10, 2012, http://edition.cnn.com/2012/07/10/world/meast/iran-detained-pastor, accessed May 2, 2013.

5. "Europe Bishops Slam Saudi Fatwa against Gulf Churches," Reuters, March 23, 2012, http://www.reuters.com/article/2012/03/23/us-saudi-christians-fatwa-idUSBRE82M1D720120323, accessed May 3, 2013.

6. U.S. Department of State, "International Religious Freedom Report 2011: Saudi Arabia," Bureau of Democracy, Human Rights, and Labor, July 30, 2012, http://www.state.gov/j/drl/rls/irf/2011/nea/192905.htm, accessed April 3, 2013.

7. Abdullah Saeed and Hassan Saeed, *Freedom of Religion, Apostasy and Islam* (Ashgate Publishing, 2004), p. 19.

8. Kevin Boyle and Juliet Sheen, *Freedom of Religion and Belief: A World Report* (Routledge Chapman & Hall, 1997), p. 73.

9. U.S. Department of State, "2011 Country Reports on Human Rights Practices—Iran," Bureau of Democracy, Human Rights, and Labor, May 24, 2012, http://www.refworld.org/docid/4fc75a92af.html, accessed April 3, 2013.

10. "Morocco Death for Apostates Fatwa Sparks Controversy," Agence France Presse, April 19, 2013, http://www.google.com/hostednews/afp/article/ALeqM5iSMC9xu-qUfsH2otkPyk8Ghep5SA?docId=CNG.c7cbe3a1e07118689fdf253a70602eb6.271, accessed April 24, 2013.

11. 'Abd ar-Rahman I. Doi and 'Abdassamad Clarke, *Shariah: Islamic Law* (Ta-Ha Publishers Ltd, 2008), p. 401.

12. Malik Ghulam Farid, ed., *The Holy Quran: Arabic Text with English Translation and Short Commentary* (Islam International Publications Ltd, 2010), 2:55, pp. 32–33.

13. Mirza Tahir Ahmad, *The Truth about the Alleged Punishment for Apostasy in Islam* (Islam International Publications, 2005), pp. 36–37.

14. Shabbir Ahmad Usmani, *Tafseer-e-Usmani*, vol. 1, translated from original Urdu (Athar Press, 2007), p. 73.

15. Malik Ghulam Farid, ed., *The Holy Quran: Arabic Text with English Translation and Short Commentary* (Islam International Publications Ltd, 2010), 2:52–53, p. 32.

16. Ibid., 4:154, p. 224.

17. Ibid., 7:150, p. 341.

18. The Holy Bible (King James Version) (American Bible Society, 1987), Exod. 32:27–28, pp. 76–77.

19. Malik Ghulam Farid, ed., *The Holy Quran: Arabic Text with English Translation and Short Commentary* (Islam International Publications Ltd, 2010), 2:55, pp. 32–33.

20. Ibid., 5:34–35, p. 244.

21. Edward William Lane, *An Arabic-English Lexicon*, part 2 (Librairie Du Liban, 1968), p. 540.

22. Ibid., part 3, pp. 1061–64.

23. Mufti Muhammad Shafi, *Ma'ariful Qur'an*, translated by Muhammad Shamim, vol. 3 (Maktaba e darul 'Uloom, 1999), pp. 134–35.

24. Mirza Tahir Ahmad, *The Truth about the Alleged Punishment for Apostasy in Islam* (Islam International Publications, 2005), p. 63.

25. Malik Ghulam Farid, ed., *The Holy Quran: Arabic Text with English Translation and Short Commentary* (Islam International Publications Ltd, 2010), 4:90, p. 208.

26. Ibid., 4:89, p. 208.

27. Ibid., 4:91, pp. 208–9.

28. Ibid., 9:12–13, pp. 379–80.

29. Edward William Lane, *An Arabic-English Lexicon*, part 5 (Librairie Du Liban, 1968), p. 1855.

30. Malik Ghulam Farid, ed., *The Holy Quran: Arabic Text with English Translation and Short Commentary* (Islam International Publications Ltd, 2010), 2:257, p. 104.

31. Ibid., 88:22–23, p. 1259.

32. Ibid., 6:108, p. 292.

33. Ibid., 10:100, p. 427.

34. Ibid., 27:93, p. 783.

35. Ibid., 10:109, pp. 428–29.

36. "Apostasy, Alcohol—Contemporary Issues—Bilal Philips," [n.d.], video clip, YouTube, http://www.youtube.com/watch?v=lBJmm-nfEow, accessed May 25, 2013.

37. Malik Ghulam Farid, ed., *The Holy Quran: Arabic Text with English Translation and Short Commentary* (Islam International Publications Ltd, 2010), 16:107, p. 540.

38. Ibid., 4:138, p. 221.

39. Abdullah Saeed and Hassan Saeed, *Freedom of Religion, Apostasy and Islam* (Ashgate Publishing Limited, 2004), p. 67.

40. Ibid., pp. 90–91.

41. Abul Ala Maududi, *Murtad Ki Saza Islami Qanun Main* [The Punishment of the Apostate according to Islamic Law], translated from original Urdu (Maktaba Jamat Islami Hind, Nazim Press Rampur, 1952), pp. 30–31.

42. Ibid, p. 47.

43. Khalid Bin Sayeed, *Western Dominance and Political Islam: Challenge and Response* (State University of New York Press, 1995), p. 33.

44. Abul Ala Maududi, *Musalman aur Maujuda Syasi Kashmakash* [Muslims and the Present Political Struggle], vol. 3, translated from original Urdu (Maktaba Jama'ati Islami, Darul Islam, 1938) p. 130.

45. Malik Ghulam Farid, ed., *The Holy Quran: Arabic Text with English Translation and Short Commentary* (Islam International Publications Ltd, 2010), 22:41, pp. 680–81.

46. Dr. Karimullah Zirvi, *The Holy Prophet of Islam* (KZ Publications, 2009), pp. 349–50.

CHAPTER 6

1. "Anti-Islam Film: Pakistan Minister Offers Bounty," BBC News, September 22, 2012, http://www.bbc.co.uk/news/world-asia-19687386, accessed June 20, 2013.

2. "Pakistan Minister Places Bounty on Anti-Islam Filmmaker," AFP, September 23, 2012, http://www.afp.com/en/node/532794/, accessed June 20, 2013.

3. "French Weekly Firebombed after It Portrays Mohammad," Reuters, November 2, 2011, http://www.reuters.com/article/2011/11/02/us-france-fire-magazine-idUSTRE7A117N20111102, accessed June 20, 2013.

4. "Muslim Cartoon Fury Claims Lives," BBC News, February 6, 2006, http://news.bbc.co.uk/2/hi/4684652.stm, accessed June 20, 2013.

5. "16 Die in Cartoon Protests in Nigeria," CNN International, February 19, 2006, http://edition.cnn.com/2006/WORLD/africa/02/18/cartoon.roundup/index.html, accessed June 20, 2013.

6. "Al-Qaeda Puts Bounties on Heads of Swedes," *The Local*, September 15, 2007, http://www.thelocal.se/8498/20070915/, accessed June 20, 2013.

7. Mirza Tahir Ahmad, *Islam's Response to Contemporary Issues* (Islam International Publications Ltd, 2007), p. 38.

8. Shahid M. Shahidullah, *Comparative Criminal Justice Systems* (Jones & Bartlett Learning, 2012), p. 514.

9. Malik Ghulam Farid, ed., *The Holy Quran: Arabic Text with English Translation and Short Commentary* (Islam International Publications Ltd, 2010), 33:58, p. 863.

10. Abdul Mannan Omar, *Dictionary of the Holy Quran* (Noor Foundation, 2003), p. 512.

11. Malik Ghulam Farid, *Dictionary of the Holy Qur'an* (Islam International Publications Limited, 2006), p. 737.

12. Malik Ghulam Farid, ed., *The Holy Quran: Arabic Text with English Translation and Short Commentary* (Islam International Publications Ltd, 2010), 24:24–25, p. 715.

13. Ibid., 5:34–35, p. 244.

14. Dr. Ahmad Lidan and Dina Lidan, *Mokhtaser Sahih Muslim: Text and Translation*, vol. 1 (Islamic Inc. Publishing & Distribution, 2000), p. 30.

15. Malik Ghulam Farid, ed., *The Holy Quran: Arabic Text with English Translation and Short Commentary* (Islam International Publications Ltd, 2010), 2:214, p. 85.

16. Ibid., 33:71, p. 865.

17. Imam Nawawi, *Riyadh as-Salihin (Gardens of the Righteous)*, translated by Muhammad Zafrullah Khan (Curzon Press Ltd, 1975), p. 18.

18. Malik Ghulam Farid, ed., *The Holy Quran: Arabic Text with English Translation and Short Commentary* (Islam International Publications Ltd, 2010), 17:54, p. 559.

19. Edward William Lane, *An Arabic-English Lexicon*, part 2 (Librairie Du Liban, 1968), p. 540.

20. Malik Ghulam Farid, ed., *The Holy Quran: Arabic Text with English Translation and Short Commentary* (Islam International Publications Ltd, 2010), 2:84, p. 42.

21. Ibid., 4:149, p. 223.

22. Imam Nawawi, *Riyadh as-Salihin (Gardens of the Righteous)*, translated by Muhammad Zafrullah Khan (Curzon Press Ltd, 1975), p. 125.

23. Joint Congressional Committee on Inaugural Ceremonies, ed., *Inaugural Addresses of the Presidents of the United States* (Cosimo, 2008), p.298.

24. Ahmadiyya Muslim Community International, "Press Release: World Muslim Leader Condemns Anti-Islam film," September 22, 2012, http://www.alislam.org/egazette/press-release/world-muslim-leader-condemns-anti-islam-film/, accessed July 5, 2013.

25. Malik Ghulam Farid, ed., *The Holy Quran: Arabic Text with English Translation and Short Commentary* (Islam International Publications Ltd, 2010), 15:7, pp. 505–6.

26. Ibid., 17:48, p. 558.

27. Ibid., 25:9, p. 732.

28. Ibid., 21:6, p. 648.

29. Ibid., 16:102, p. 539.

30. Ibid., 16:104, p. 539.

31. Ibid., 41:27, p. 966.

32. Ibid., 33:49, p. 859.

33. Ibid., 43:8, p. 984.

34. Ibid., 20:131, p. 644.

35. Ibid., 38:18, p. 921.

36. Ibid., 4:141, p. 221.

37. Ibid., 25:64, p. 741.

38. Ibid., 5:9, p. 238.

39. "Haatprediker roept op tot doden Wilders" ("Hate preacher calls for killing Wilders"), De Telegraaf (September 3, 2010), http://www.telegraaf.nl/binnenland/article20340673.ece, accessed June 21, 2013.

CHAPTER 7

1. Karen Armstrong, *Muhammad: A Biography of the Prophet* (Harper Collins, 1993), p. 191.

2. U.S. Department of Justice Bureau of Justice Statistics, "Female Victims of Sexual Violence, 1994–2010," Office of Justice Programs, March 2013.

3. Senator Robert Torricelli, *In Our Own Words: Extraordinary Speeches of the American Century* (Washington Square Press, 1999) p. 238.

4. Emory Adams Allen, *History of Civilization*, vol. 3 (Central Publishing House, 1891), pp. 544–45.

5. Day Otis Kellogg, *The Encyclopaedia Britannica*, vol. 24 (The Werner Company, 1902), p. 638.

6. "Interview with Montgomery Watt," *Review of Religions* 99, no.11 (November 2004), p. 45.

7. Malik Ghulam Farid, ed., *The Holy Quran: Arabic Text with English Translation and Short Commentary* (Islam International Publications Ltd, 2010), 4:2, p. 181.

8. Ibid., 78:9, p. 1219.

9. Ibid., 51:50, p. 1056.

10. Ibid., 4:33, p. 195.

11. Ibid., 33:36, p. 855.

12. Ibid., 85:11, p. 1249.

13. Ibid., 24:32, p. 717.

14. Edward William Lane, *An Arabic-English Lexicon*, part 2 (Librairie Du Liban, 1968), p. 809.

15. Ibid.

16. Ibid.

17. *The Holy Quran with English Translation and Commentary*, vol. 4 (Islam International Publications Limited, 1988), 33:60, p. 2134.

18. Edward William Lane, *An Arabic-English Lexicon*, part 2 (Librairie Du Liban, 1968), p. 440.

19. Ibid., part 1, p. 44.

20. *The Holy Quran with English Translation and Commentary*, vol. 4 (Islam International Publications Limited, 1988), 24:31, p. 717.

21. Courtney E. Martin, *Perfect Girls, Starving Daughters* (Simon and Schuster, 2007), p. 29.

22. "Girls Do Better without Boys Study Finds," *The Guardian*, March 17, 2009, http://www.theguardian.com/education/2009/mar/18/secondary-schools -girls-gcse-results, accessed September 1, 2013.

23. "Home Porn Gives Industry the Blues," *The Observer*, December 15, 2007, http://www.theguardian.com/world/2007/dec/16/film.usa, accessed September 1, 2013.

24. Field listing—GDP, CIA World Factbook, https://www.cia.gov/library/ publications/the-world-factbook/rankorder/2001rank.html, accessed September 1, 2013.

25. Holy Bible (New American Standard Bible) (Foundation Publications, 1997), 1 Tim. 2:9.

26. Leonard J. Swidler and Arlene Swidler, *Women Priests: A Catholic Commentary on the Vatican Declaration* (Paulist Press, 1977), p. 41.

27. Holy Bible (New American Standard Bible) (Foundation Publications, 1997), 1 Cor. 11:5–6.

28. Ibid., 11:7–10.

29. *The Holy Quran with English Translation and Commentary*, vol. 4 (Islam International Publications Limited, 1988), 17:24–25, pp. 553–54.

30. Ibid., 46:16, p. 1012.

31. Mohammad Abdalla and Ikebal Mohammed Adam Patel, "An Islamic Perspective on Ageing and Spirituality," in *Ageing and Spirituality across Faiths and Cultures*, edited by Elizabeth MacKinlay (Jessica Kingsley Publishers, 2010), p. 119.

32. Muhammad Zafrulla Khan, *Islam: Its Meaning for Modern Man* (Routledge and Kegan Paul, 1962), p. 130.

33. Malik Ghulam Farid, ed., *The Holy Quran: Arabic Text with English Translation and Short Commentary* (Islam International Publications Ltd, 2010), 9:71–72, p. 393.

34. Ibid., 4:35, p. 195.

35. National Institute of Justice and Centers for Disease Control and Prevention, "Extent, Nature, and Consequences of Intimate Partner Violence," U.S. Department of Justice, July 2000, https://www.ncjrs.gov/pdffiles1/nij/181867.pdf, accessed March 2, 2014.

36. Malik Ghulam Farid, ed., *The Holy Quran: Arabic Text with English Translation and Short Commentary* (Islam International Publications Ltd, 2010), 4:33, p. 195.

37. James Q. Wilson, *American Politics, Then & Now: And Other Essays* (American Enterprise Institute Press, June 2010), p. 186.

38. Edward William Lane, *An Arabic-English Lexicon*, part 8 (Librairie Du Liban, 1968), p. 2795.

39. Ibid.

40. Malik Ghulam Farid, ed., *The Holy Quran: Arabic Text with English Translation and Short Commentary* (Islam International Publications Ltd, 2010), 2:227, p. 91.

41. Amina Wadud, *Qur'an and Woman: Rereading the Sacred Text from a Woman's Perspective* (Oxford University Press, 1999), p. 76.

42. Ibid.

43. "Why Are Hindu Honor Killings Rising in India?," *Time Magazine*, May 25, 2010, http://content.time.com/time/world/article/0,8599,1991195,00.html, accessed September 13, 2013.

44. Felix Bryk, *Circumcision in Man and Woman: Its History, Psychology and Ethnology* (University Press of the Pacific, 2001), pp. 45–46.

45. Anika Rahman and Nahid Toubia, *Female Genital Mutilation: A Guide to Laws and Policies Worldwide* (Zed Books, 2000), p. 6.

46. "Islam's Authority Deficit," *The Economist*, June 28, 2007, http://www.economist.com/node/9409354, accessed September 14, 2013.

47. "Egypt Clerics: Female Circumcision Un-Islamic," Middle East Online, July 4, 2007, http://www.middle-east-online.com/english/?id=21307, accessed September 14, 2013.

48. "Islam Does Not Support Female Circumcision—Expert," GhanaWeb, March 16, 2005, http://www.ghanaweb.com/GhanaHomePage/NewsArchive/ artikel.php?ID=77396, accessed September 14, 2013.

49. *The Holy Quran with English Translation and Commentary*, vol. 4 (Islam International Publications Limited, 1988), 17:24–25, pp. 553–54.

50. Karen Armstrong, *Muhammad: A Biography of the Prophet* (Harper Collins, 1993), p. 190.

51. Lord Headley, *Three Great Prophets of the World: Moses, Jesus and Muhammad* (The Islamic Review, 1923), p. 58.

52. Ronak Husni and Daniel Newman, *Muslim Women in Law and Society: Annotated Translation of al-Tahir al-Haddad's* Imra'tuna fi 'I-sharia wa 'I-mujtama (Routledge, 2007), p. 159.

53. "Full Text of Malala Yousafzai's Speech at UN," *Pakistan Today*, July 13, 2013, http://www.pakistantoday.com.pk/2013/07/13/news/national/full-text -of-malala-yousafzais-speech-at-un/, accessed September 14, 2013.

54. Lynne E. Ford, *Encyclopedia of Women and American Politics* (Facts On File, 2008), p. 346.

55. James Peggs, *India's Cries to British Humanity*, 2nd ed. (Seely and Son, 1830), p. 113.

56. "India Has Killed 10 Million Girls in 20 Years," ABC News, December 15, 2006, http://abcnews.go.com/Health/story?id=2728976, accessed September 1, 2013.

57. John Wroath, *Until They Are Seven: The Origins of Women's Legal Rights* (Waterside Press, 1998), p. 16.

58. Mirza Masroor Ahmad, "Islam and Women's Rights," *Review of Religions* 104, no. 3 (March 2009), p. 14.

59. Peter Ward, *Courtship, Love, and Marriage in Nineteenth-Century English Canada* (McGill-Queen's University Press, 1990), p. 40.

CHAPTER 8

1. Pamela Geller, "Islam: This Is Defamation of Religion," December 2009, http://atlasshrugs2000.typepad.com/atlas_shrugs/2009/12/islam-this-is -defamation-of-relgion.html, accessed July 27, 2013.

2. Malik Ghulam Farid, ed., *The Holy Quran: Arabic Text with English Translation and Short Commentary* (Islam International Publications Ltd, 2010), 3:36, pp. 131–32.

3. Ibid., 3:37, pp. 132–33.

4. Ibid., 3:43, p. 135.

5. Ibid., 66:13, p. 1158.

6. Ibid., 19:17–22, pp. 605–7.

7. Ibid., 2:260, p. 328.

8. Ibid., 21:108, p. 1725.

9. Ibid., 3:46, p. 136.

10. Ibid., 19:23, p. 607.

11. Ibid., 19:25–27, pp. 608–10.

12. The Holy Bible (King James Version) (American Bible Society, 1987), Luke 2:8.

13. Malik Ghulam Farid, ed., *The Holy Quran: Arabic Text with English Translation and Short Commentary* (Islam International Publications Ltd, 2010), 3:47, p. 137.

14. Ibid., 3:49–50, pp. 138–39.

15. Edward William Lane, *An Arabic-English Lexicon*, part 5 (Librairie Du Liban, 1968), p. 1906.

16. Malik Ghulam Farid, ed., *The Holy Quran: Arabic Text with English Translation and Short Commentary* (Islam International Publications Ltd, 2010), 6:105, p. 292.

17. Ibid., 22:47, pp. 681–82.

18. Ibid., 8:25, p. 363.

19. Holy Bible (New American Standard Bible) (Foundation Publications, 1997), Isa. 27:13.

20. Ibid., Isa. 11:11–12.

21. Ibid., Ezek. 34:11–14.

22. Ibid., Matt. 15:24.

23. Ibid., Matt. 10:5–6.

24. Ibid., John 10:16.

25. Ibid., Matt. 19:28.

26. Ibid., Luke 19:10.

27. Malik Ghulam Farid, ed., *The Holy Quran: Arabic Text with English Translation and Short Commentary* (Islam International Publications Ltd, 2010), 3:52, p. 140.

28. Ibid., 19:31, p. 611.

29. Ibid., 112:2–5, pp. 1322–23.

30. Ibid., 19:89–93, p. 621.

31. Holy Bible (New American Standard Bible) (Foundation Publications, 1997), Mark 12:29–30.

32. Ibid., Mark 12:32.

33. The Holy Bible (King James Version) (American Bible Society, 1987), Matt. 19:16–17.

34. Ibid., John 10:31–36.

35. Ibid., Psalm 82:6.

36. Ibid., Luke 3:38.

37. Ibid., Exod. 4:22.

38. Ibid., Hosea 11:1.

39. Ibid., Psalm 82:6.

40. Ibid., Jer. 31:9.

41. Ibid., Psalm 89:27.

42. Ibid., Psalm 2:7.

43. Ibid., 1 Chron. 22:9–10.

44. Ibid., 2 Sam. 7:13–14.

45. Ibid., Rom. 8:14.

46. Ibid., Matt. 5:9.

47. Ibid., Deut. 21:23.

48. Malik Ghulam Farid, ed., *The Holy Quran: Arabic Text with English Translation and Short Commentary* (Islam International Publications Ltd, 2010), 4:158, p. 225.

49. Abdullah Yusuf Ali, trans., The Holy Qur'an (Wordsworth Editions Limited, 2000), 4:157, p. 78.

50. Mohammed Marmaduke Pickthall, trans., *The Glorious Qur'an: The Arabic Text with a Translation in English* (Tahrike Tarsile Quran Inc., 2006), 4:157, p. 86.

51. Malik Ghulam Farid, ed., *The Holy Quran: Arabic Text with English Translation and Short Commentary* (Islam International Publications Ltd, 2010), 4:159, p. 226.

52. Abdullah Yusuf Ali, trans., The Holy Qur'an (Wordsworth Editions Limited, 2000), 4:158, p. 78.

53. Mohammed Marmaduke Pickthall, trans., *The Glorious Qur'an: The Arabic Text with a Translation in English* (Tahrike Tarsile Quran Inc., 2006), 4:158, p. 87.

54. Saiyed Jafar Reza, *The Essence of Islam* (Concept Publishing Company, 2012), p. 19.

55. Yasin T. Al-Jibouri, *Mary and Jesus in Islam* (AuthorHouse, 2011), p. 153.

56. Ibid., p. 153 (n. 1).

57. Malik Ghulam Farid, ed., *The Holy Quran: Arabic Text with English Translation and Short Commentary* (Islam International Publications Ltd, 2010), 3:56, p. 140.

58. Andrew J. Lane, *A Traditional Mu'tazilite Qur'an Commentary* (BRILL, 2006), p. xiv.

59. Muhammad Farooq-i-Azam Malik, *English Translation of the Meaning of Al-Qur'an* (The Institute of Islamic Knowledge, 2001) p. 166.

60. Mohammed Marmaduke Pickthall, trans., *The Glorious Qur'an: The Arabic Text with a Translation in English* (Tahrike Tarsile Quran Inc., 2006), 3:55, p. 59.

61. Mirza Tahir Ahmad, *Christianity: A Journey from Facts to Fiction* (Islam International Publications Ltd, 2006), p. 67.

62. The Holy Bible (King James Version) (American Bible Society, 1987), Luke 22:42.

63. Ibid., Luke 22:44.

64. Ibid., Mark 14:34.

65. Ibid., Mark 11:24.

66. Ibid., John 11:41–42.

67. Holy Bible (New American Standard Bible) (Foundation Publications, 1997), Heb. 5:7.

68. Ibid., Matt. 27:19.

69. Ibid., Luke 23:14–16.

70. Flavius Josephus, *The Works of Flavius Josephus: The Learned and Authentic Jewish Historian and Celebrated Warrior* (Lackington, Allen & Co, 1806), p. 242–43.

71. Holy Bible (New American Standard Bible) (Foundation Publications, 1997), John 19:31–33.

72. Ibid., John 19:34.

73. Ibid., Matt. 27:57–60.

74. Haim Hermann Cohn, *The Trial and Death of Jesus* (Ktav Pub. House, 1977), p. 238.

75. The Holy Bible (King James Version) (American Bible Society, 1987), Matt. 27:64.

76. Ibid., John 19:39.

77. Hadhrat Mirza Ghulam Ahmad, *Jesus in India* (Islam International Publications Ltd, 2003) p. 69.

78. Holy Bible (New American Standard Bible) (Foundation Publications, 1997), Matt. 12:39–40.

79. Ibid., Matt. 28:10.

80. Hadhrat Mirza Ghulam Ahmad, *Jesus in India* (Islam International Publications Ltd, 2007).

81. *The Ulama of Egypt on the Death of Jesus Christ: A Fatwa*, Introduction by Shaikh Muhammad Tufail (Ahmadiyya Anjuman Isha'at-i-Islam Lahore, 1947).

82. Malik Ghulam Farid, ed., *The Holy Quran: Arabic Text with English Translation and Short Commentary* (Islam International Publications Ltd, 2010), 3:145, p. 162.

CHAPTER 9

1. Vartan Gregorian, *Islam: A Mosaic, Not a Monolith* (Brookings Institution Press, 2004), p. 2.

2. Edward William Lane, *An Arabic-English Lexicon*, part 2 (Librairie Du Liban, 1968), p. 792.

3. Imam Jalaluddin Al-Suyuti, *Al-Khasais-ul-Kubra*, part 2, translated from original Arabic, p. 115.

4. Malik Ghulam Farid, ed., *The Holy Quran: Arabic Text with English Translation and Short Commentary* (Islam International Publications Ltd, 2010), 24:56, p. 726.

5. Hadrat Mirza Bashir-ud-Din Mahmud Ahmad, *The Outset of Dissension in Islam* (Islam International Publications Ltd, 2013), p. 12.

6. Maulana Muhammad Ali, *The Early Caliphate* (AAIL, 1932), p. 177.

7. Ibid., pp. 180–81.

8. Shah Ismail Shaheed, *Al-Arba'in fi Ahwal-al-Mahdiyin*, p. 9.

9. Pew Forum on Religion & Public Life, "Mapping the Global Muslim Population," (Pew Research Center, October 2009), p. 1.

10. Ibid.

11. Abdul Ali, *Islamic Dynasties of the Arab East* (M.D. Publications Pvt. Ltd, 1996), p. 97.

12. Ibid., p. 98.

13. Yaron Friedman, *The Nusayri-'Alawis: An Introduction to the Religion, History, and Identity of the Leading Minority in Syria* (Koninklijke Brill NV, 2010), pp. 7–8.

14. "Alawite Stronghold In Syria a Haven amid War," The Associated Press, August 30, 2013, http://news.yahoo.com/alawite-stronghold-syria-haven-amid-war-053606311.html, accessed September 19, 2013.

15. Vali Nasr, *The Shia Revival: How Conflicts within Islam Will Shape the Future* (W. W. Norton & Company Inc., 2006), pp. 54–55.

16. Valerie J. Hoffman, *The Essentials of Ibadi Islam* (Syracuse University Press, 2012), p. 4.

17. Imam Nawawi, *Riyadh as-Salihin (Gardens of the Righteous)*, translated by Muhammad Zafrullah Khan (Curzon Press Ltd, 1975), p. 249.

18. "The Roar of Rumi—800 years On," BBC News, September 30, 2007, http://news.bbc.co.uk/2/hi/south_asia/7016090.stm, accessed September 26, 2013.

19. Andrew Rippin, *World Islam: Critical Concepts in Islamic Studies*, vol. 4 (Routledge, 2008), p. 287.

20. Arthur John Arberry, *Tales from the Masnavi* (Curzon Press Ltd, 1993), p. 11.

21. Madawi al-Rasheed, *A History of Saudi Arabia* (Cambridge University Press, 2002), p. 18.

22. Mirza Ghulam Ahmad, *The British Government and Jihad* (Islam International Publications Ltd, 2006), p.7.

23. Ibid., p. 11.

24. Ibid., p. 17.

25. Mirza Ghulam Ahmad, *Malfoozat*, vol. 1 (al-Shirkatul Islamiyyah Limited, 1984), pp. 44, 59.

INDEX

ABOUT THE AUTHOR

Harris Zafar is a public speaker, writer, and activist, as well as a commentator on Islam, human rights, pluralism, and freedom of religion. As national spokesperson for Ahmadiyya Muslim Community USA—among the oldest Muslim organizations in America—Harris addresses issues facing Islam and the Muslim world, in various media. A staunch advocate for universal human rights, Harris was praised in a March 2012 motion raised on the floor of the House of Commons in Great Britain for his work in defending religious freedom.

A frequent speaker and lecturer on Islam at conferences, universities, schools, interfaith services, churches, and other public events, Harris has spoken across the United States and even internationally. He is an adjunct instructor of Islamic Studies at two colleges, where he instructs courses on the teachings of Islam and the history of both the religion and its Prophet Muhammad. He regularly appears on national and local news programs in print, on TV, and on radio to provide commentary on current issues from an Islamic perspective and to condemn intolerance and abuses of human rights, especially when done in the name of religion.

Harris is also a freelance writer whose work has been published in *USA Today*, the *Washington Post*, the *Christian Science Monitor*, the *Huffington Post*, the *New York Daily News*, BeliefNet, the *Oregonian*, Fox News, the *Review of Religions*, and the *Muslim Sunrise*.

Harris serves the Ahmadiyya Muslim Youth Association as national director of Faith Outreach, encouraging Muslim youth to understand and speak out about the true teachings of Islam. He previously served as national director of Community Service and as local president of the Portland chapter. Harris continues his dedicated work toward peace, education, and pluralism through his lectures, writings, interfaith dialogues, and media appearances.

The son of Pakistani parents, Harris was born and raised in the United States and maintains his identity as a Muslim and an American by following Islam's commandment to be a loyal citizen of the country in which one resides. He is married, has three beautiful children, and currently resides in Portland, Oregon.